# Market Centers
# and Retail Location
## Theory and Applications

# Market Centers and Retail Location
## Theory and Applications

BRIAN J. L. BERRY
*The University of Texas at Dallas*

JOHN B. PARR
*University of Glasgow*

*with*
BART J. EPSTEIN
*Kent State University*

AVIJIT GHOSH
*New York University*

ROBERT H. T. SMITH
*University of Western Australia*

*Prentice Hall, Englewood Cliffs, New Jersey 07632*

*Library of Congress Cataloging-in-Publication Data*

Berry, Brian Joe Lobley, (date)
   Market centers and retail location.

   Bibliography: p.
   Includes index.
     1. Shopping centers—United States—Location.
2. Central business districts—United States.  3. Store
location—United States.  I. Parr, John B.  II. Title.
HF5430.3.B47  1988      381'.1      87-29098
ISBN  0-13-556184-1

Editorial/production supervision
   and interior design: *Kathleen M. Lafferty*
Cover design: *Wanda Lubelska Design*
Manufacturing buyer: *Paula Benevento*

 © 1988 by Prentice-Hall, Inc.
A Division of Simon & Schuster
Englewood Cliffs, New Jersey 07632

A version of this text was previously published (1967) under the
title *The Geography of Market Centers and Retail Distribution*.

Printed in the United States of America

10  9  8  7  6  5  4  3  2  1

ISBN   0-13-556184-1   01

PRENTICE-HALL INTERNATIONAL (UK) LIMITED, *London*
PRENTICE-HALL OF AUSTRALIA PTY. LIMITED, *Sydney*
PRENTICE-HALL CANADA INC., *Toronto*
PRENTICE-HALL HISPANOAMERICANA, S.A., *Mexico*
PRENTICE-HALL OF INDIA PRIVATE LIMITED, *New Delhi*
PRENTICE-HALL OF JAPAN, INC., *Tokyo*
SIMON & SCHUSTER ASIA PTE. LTD., *Singapore*
EDITORA PRENTICE-HALL DO BRASIL, LTDA., *Rio de Janeiro*

# Contents

# Preface

That a new text updating the original should be warranted twenty years after *The Geography of Market Centers and Retail Distribution* was first written is a gratifying testament to the continuing use of an original volume more focused than usual.

The original volume's strong thesis stated the following:

> . . . that the geography of retail and service business displays regularities over space and through time, that central-place theory constitutes a deductive base from which to understand these regularities, and that the convergence of theoretical postulates and empirical regularities provides substance to marketing geography and to city and regional planning. . . .

The order of presentation mirrored this thesis. Terms and regularities were introduced by examining several case studies in the United States in both historical and cross-sectional detail. Central-place theory was then developed in its classical and contemporary forms. A study of origins and of cross-cultural contrasts was added, followed by brief treatments of the predictive procedures of applied marketing geography and of the prescriptive aspirations of the planner. This sequence of presentation was the result of several years of experimenting with various ways to present quickly, yet rigorously, both classical and contemporary ideas to beginning students. Students were admonished to proceed slowly and carefully, paying particular attention to the maps and diagrams, because the presentation was cumulative. Understanding later parts depended upon understanding initial parts: If students understood the diagrams they would understand the equations.

In preparing this new edition, we see no need to change the original thesis nor to modify the essential organization of the book or the advice to students. In the past twenty years, however, significant advances have been made in the formalization of central-place theory. A theory of periodic marketing systems has emerged, and marketing geography has progressed as an applied field. The broad outlines of marketing geography's convergence with the store-choice modeling procedures of marketing scientists seem clear. Moreover, central-place ideas have assumed an increasingly important role in the formulation of national spatial strategies for economic development. We therefore have replaced and extended substantial parts of the original book, while attempting to preserve the qualities that assured its longevity.

This was not a task for the original author alone. Several contributors to the developments of the past twenty years joined with me to prepare this new version. John Parr undertook Chapters 3 and 4 as his prime responsibility, and he also worked on the integrity and consistency of the volume as a whole. Robert Smith and Avijit Ghosh contributed a new Chapter 5 on periodic marketing systems. Bart Epstein provided sections on marketing geography. All four of my colleagues critiqued the entire draft. There are many strings left untied in this field, however, for this remains an active arena for both creative research and application. The definitive statement of a dynamic general central-place theory remains to be made. The links between that theory, store-choice modeling, and marketing geography remain unspecified. Uses of central-place theory concepts in national spatial planning have yet to progress beyond articles of faith. Thus, while comparison of this volume with the original will reveal that substantial progress has been made, the gap between present accomplishments and the models to which we aspire remains large. The need remains for that overarching statement of a general theory that will provide conceptual unity while informing practice. It is hoped that this edition may provide a base from which progress towards that statement can be made.

*Brian J. L. Berry*

# 1

# Market Centers
# and Retail Location

## INTRODUCTION

In market economies we are accustomed to thinking of the division of labor, differentiating among the activities of production, distribution (exchange), and consumption. It is in the system of *exchange*, through the activity of *distribution*, that the supplies of producers and the demands of consumers are brought together. In this sense, the interconnections of the exchange network are the strands that hold society together.

Exchange takes place in *markets*. Markets exist where a number of sellers and buyers communicate, and the prices offered by the sellers and paid by the buyers are affected by the decisions of each group. A market, then, is a system which produces self-regulating prices; the prices, in turn, are the mechanisms connecting individual actions of choice or decisions.

In this general sense there are *world markets*, for example, the wheat or copper markets. Most types of exchange, however, involve a specific *marketplace*.

> Market places are sites with social, economic, cultural and other referents where there are a number of buyers and sellers, and where price offered and paid by each is affected by the decisions of the others. (Belshaw, 1965, p. 8)

The Chicago wheat pit and the London metals exchange are dramatic examples of marketplaces of international significance, yet equally important are the hundreds of thousands of small market centers that dot the globe (Claval, 1962). Although they are seldom imposing, it is in these market centers that the daily process of exchange takes place. Whether they be periodic markets in the rural areas of Asia or North Africa, or markets in the villages and towns of the American Midwest, or a dramatic new shopping center, or a decaying central business district, these market centers are the places to which consumers travel to complete the exchange process. It is in market centers that demands and supplies must ultimately be brought into balance through the price mechanism. In effect, producers and consumers come face to face in retail stores. Retail and service businesses are the end of the chain of production and distribution and the beginning of the process of consumption. It is thus in the geography of retail and service business that we find the equilibrating interface between the geography of production, long a topic of professional interest and study, and the relatively neglected geography of consumption. We need to understand the organizing principles of this interface, and we need to appreciate the socio-economic and cultural factors that produce variation in organization as well as the spatial invariants.

The intermeshing of the geographies can be conceived in this way. Any economic system comprises a set of individuals who are the consumers of what is produced and, at the same time, the producers of what is demanded. In contemporary societies there is extreme division, or specialization, of labor. People specialize and regions specialize, yet individuals of similar income levels within a given society tend to demand similar arrays of goods and services (market baskets). Whereas the geography of production is marked by extreme regional specialization, the geography of consumption involves demands for similar baskets of goods that repeat themselves from region to region. A problem of coordination results, and it is dealt with by the system of exchange and distribution. Local collection points assemble the specialties of producing regions. Local distribution points import the many goods consumers need from collection points in other locales. Collection and distribution points interlock in a complex web of exchange. Collection may involve several steps, but ultimately metropolitan centers provide the points of focus. Similarly, distribution takes several steps, including both wholesaling and retailing, but metropolitan centers ultimately have this role, too. Metropolitan centers are also producers of regional specialities and assembly points for the goods demanded by their surrounding regions. They are also major consumers themselves. Intermetropolitan exchanges are the connecting strands of modern economies; metropolitan regions are the foci about which such economies are organized. It is in the metropolitan regions that the geographies of production and consumption interlock (Duncan, 1960).

Major metropolitan centers wholesale many of the products that they have assembled to smaller surrounding urban places, which, in turn, ship them to even smaller places. These market centers are visited by consumers to purchase needed goods and services. The essence of the geography of retail and service business is the clustering of establishments in market centers visited by surrounding consumers; the size and composition of the cluster is dependent upon the aggregate demand of the consumers in the region that looks to the market center as a point of focus.

*Centrality* is the essence of the point of focus. Consumers who must visit the market center on a regular basis want a location that permits them to conduct their business with a minimum of effort. Yet their business trips are varied. They are willing to travel only short distances to obtain items they need frequently. Less-frequent purchases can often be postponed so that a single longer trip can accomplish several things—not only shopping, but also socializing, seeking entertainment, participating in politics, and doing other activities. Centrality, therefore, has meaning at different scales. In any area a variety of ''central places'' will thus exist. Businesses located in some centers will attract consumers on a frequent basis, but only over short distances. In centers such as these, centrality means superior access to a local market area, but a small market means that a limited array of goods and services will be provided. Other central places will be able to provide a greater variety of goods to much wider areas. In these centers, centrality means accessibility to a larger region.

*Central-place theory* attempts to explain the location, size, functional characteristics, and spacing of these clusters of activity. It is, therefore, the descriptive and theoretical base of the geography of retail and service business. In the balance of Chapter 1 and in Chapter 2 we will attempt to describe the basic ideas of this theory through the use of examples. By following the examples, you will come to appreciate why the central-place theory, spelled out in Chapters 3 and 4, has such intellectual and practical significance.

Figure 1.1 identifies the areas of the United States to be used as the empirical base of our study. These areas provide a cross section of mid-continent America. Area 1 on the map spans the city and suburbs of the Chicago metropolitan area. Area 2 typifies the corn-growing, meat-fattening Midwest, lying between Omaha, Nebraska, and Council Bluffs, Iowa, to the west and Des Moines, Iowa, to the east. Areas 3 and 4 are in South Dakota. Area 3 includes wheat-growing and cattle-raising counties centering on Aberdeen in the northeast, while Area 4 spans

**Figure 1.1**   Areas investigated in 1960.

both rangelands to the north and east and the mining, forest, and recreation areas of the Black Hills to the west of Rapid City.

Each of these areas was analyzed in detail in 1960 in a study designed to evaluate and to compare the properties of central-place systems in a variety of different locations. An initial report was made on these studies in 1962 (Berry, 1962). Subsequently, both the city of Chicago and its metropolitan area were examined in much greater depth (Berry, 1963 and 1965).

Most of the terms and concepts of central-place theory can be introduced by looking at the southwestern corner of Iowa (Area 2, shown in more detail in Figure 1.2). Several reasons exist for examining this area in some detail. First, Iowa has been the classic region for study of central places in the United States because scholars thought that it satisfied the assumptions of central-place theory more nearly than any other region in North America. Second, to complete the picture we have available not only the field investigations on 1960, but also a study of the historical development of market centers in the area (Laska, 1958). And we also have a unique record of farmers' shopping preferences in 1934 in a form making possible comparisons with the 1960 data (Bureau of Business and Economic Research, 1934).

In his historical study, Laska used Dun and Bradstreet reference books to identify centers with retail stores. Because of the limitations of the data, he had to restrict himself to places with grocery and clothing stores. The 1934 studies

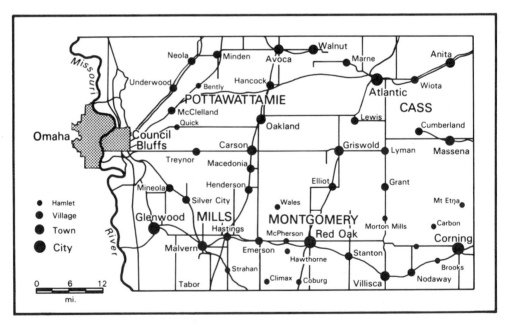

**Figure 1.2**   Status of market centers in southwestern Iowa in the summer of 1960. The area coincides with that investigated by Laska in 1958, as shown in Figures 1.3 to 1.7.

were completed by Works Progress Administration workers and record where farmers shopped for a variety of different goods and services, plus their preferences for particular market centers. What we learn from these comparisons is that, at any historical moment, the geographic distribution of retail and service business in central places approximates an equilibrium adjustment to the geographic distribution of consumers. However, through time there have been continual changes in the distribution and characteristics of consumers, in modes of travel, and in the technology of retailing; therefore, there have been adjustments in the patterns of business and centers. Settlement of the area was accompanied by the spread of centers and by increases in population and numbers of centers, reaching a population zenith around 1900. Subsequently there was a thinning of the system of centers because of changes in agriculture, loss of farm population, changes in consumer mobility, and changes in the technology of retailing.

Central places for the farming population were provided by points of focus that initially were not associated with retailing. Grist mills, post offices, county seats, and railroad stations created a variety of meeting places for farmers; enterprising businesses could take advantage of the superior accessibility to the consuming population that such locations provided. Combinations of the elements led to greater centrality for some of the initial meeting places, and these places provided excellent location opportunities for businesses serving less frequent demands. Competition among emerging retail centers, in the framework of these differential opportunities, created the central-place system.

## EMERGENCE OF THE CENTRAL-PLACE SYSTEM
## IN SOUTHWESTERN IOWA UP TO 1960

We are fortunate to have data for a long period of southwest Iowa's history, and it will be possible to tell the story in detail of the emergence of the central-place system, gradually becoming more specific about the area and more precise about the ideas and terms to be used subsequently. Such a study will be rewarding, for the story must have repeated itself many times as the frontier expanded westward. Thus, Figures 1.3 to 1.8 contain only those features essential to the narrative. They cover the area seen in Figure 1.2 east of the bluffs overlooking the Missouri River, so that all centers, except Glenwood and Omaha–Council Bluffs, ultimately appear.

Although traders, agents, and missionaries had been in the area prior to 1846, the first white settlers did not arrive until the land was ceded to the United States by the Pottawattamie Indians in June of that year. The first settlers were Mormons, who established the trail west from Des Moines to what is now Council Bluffs. They created Omaha as their 1846–1847 winter quarters. When Brigham Young pushed further west, many of the Mormons remained in the area and established the first farms. In 1852 about half the Mormons in the area answered his call and left to join Young in Utah, but the other half remained in the area, forming the Reformed Mormon Church. Other white settlers also arrived in the period from 1846 to 1851. These pioneer families provided most of their own needs. The first land plowed for farms was close to the woodlands which banded the area from north to south. These families were not completely self-sufficient. In the early years many of them obtained corn and other necessities by traveling 100 miles south to St. Joseph, Missouri, or back east to Des Moines. Stores were built in Council Bluffs from 1847 to 1849 to cater to the increasing flow of westward migrants, and after 1849 there was rapid growth in Council Bluffs and Omaha as gold seekers streamed towards California. The first center serving the pioneer farmers was constructed in 1851—a general store selling dry goods and groceries. By 1868, on the eve of the opening of the railroads, a rudimentary set of centers had developed (Figure 1.3). The woodland locations mirror the settlement patterns of the pioneers and provide a good example of the first principle of central-place location: *consumer orientation* of retail facilities. Centers conform in their spatial pattern to that of consumers because only those located centrally can attract trade from consumers eager to satisfy their needs and, simultaneously, to economize on the cost of travel.

Often, in the early years, several stores would be established within a mile or so of one another, each providing approximately the same goods and services. Competition would be intense, and success was often based upon the acquisition of some additional attribute that enhanced centrality. All centers that survived were the sites of grist mills, which were basic points of focus for the pioneer economy. Perhaps the most important additional factor determining survival of a center was designation as the county seat; political centrality provided added reasons for farmers to visit a particular center rather than another. Iranistan, Indiantown, and Lewis were founded in 1853 and 1854 within a mile of each other, but the first two were abandoned when Lewis was designated as Cass County

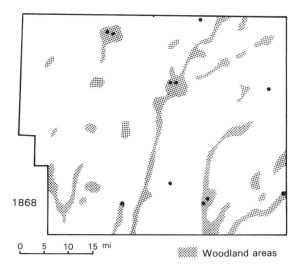

1868

0   5   10   15 mi

▓▓ Woodland areas

**Figure 1.3**  Rudimentary pattern of centers of 1868.

seat. Similarly, Frankfort flourished as the county seat from 1855 to 1865, but was deserted after the seat of Montgomery County was transferred in 1865.

The pioneer rural economy of the first quarter-century of settlement was transformed by the completion of railroads to Council Bluffs in 1868 and 1869. Railroads provided the area with access to the market economy of the nation, and the railroad stations were the collection and distribution centers through which the connections were maintained. Farmers began to specialize, using the railroad to ship their products to eastern markets. Other entrepreneurs were sensitive to the changes in farmers' behavior. Centers, built in anticipation of the railroad, competed for railroad stations because of the centrality to farmers that the stations would provide. It was the railroad officials who most clearly saw the advantages a center would have with the addition of a railroad station. Many of these officials were active in the promotion of centers, and since they determined the precise location of stations, they were all too often the ones who profited most. Atlantic and Red Oak were both built in this way. Other centers in the vicinity of centers with railroads were abandoned as businesses transferred their activities closer to the stations. Thus, Grove City vanished after the railroad's benefits accrued to Atlantic. Size differences emerged among the station centers when some were designated county seats and when others added processing activities to their collection and distribution functions. By 1879 the system of centers was almost completely railroad-oriented. (In Figure 1.4, as in Figures 1.5, 1.6, and 1.7, the different dot sizes identify towns with 1, 2–4, 5–9, and more than 10 grocery and clothing stores.) The most densely settled areas followed the railroads, and gaps in the pattern of centers corresponded to gaps in the settlement pattern caused by inaccessibility to the railroads.

After 1879 the settlement pattern filled in as more settlers came to the area,

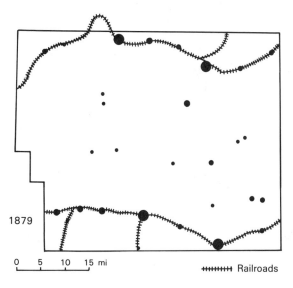

1879

0   5   10   15 mi

┼┼┼┼┼┼ Railroads

**Figure 1.4**  Distribution of centers in 1879.

as branch railroad lines were constructed linking the larger main-line towns, and as a system of rural roads emerged linking farms to markets and markets to each other. The number of centers increased as the population expanded and increased and as previously inaccessible interstices between the railroads were filled.

The patterns of 1904 and 1914 are seen in Figures 1.5 and 1.6. Many of the centers created after 1879 were associated with new railroad stations. Griswold, for example, was built at the Atlantic–Red Oak midpoint, and Elliot at the station halfway between Griswold and Red Oak. Wilson vanished when its post office was transferred to Elliot. Lewis was fortunate enough to acquire the Atlantic-Griswold midpoint station. Railroad centers with branch lines radiating from them grow more rapidly than those without. Growth was even more rapid if the center was a county seat.

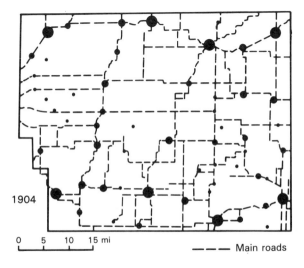

1904

0  5  10  15 mi

－ － － Main roads

**Figure 1.5**  Relative importance of centers in 1904.

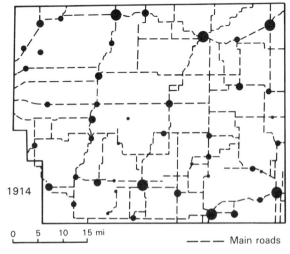

1914

0  5  10  15 mi

－ － － Main roads

**Figure 1.6**  The pattern of centers in 1914.

Yet the period 1904 to 1914 saw the onset of new trends. Although some new centers were established after 1900, the number of centers had actually reached its peak by this time. The story changed from one of different factors shaping expansion, growth, and new center location to one of competition, differential growth, and decline within the existing set of centers. All the existing centers possessed some modicum of centrality in the local economy, as provided by the railroads or the county political system. The location of a grist mill declined in importance. The introduction of rural free delivery after 1900 eliminated many small post offices and made continuation of the stores associated with them unprofitable. Comparison of Figures 1.5 and 1.6 will reveal a thinning of the pattern of centers through elimination of the smaller centers.

Tendencies toward differential growth and the thinning of the center pattern latent before 1914 were released by the coming of the automobile and the paving of roads. Roads paved to make farms more accessible to their local market centers enabled farmers to bypass the smaller centers and patronize larger centers. Use of trucks made possible centralization of railroad collecting and distributing operations in the larger stations, eliminating the centrality provided by stations in smaller towns. A process of differential growth started in which the smallest centers vanished, the intermediate-sized centers suffered a relative decline, and only the larger centers grew. In the period from 1914 to 1956 all the centers that were abandoned lay on inferior roads within nine miles of a major center. The few new centers to be established were located at previously unoccupied paved highway intersections. The centralization process was fostered by increased scale of retailing and the emergence of chain-store operations. Chain-stores preferred larger centers, and bigger stores had to locate in larger centers to be able to reach the larger market area necessary for profitable operations. Figure 1.7 shows the resulting pattern in 1956. The largest centers were those which were able to com-

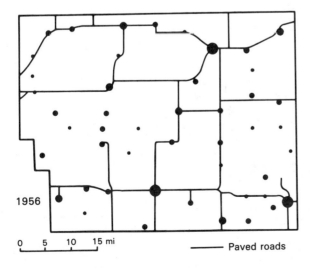

1956

0   5   10   15 mi

———— Paved roads

**Figure 1.7** Relative importance of centers in 1956.

bine all elements of local centrality: first, political (the county seats); second, railroads (the main stations); and third, market attractions (the greatest variety of the largest-scale retail and service facilities, offering a more powerful appeal to consumers than their smaller competitors).

What can be seen in these shifts is the "guiding hand" of a changing market economy. Although a few individuals (for example, the railroad officials) had been able to use prior knowledge to locate successful enterprises before technology changed, many who attempted to establish market centers failed in the competitive process because others were lucky enough to select locations with greater centrality. Figure 1.8 locates the many centers that failed. Over the century just reviewed, the centers that survived were those that best satisfied the rules of consumer-orientation by occupying locations of maximum accessibility. As accessibility changed, so did patterns of survival. And given the large number of alternatives in Figure 1.8, if accessibility had changed in a different way, the pattern of centers would have changed differently too.

The key consideration is consumer-orientation. What do different and cumulative definitions of centrality mean in terms of the behavior of consumers? Evidence is available for 1934, when a detailed survey was made of farmers' shopping habits in a portion of the area shown in Figure 1.20. Responses to the question "Where do you obtain your . . . ?" were recorded on manuscript maps for a great many goods and services; seven of these maps are presented as Figures 1.9a through g. The mapping device used is the *desire-line*, a straight line drawn between farm and market to indicate the farmers' shopping habits.

The first maps (Figures 1.9a and b) exemplify the very local market areas for those goods and services for which consumers were unwilling to travel far, either because of frequency of demand, bulk of the commodity, or the scale of the social community being served. Later maps (Figures 1.9c through g) show

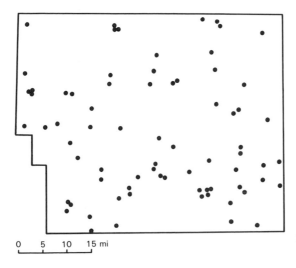

0   5   10   15 mi

**Figure 1.8** Centers that failed between 1851 and 1856.

how centers with superior centrality extend their market areas by capturing the trade of surrounding smaller centers for different goods and services. These are the goods and services that must be provided at greater scale if the businesses providing them are to be profitable, and these are goods and services for which consumers are willing to travel longer distances. Thus, in Figures 1.9e and f only the cities (county seats), with their many cumulative advantages, have significant market areas, and in Figure 1.9g even they defer to the regional capitals of Omaha–Council Bluffs to the west and Des Moines to the east when consumers seek a daily newspaper.

Several facts are notable about the successions of market areas. First, they seldom overlap, except in a limited, peripheral "zone of indifference," so that consumers appear to be making systematic choices of the centers offering the goods they need. (Generally consumers chose the closest center, although in Figure 1.9c, for example, the larger places with greater cumulative accessibility draw in consumers from longer distances.) Second, centers are, indeed, close to the geometric centers of their respective market areas. Third, small centers perform only a few limited-scale activities, whereas large centers perform a range of activities and serve a variety of areas of different sizes. If a *system* is defined as an entity comprising interacting interdependent elements, then we certainly seem to be dealing with "central-place system" of markets, consumers, and the multiple interactions and interdependencies among them. (Note that synonyms are often used for the term "market area," namely, trade area, service area, hinterland, or complementary region.)

## SOUTHWESTERN IOWA'S CENTRAL-PLACE SYSTEM IN 1960

The features of this central-place system must now be spelled out more rigorously, making use of many kinds of interlocking data collected in 1960. These data include information on the retail and service activities performed by the centers, information about their market areas, and data concerning consumer shopping and travel behavior. The area covered is slightly smaller than that for the 1934 and 1956 studies (compare Figures 1.2, 1.9, and 1.10). Although surveys were made of the kinds of retail and service business provided by all the centers shown in Figure 1.10, and although sample studies were conducted of the market areas of businesses in each of them, limitations of time and funding dictated that interviews of farmers and urban residents about their shopping habits and preferences be restricted to the area that has been shaded in Figure 1.10.

A 10 percent random spatial sample of the farmers and a 5 percent random spatial sample of the urban households in the area were asked about the centers from which they obtained many different kinds of goods and services. Four of these goods and services have been selected for presentation here: clothing, furniture, dry cleaning, and food. Separate maps are presented for shopping habits of the urban and rural residents; see Figures 1.12 through 1.19. Figure 1.11 is a

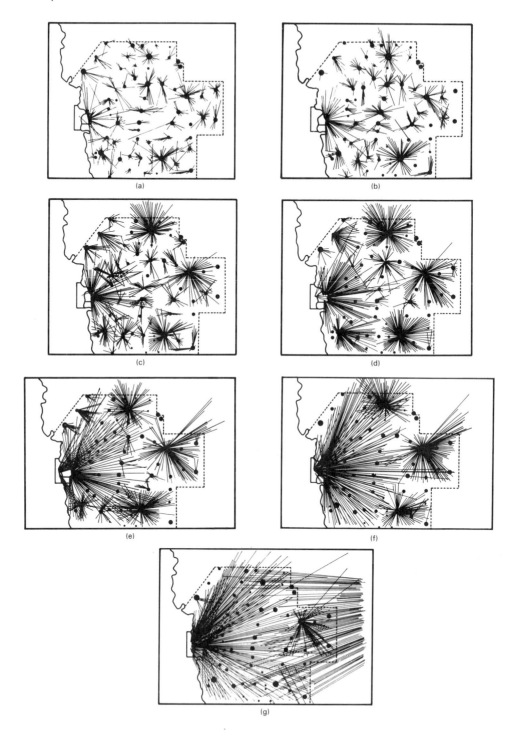

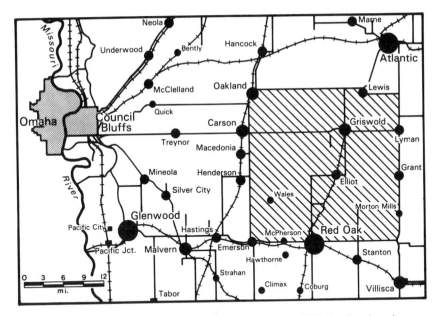

**Figure 1.10**   The area studied by Berry's research team in 1960. Retail and service businesses were inventoried in all the centers shown. The shaded portion is that segment of the total study area within which farmers and urban residents were interviewed about their shopping habits. It is this segment that is highlighted in Figures 1.12 through 1.19.

legend of the cartographic conventions used in these maps and the map in Figure 1.10. Desire-lines depict farmers' center choices. Centers are scaled into five sizes (hamlet, village, town, city, and the regional capital), corresponding to the levels of the central-place hierarchy. Preferences of urban residents are shown by "wheels." If the commodity is purchased by one of the sample respondents in his or her center of residence, a spoke is added to the wheel. If another central place is visited, an arrow is shown from one wheel to another.

The purpose of this series of maps is the following: first, to show the successive parceling of the area into a "hierarchy of central places"; second, to show the "levels" of the hierarchy; third, to examine the size of market areas and the nature of market-area boundaries for each of these levels; and fourth, to explore the locations of lower-level centers relative to the locations of higher-level centers and their market areas. These four features of central-place systems provide a

**Figure 1.9**   (a) Where farmers went to church in 1934. (b) Grocery stores' market areas in 1934. (c) Patronage of physicians in 1934. (d) Where farmers went for legal advice in 1934. (e) Centers visited to purchase women's coats and dresses in 1934. (f) Hospital service areas in 1934. (g) Which center's daily newspapers were read by farmers in 1934.

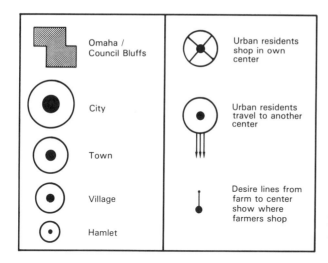

**Figure 1.11** Cartographic conventions and symbols used in Figures 1.12 to 1.19.

basic organizing scheme for understanding the geography of retail and service business.

Refer back to Figure 1.10. It shows several dot sizes corresponding to the levels of the central-place hierarchy. The *villages* of Elliot, Lewis, and Stanton, for example, had populations of 459, 501, and 514, respectively, in 1960. In them were found, respectively, 26, 24, and 21 different types of retail and service business, and 42, 43, and 28 different establishments. (The difference between establishments and business types is a simple one. A village may have several gas stations. This is one business type but several establishments.) Villages had a maximum "reach" of over 5 miles—this was the maximum distance consumers traveled to villages—involving a maximum market area of approximately 90 square miles. Within this area they supplied another 500 to 600 people, so that the total population served was 1100 to 1200. This maximum reach of a village is equivalent to the *real range* of a good or service provided by the village. (This concept is discussed in Chapter 3.) Examples of the activities locating in each of the villages are the following: grocery store, gas station, bar, restaurant, post office, farm elevator, and church.

*Towns* such as Griswold, Villisca, or Oakland formed the next level of the hierarchy. They had populations of 1207, 1340, and 1690, respectively. These towns provided, respectively, 50, 43, and 49 different kinds of business with 102, 90, and 97 business establishments. Total taxable sales in 1960 were $2 million to $2.5 million. Their maximum reach extended outward to 10 miles and comprised a market area of 300 square miles containing an additional 2500 to 3500 consumers, for a total of 4000 to 4200 people served. In addition to the business activities of the villages, they provided others, such as: hardware store, furniture and appliance store, complete drug store, doctor, dentist, dry cleaners, bank, insurance agent, and funeral parlor. These activities could not be provided profitably in the villages, whose shorter reach encompasses too few consumers. They therefore are said to have greater "conditions of entry" or "threshold requirements" than the activities locating in the villages, or to be a "higher level" than those provided by the villages.

The third level was occupied by *cities* such as Atlantic and Red Oak. These had populations of 6890 and 6421, respectively. There were, respectively, 92 and 90 kinds of business, and 411 and 312 establishments. The cities had maximum reaches of 20 miles with market areas of 1000 square miles containing more than 20,000 additional consumers. The total population served approached 30,000. Sales in 1960 were $16 million in Atlantic and $14 million in Red Oak. In addition to the activities provided by the towns and villages, the cities offered others such as: county government offices, jewelry stores, shoe stores, clothing stores, specialized stores, junior department stores, florists, liquor stores, pharmacies, movie theatres, newspaper publishers, new and used auto dealerships, and auto accessory stores.

Two other levels of central place are noted on the illustration: hamlets and the regional capital. The *hamlets* had less than 100 population, usually only one or two stores, such as a general store, a farm elevator, a gas station, a roadside restaurant, or a bulk fuel depot. The *regional capital* of Omaha–Council Bluffs reached out for almost 40 miles on the Iowa side of the Missouri River, to an area containing more than 100,000 people. (Within this area those to the north preferred Council Bluffs, but those to the south, who could reach Omaha without having to pass through Council Bluffs, preferred the larger city, Omaha, although there were no differences in the eastward reach between the two.) Sales in Council Bluffs alone approached $70 million in 1960. There were over 1100 retail and service establishments, including an array of department stores and specialty shops, professional services, and cultural facilities.

These are the levels of the hierarchy. Figures 1.12 through 1.19 reveal how they interlock in a *spatial system*, and Table 1.1 shows how they relate in an accumulative fashion. Figures 1.12 and 1.13 show how the two county seats, Red Oak and Atlantic, and the regional capital attracted clothing customers from surrounding areas. The residents of the different central places showed clear and

**TABLE 1.1**  STEPS OF THE HIERARCHY

| Level of goods and services provided by center | Level of center | | | | |
|---|---|---|---|---|---|
| | Hamlet | Village | Town | Small city | Regional capital |
| Lowest | * | * | * | * | * |
| 2 | | * | * | * | * |
| 3 | | | * | * | * |
| 4 | | | | * | * |
| 5 | | | | | * |

* Indicates that a center provides this group of functions.

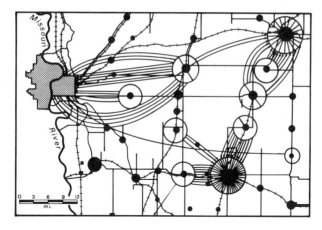

**Figure 1.12** Where the urban residents bought their clothing in 1960.

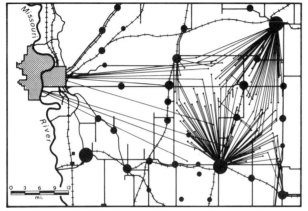

**Figure 1.13** Where the farmers bought their clothing in 1960.

mutually exclusive preferences, so that there is no difficulty in identifying the market areas dominated by each central place (Figure 1.12). Much the same can be said of the rural residents. Within the market areas traced out on the map of urban shopping habits, the farmers made the same clear choices (Figure 1.13). There was only a little crossing over along the market-area boundaries. Along the boundaries, farmers said that they visited both centers, indicating that market-area boundaries trace out real lines of "indifference in choice," the geographic equivalent of the economist's "indifference curves."

Two final points should be noted: First, the regional capital drew consumers from somewhat further than the cities (county seats); and, second, most towns, villages, and hamlets did not have clothing stores because their maximum market areas embraced too few customers for this type of store to be profitable. In Figure 1.13 one or two trips to smaller centers to purchase clothing are recorded. These all involve older people who bought work clothes sold by variety or general stores.

What happens to consumer behavior when the reach of the smaller towns is sufficient to support a store? Figures 1.14 and 1.15 provide the answer. Figures 1.14 and 1.12 are identical, except that Griswold consumers shop in their own town for furniture. In Figure 1.15, Griswold is seen to attract farmers at the expense of both Atlantic and Red Oak. And to the southeast, Villisca does the same at the expense of Red Oak (in the interview area) and Corning (not in the study area map of 1960).

Drawing power for furniture sales is again related to size. First, the drawing power of Omaha–Council Bluffs is greatest. The variety and scale of offerings in Omaha–Council Bluffs is powerful enough to override towns such as Oakland, which draw in some consumers although they are unable to secure the more exclusive trade area of Griswold or Villisca. Second, the county seats of Atlantic and Red Oak have smaller market areas for furniture than for clothing because a merchant in Griswold, located on the "watershed" between their market areas, was able to attract by aggressive merchandising and competitive prices enough of the local farmers in that watershed zone to make the selling of furniture prof-

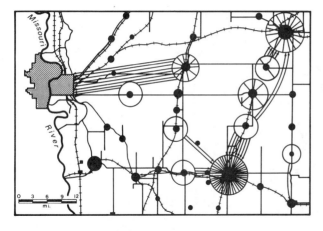

**Figure 1.14** Furniture stores preferred by urban residents in 1960.

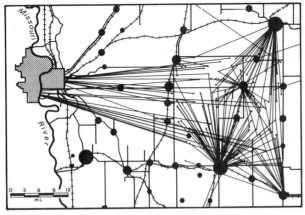

**Figure 1.15** Furniture stores preferred by farmers in 1960.

itable. And third, the towns of Griswold and Villisca now appear as central places, but with the lowest drawing power.

Dry cleaning is also an activity that can be supported by the intermediate-sized towns. Thus Figure 1.16 is a repetition of Figure 1.14, except for one or two long-distance arrows related to a weekly dry-cleaning pick-up service operating out of Glenwood. In fact, if *any* of the activities listed earlier as being provided by the towns had been selected, the maps would have been *identical.* This is so because *the levels of the central-place hierarchy are the result of the common behavior of consumers with respect to goods and services of the same type.* Similarly, the types of businesses listed along with the description of the cities (county seats) would have produced maps identical to Figures 1.12 and 1.13.

One difference is to be noted between Figures 1.15 and 1.17, however. The market areas of Atlantic, Red Oak, and Griswold are unchanged, but the reach of the regional capital, Omaha–Council Bluffs, into the western part of the interview area has been replaced by exclusive market areas of towns such as Oakland. The difference stems from the nature of the two goods, furniture and dry

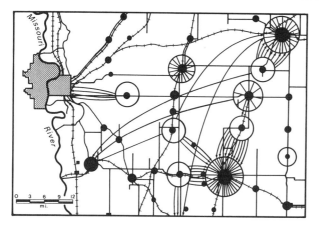

**Figure 1.16**  Dry cleaners used by residents in 1960.

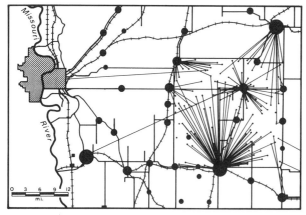

**Figure 1.17**  Dry cleaners used by farmers in 1960.

cleaning. The former is demanded infrequently, and people like to do comparison shopping in stores which offer great variety. Furniture is a "shopping good." Dry cleaning, on the other hand, is a "convenience service," needed frequently and not requiring comparison buying. The regional capital is able to extend its reach to 40 miles for shopping goods, but for convenience goods the advantages of proximity afforded by such towns as Oakland and Carson are critical to their success, and these towns are able to attract enough consumers to make dry cleaning a profitable venture.

Figures 1.18 and 1.19 show purchasing patterns for foodstuffs, a village-level good. Villages such as Lewis, Elliot, Emerson, and Stanton, located on the watersheds of the market areas described earlier for higher order goods, are all able to reach out for consumers and, by offering the advantages of proximity, attract enough of them to make grocery stores profitable. Note, also, that urban residents most often prefer to shop for groceries in the center in which they live (Figure 1.18).

Figure 1.19 shows, in addition, that the reach into rural areas of city-level

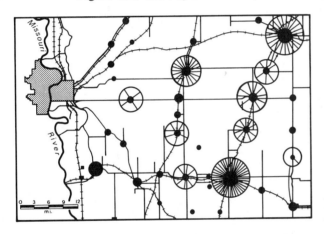

**Figure 1.18**  Travel to purchase groceries in 1960: urban residents.

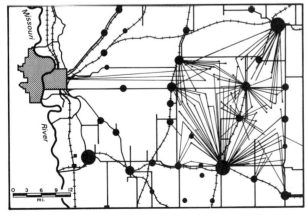

**Figure 1.19**  Travel to purchase groceries in 1960: farmers.

centers is a function of size (the economies of scale and technology) that comes with the larger and more sophisticated food stores. Villages attract fewer farmers over shorter distances than do towns, and towns, in turn, have shorter reaches than county seats. This corresponds neatly to the historical view that the cumulative advantages of the different places determine their importance as foci for rural life. Careful examination of Figure 1.19 will also show the towns to have about the same market areas as in Figures 1.15 and 1.17, indicating that the villages have established market areas largely at the expense of the county seats.

## A CENTRAL-PLACE HIERARCHY AS A SPATIAL SYSTEM

What may be concluded from the foregoing? First, a central-place hierarchy is composed of distinct levels of centers providing particular groups of goods and services to distinct market areas. Second, the interdependent spatial patterns of centers (of both the same and different levels) and the interlocking market areas of goods and services of related levels weld the hierarchy into a central-place system. Central-place theory is of great importance since it both explains and predicts these patterns and relationships.

To review these patterns and relationships: Towns are located midway between the cities (county seats), and villages midway between towns and cities. As one travels along the highways between two cities, a very regular progression of centers is encountered: city, village, town, village, city—all approximately evenly spaced (actually, the villages are likely to be a little closer to the towns than they are to the cities).

At the level of goods and services appearing first in villages (i.e., those activities which can be performed profitably serving the consumers within the maximum reach of villages), centers of all levels have market areas. Market areas of villages are smaller than those of towns and cities. The market-area boundaries lie approximately 5 miles from the village centers, 8 miles from the town centers, and 10 to 15 miles from the city centers. The villages no longer have market areas when the next level of activities is examined, however, because they attract too few people to satisfy the minimum profitable market size (threshold requirements) of furniture stores or dry cleaners. The people who shop for groceries in the villages turn to the nearest cities (county seats) so that market areas of towns still reach out 8 miles whereas those of the county seats reach out 15 miles and more. The market areas of regional capitals reach out 30 miles for convenience services and 40 miles for shopping goods of the town level. Finally, the towns no longer participate in the sales of such commodities as clothing, shoes, and jewelry; their reach is too small to satisfy the conditions of entry of retail businesses of that kind. The cities and the regional capital reach out to embrace the market areas of the towns, to distances of 20 miles and 40 miles, respectively.

Are the market areas of the cities (county seats) ever captured by the regional capital in the provision of yet higher-level goods or services? Figure 1.9g shows how, in 1934, Omaha–Council Bluffs from the west and Des Moines from the east reached across the study area to sell their daily newspapers. At that time, Atlantic remained the only county seat to publish a daily newspaper, although other county seats did publish biweeklies or weeklies.

The levels thus proceed upwards, and for the United States as a whole, the complete hierarchy includes the hamlet, village, town, city (county seat), regional capital, and national metropolis (Borchert and Adams, 1963). Sizes of the centers at each level vary from one part of the country to another, and the size characteristics of the centers are disturbed by the presence of manufacturing and other nondistributive activities. (These disturbances, as we shall see later, are *relatively* greater for the smaller centers in such situations.) However, from the Iowan base, the sequence of population sizes was, in 1960, approximately 100, 500, 1500, 6000, 60,000, and over 250,000 persons.

These are, of course, statistics that are a quarter-century old. The numbers are different today because populations, incomes, accessibility, retailing technology, and development styles have continued to evolve. Such changes offer many opportunities for research into the ways market centers and retail locations adjust to maintain balance with population distribution, purchasing power, and travel patterns. In conducting such research, an understanding of the principles that have guided past changes is critical, for it is these principles that reveal the underlying forces guiding contemporary shifts. These principles are the concern of the subsequent chapters.

## REFERENCES

BELSHAW, C. S. (1965) *Traditional Exchange and Modern Markets*. Englewood Cliffs, N.J.: Prentice-Hall, Inc.

BERRY, B. J. L. (1962) *Comparative Studies of Central-Place Systems*. Washington, D.C.: Office of Naval Research, Geography Branch.

BERRY, B. J. L. (1963) *Commercial Structure and Commercial Blight*. Chicago: University of Chicago.

BERRY, B. J. L. (1965) *Metropolitan Planning Guidelines: Commercial Structure*. Chicago: Northeastern Illinois Planning Commission.

BORCHERT, J. R., and R. B. ADAMS (1963) *Trade Centers and Tributary Areas of the Upper Midwest*. Minneapolis, Minn.: University of Minnesota.

BUREAU OF BUSINESS AND ECONOMIC RESEARCH (1934) *Community Service Survey Maps*. Iowa City, Iowa: University of Iowa.

CLAVAL, P. (1962) *Géographie Générale des Marchés*. Paris: Les Belles Lettres.

DUNCAN, O. D. (1960) *Metropolis and Region*. Baltimore, Md.: Johns Hopkins University.

LASKA, J. A., JR. (1958) "The Development of the Pattern of Retail Trade Centers in a Selected Area of Southwestern Iowa." Chicago: University of Chicago. Unpublished M.A. Thesis.

# 2

# Some Properties of Central-Place Hierarchies

In Chapter 1 it was established that retail and service businesses cluster into levels based upon the sizes of market areas required for profitable operation. It was also seen that centers form levels based upon the economic reach provided by their centrality and that the levels of services and levels of centers interlock in a spatial system (the central-place hierarchy). In reaching those conclusions, however, we have only begun to develop a picture of the geography of retail and service business. There are many features of the system still to be explored. How, for example, does this system vary from one part of the United States to another? How does it undergo changes in form at high population densities within cities? It is these systematic variations that are the concern of this chapter: the organization of retail activity and of central places across the larger landscape in terms of systematic regularities.

## VARIATIONS IN MARKET AREAS

For all the market areas of all the goods and services presented in Figures 1.12 to 1.19, we calculated the total area served by each center and the total population residing in that area. These numbers were used to plot points in a graph, noting whether the central place in question was a village, town, city, or regional capital. For any given center, there are several points in the graph, one for each good or service for which the market area was calculated. The scatter diagram shown in

Figure 2.1 resulted. Since the graph has a logarithmic scale on both axes, straight lines drawn upward to the right at an angle of 45° trace out equal population densities (see Figure 2.8 for the addition of the density scale).

Note in Figure 2.1 how the set of points slopes upward, tracing out the average level of population density of southwestern Iowa. Distinct parts of the swarm, however, are occupied by centers of each level in lines of points inclined in excess of 45°. Larger lower-density market areas are near the top of each line, and smaller higher-density market areas are below each line. This pattern is created because rural population densities decline with distance from centers; and, therefore, the larger the market area, the lower the average population density of the area, other things being equal.

Examine the points marked "V". Each is the market area of a village-level center for some good or service. The largest area is nearly 90 square miles; this is the maximum "reach" of a center of this level. Similarly, the maximum reach of towns ("T" in the graph) is a 300-square-mile market area and that of the cities ("C" in the graph) is over 1000 square miles. In other words, the largest village-level market area has a radius of a little over 5 miles. The market-area radius of towns is approximately 10 miles for any kind of good or service provided at this level of the hierarchy. The market-area radius for cities is about 20 miles.

Figure 2.2 adds another perspective. It repeats the scatter of points in Figure

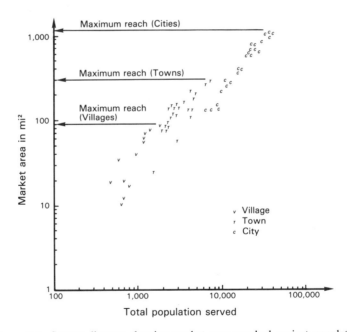

**Figure 2.1**  Scatter diagram showing market area graphed against population served in order to show levels of the hierarchy.

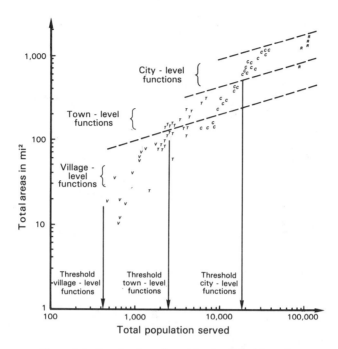

**Figure 2.2**    Levels of goods and levels of the hierarchy.

2.1, but separates the market areas of the lowest-level functions (such as groceries) provided by villages, towns, and cities from the next level of activities (such as dry cleaning) provided by the towns and cities, but not by the villages. These, in turn, are separated from the highest-level activities (such as clothing stores) provided only by the small cities and by the regional capital. The graph enables the *threshold* or minimum-sized market area for each level of function to be identified: about 425 people for village-level activities; 2500 for town-level functions; and close to 20,000 for city-level functions.

The market areas of higher-level centers are greater than those of lower-level centers for the same type of good or service, reflective of economies of scale and the greater range of style and quality of merchandise that can be offered to a larger clientele. This may also be noted in Figure 2.3. A point is plotted for each farmer, showing (for trips to buy food and clothing) how the maximum distance that consumers travel depends upon the level of the hierarchy visited. Level in the hierarchy is indexed in the graph by the number of "central functions" (i.e., the number of different kinds of retail and service businesses) provided. Therefore, a dot plotted for each farmer interviewed identifies the level of center visited and the distance traveled to obtain a particular function. The maximum distance traveled to a center of a given level is called the *real range* of a function.

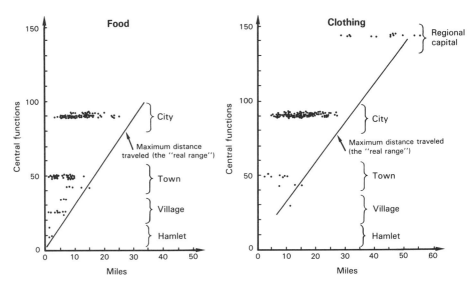

**Figure 2.3**  Real ranges of food and clothing at different levels of the hierarchy.

It will be seen that this real range of a function varies according to the level of center from which it is obtained. Thus, the real range of food stores is just over 5 miles for villages but about 10 miles for towns. Similarly, the real range of clothing stores is just over 10 miles for towns but well over 20 miles for cities. The diagonal line in Figure 2.3 represents an "envelope" curve that traces out variations in the real range (the maximum distances traveled to centers) for different levels of the hierarchy.

Total consumer travel to and from the central places varies in a related way. Data were obtained from the Iowa State Highway Commission on the point of origin and destination of automobiles traveling in the study area during an average summer day in 1960. Data were also obtained for the number of miles of travel involved. Figures 2.4 and 2.5 summarize the evidence. Atlantic was the point of arrival for 1912 trips and the point of departure for 1994. The vehicle-miles of travel involved were 46,900 for vehicles arriving in Atlantic and 44,600 for vehicles departing, or a total in excess of 90,000. For the town of Villisca the figures were: trips in, 433; trips out, 422; vehicle-miles in, 8010; out, 8490. For villages, inbound and outbound trips averaged 200, with perhaps 2500 vehicle-miles of total travel each way. Note in both Figure 2.4 and Figure 2.5 the following: First, the approximate straight-line (semi-logarithmic) relationships between the trip variables and central functions; and second, the clusters of points relating to the levels of the hierarchy. Use will be made later of the statement inserted on Figure 2.4 to the effect that the levels of the hierarchy fall at approximately 24, 48, and 96 functions, or $24 \times 2^0$, $24 \times 2^1$, and $24 \times 2^2$.

The scope of the investigation is now enlarged to include two study areas in South Dakota (Figures 2.6 and 2.7) and the central city and suburbs of Chicago.

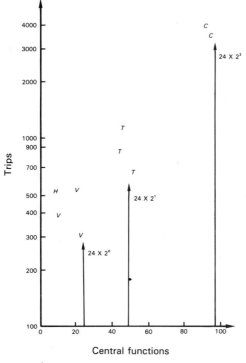

**Figure 2.4** Relation between total inbound and outbound trips and the size of center.

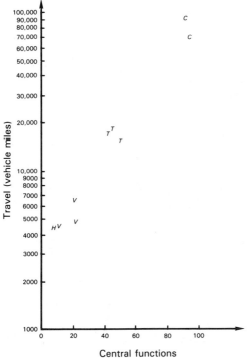

**Figure 2.5** Relation between total vehicle-miles of travel and size of center.

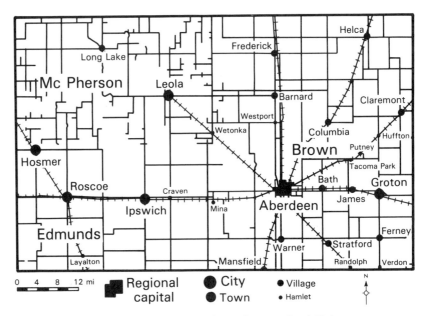

**Figure 2.6**   The study area in northeastern South Dakota.

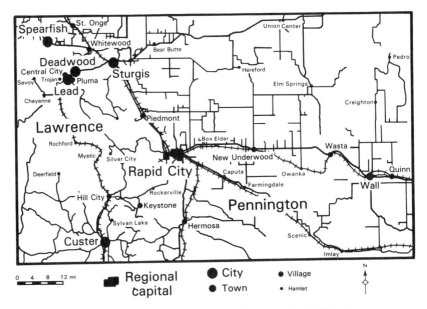

**Figure 2.7**   The study area in southwestern South Dakota.

Market areas were obtained by field survey in each of these areas and added to the Iowa pattern to produce Figure 2.8. Note the systematic increase of trade-area size with decreasing population densities. The only irregularities are in south-

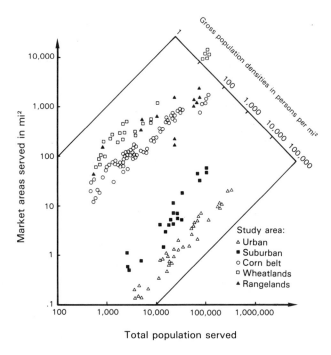

**Figure 2.8**  Market areas expand as population densities drop.

western South Dakota, which includes not only rangeland but also higher-density mining and recreational areas in the Black Hills. In this area there are clusters of urban centers amidst the broken terrain, supported by activities other than those of central places.

If the levels of the hierarchy are added, as in Figure 2.9, other important features emerge. First, the different levels of the central-place hierarchy in each of the rural areas and the levels of a hierarchy of business centers within the Chicago metropolitan area were so consistent that straight lines could be drawn linking the upper limits of the points. These points correspond to similar levels under different conditions of population density. Corresponding to the differentiation of centers into villages, towns, and cities in rural areas is a differentiation of urban shopping facilities into street-corner convenience clusters, neighborhood, community, and regional shopping centers.

If the effects of decreases in population density were simply to "stretch out" the central-place hierarchy in a consistent manner—if one could map the pattern of centers in the city on a rubber sheet, stretch it out, and call it "Iowa"—Figure 2.9 would be less interesting than it is. If this were the case the breaks between levels of centers would be vertical straight lines, keeping populations of the market

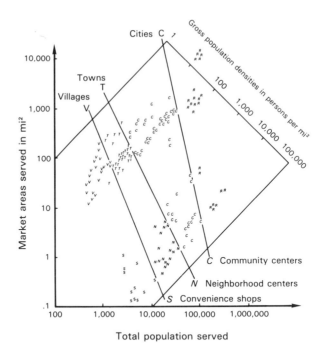

**Figure 2.9**   Relationship of levels of the hierarchy to levels of density: As densities decline, centers of a given level serve fewer people.

areas constant and allowing only the square mileage of the market areas to increase or decrease proportionately with density shifts. But this is not so; the lines separating levels slope backward to the left, indicating that market areas increase in size as densities drop, but not as fast as the densities decline. Therefore, the populations that are servved within the range of centers of each level of the hierarchy decrease systematically. Correspondingly, functions with the greatest threshold requirements (minimum numbers of consumers to guarantee profitability) have to move up a level in the hierarchy to be able to reach a population of sufficient size to guarantee economic survival. As a result, populations of central places fall because the economic base of the market towns is eroded by loss of higher-threshold stores to larger centers, and there are therefore fewer jobs to support the center populations.

Figure 2.10 shows (by numbers scaled along the lines marking upper limits of levels) how the populations of centers at each level decline with densities. Thus, towns drop from 1600 to 400 population, villages from 700 to 50, and cities from 8000 to 1500. Comparing the functions of centers in Iowa and South Dakota, we found that towns in the latter area, at lower densities of population, could no longer provide the following types of businesses: furniture stores, appliance

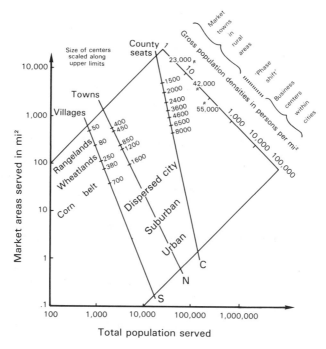

**Figure 2.10**   Populations of centers shown in relation to levels of the hierarchy, to market-area sizes, to total populations served, and to changing population densities.

stores, variety stores, insurance and real-estate brokers, movers and haulers, funeral homes, doctors, and dentists. These moved up to the city level in the hierarchy. Similarly, the simplest facilities of local government, farm implement dealers, and barber and beauty shops were no longer found in the villages but moved or centralized to the towns.

The reason for this upward shift of functions to centers at higher levels of the hierarchy as population densities drop is as follows. To maintain a given array of activities, market areas must increase in size in direct proportion to the decrease in population densities. Furthermore, the maximum distance consumers travel to the center must increase in similar proportion to the density decline. Evidently consumers travel further where densities are lower, for movement will generally be easier where congestion is less, so that the reach of centers does increase. The change is less than proportionate to the fall in densities, however, so that increasing market-area size is accompanied by decreasing market-area populations. The centers' functions must adjust to the declining numbers of consumers reached within these market areas of increasing radius; the only way to do this is to move to higher-level centers serving wider regions. Similarly, at very high densities, congestion will not completely localize consumer movements, so that business centers of any given level within cities reach more consumers and are functionally more complex than their rural counterparts.

In Figure 2.4 it was noted that the progression of central functions in the villages, towns, and cities of Iowa was approximately 24, 48, and 96. This could also be written as $24 \times 2^0$, $24 \times 2^1$, $24 \times 2^2$, where the 0, 1, and 2 are exponents describing the level of centers in the hierarchy (less 1), beginning with level 1 for the villages and proceeding upward. This is an example of the mathematical regularity that accompanies the geometric regularity of central-place hierarchies, and it forms the basis for the modern theories discussed in Chapter 4.

The Aberdeen region of South Dakota displays a similar mathematical progression: approximately 15, 30, and 60, or $15 \times 2^0$, $15 \times 2^1$, and $15 \times 2^2$. It appears that a more general expression for the progression of central functions (business types) at the different levels of the hierarchy is $\eta 2^{m-1}$ where $m$ is the level of the hierarchy and $\eta$ is a parameter that varies from area to area. Since we have also noted the "slippage" of the functions of centers as population densities drop, we must conclude that $\eta$ varies with population densities, indicating that businesses present at lower levels of the hierarchy have moved up to the next level of the hierarchy in areas with lower densities. Even more generally, we may write the expression as $\eta \rho^{m-1}$ where $\rho$ is a second parameter. A hypothesis that might be explored is whether $\rho$ takes on values that relate to the spatial arrangement of centers (for example, 2 or 4 on a rectangular lattice, or 3, 4, or 7 on a triangular lattice). More on this question will be found in Chapters 3 and 4.

## CORRELATES OF CENTER SIZE

The foregoing implies that if the reaches of centers were to increase proportionately to the declines in population density, the upward shift of higher-threshold activities would be unnecessary. This suggests that there are some constant correlates of center size; for example, that a given number of consumers will be served by a given mix and number of retail establishments, and, in turn, that the jobs created by a given number of retail and service businesses will support a given size of center population. Figures 2.11, 2.12, and 2.13 illustrate this point in rural cases. The resident population, number of business types, and number of establishments of each center have been graphed against one another. Figure 2.11 shows that the population of centers is dependent upon the number of different kinds of business that they provide to their market areas; the coefficient of correlation is 0.95. The number of business types indicates level in the hierarchy, and therefore also indexes the degree of centrality. Note how the different study areas all have the same pattern; their points are completely intermixed in the curve. Figure 2.12 shows, for the Iowa case, how total population within the maximum reach of centers varies with the functions performed by those centers,

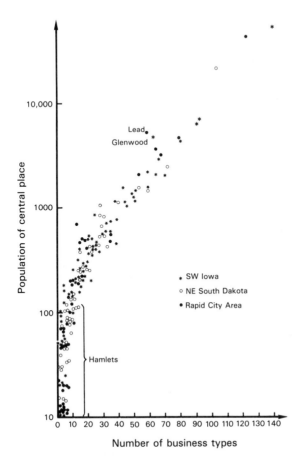

**Figure 2.11**  Populations of central places related to the number of types of business provided. Data for the three rural study areas have been combined in this graph to show the consistencies in the relationship.

reemphasizing the regularity of the progression. The graph contains a point for each center studied, and the separation of the clusters of points reinforces the idea of levels of the hierarchy. Finally, Figure 2.13 states that the total number of retail and service establishments located in a center is a function of center population. It should be seen that a center's population, while supported by its central-place functions, also places demands upon those functions as it seeks to supply its own needs. The responses will be varied. Some stores will just grow in size, others will duplicate identical units, yet others will begin to specialize. In any case, Figure 2.13 shows the rate of growth of establishments to be proportional to the rate of growth of center population. Because both center population and total population served are related in the same manner to types of business (Figures 2.11 and 2.12), the rate of growth of establishment is also proportional to growth of total population served.

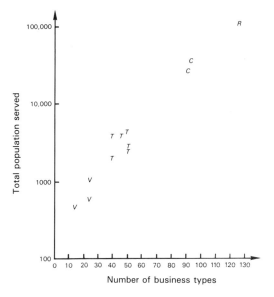

**Figure 2.12**  Relationship between the total population served by central places in southwestern Iowa and the number of types of business provided by the center.

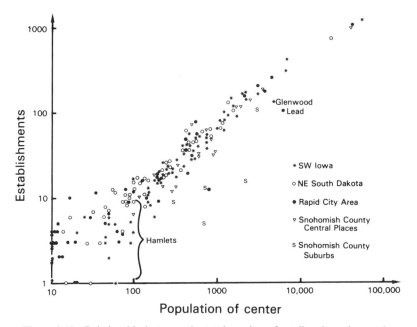

**Figure 2.13**  Relationship between the total number of retail and service establishments in a central place and the center's population. Data for four different study areas are included in the graph.

A few centers deviate from this pattern, however, such as Lead in the Black Hills of South Dakota and Glenwood in Iowa, but the deviations reinforce the principle. These centers perform *specialized functions* in addition to their role as market centers, so their resident populations are greater than would be predicted using either their market-area size or the numbers and types of business located in them. Lead is a mining center, and Glenwood has a state mental institution. If the 1800 residents of that institution were subtracted from Glenwood's reported population in Figure 2.11, then the center would have almost exactly the population which might be expected from its retail and service offerings.

A similar situation exists if a center lies within commuting radius of a larger metropolis, becoming part of the metropolitan labor and housing markets. Such centers become commuting suburbs, which have higher populations than might be predicted from their retail activities, as with the Seattle suburbs in Snohomish County, Washington—identified by an "S" in Figure 2.13.

This leads us to an important conclusion: Central-place principles provide a complete statement of urban location only when urban centers are supported as market centers by the retail and service functions that they provide for surrounding regions (market areas). Wide deviations in urban population from that predicted by marketing geography will result if a center has specialized functions. These functions may be related to the geography of production, for example, if one is dealing with a mining town in a region of primary production, a factory town in the manufacturing belt, a railroad town at a classification yard, or a port in a shipping region. Of course, such specialized functions do support a residential population, which in turn supports retail and service activities within the town. But this retail and service provision is less than in a central place of similar population size because purchases made by the resident population are not matched by those of the residents of a corresponding outlying market area.

## THE URBAN CASE

Figure 2.10 shows that the hierarchy of business centers within cities is consistently related to the hierarchy of market centers in rural areas. The expectation is that, because of higher population densities within cities, centers of comparable level in the hierarchy will be functionally more complex than their rural counterparts.

The urban case differs in significant ways from the rural, however, and the differences increase with increasing size of center. The functions performed by a village in Iowa will group somewhat loosely in a single business area, although a gas station, bulk fuel-oil depot, or church may be located on the outskirts of the settlement. A town in Iowa has a much better defined central business core and may have several additional clusters of business on the main highways at the edges of town, one or more of them catering to highway traffic. Others, such as lumber yards, may include services that demand more space than can be afforded in the central business area. Cities (county seats) such as Atlantic had definite central business districts (CBDs) in 1960, in which the highest-threshold functions were located. Within these CBDs there was structure and pattern, for the different kinds of business sorted themselves out according to the amounts they were willing to pay for the most central location, usually the main highway intersection. Each CBD was therefore characterized by a cone of land value which was highest at the main intersection. Land value declined as centrality declined away from the intersection. In addition, the small cities had peripheral highway-oriented business strips of restaurants, motels, and gas stations, and business "ribbons" along which were located the space-consuming businesses which could not afford CBD sites. Also located in the peripheral areas were service businesses such as plumbing and electrical companies, which did not need proximity to the CBDs. The population of these small cities had grown large enough to make it profitable for enterprising businesses to locate in the several residential neighborhoods and to supply these areas with village-level goods and services, thereby competing with the CBD. The cities showed the first explicit emergence of a hierarchy of business centers within the urban area.

Figure 2.14 gives some indication of how the number of separate business areas varied with the size of centers in Iowa in 1960. In this diagram, a business area is defined as a group of contiguous business establishments or as a single store located beyond reasonable walking distance of another store.

At the city (county seat) level the complexity of business structure within cities increases. The regional capitals had larger and more complex highway-oriented strips and business ribbons and additional types of specialized business

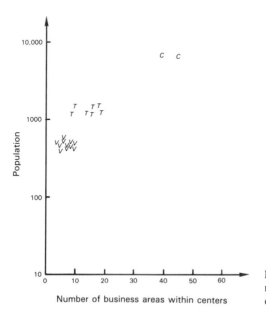

**Figure 2.14** Relationship between number of business areas within centers and the centers' populations.

areas. Their regional functions were provided from their own CBD, but the urban residents obtained lower-level goods from outlying business centers of at least two lower levels.

This successive elaboration culminated within major metropolitan centers like Chicago, in which seven million people spread across nine counties in two states. In 1960, the overall pattern of consumer-orientation of business land use remained unchanged, as indicated by the shaded areas showing nonresidential land in Figure 2.15. However, the structure of business areas had become significantly more complex, as the typology in Figure 2.16 indicates. Figure 2.16 comprises the following:

**A hierarchy of business centers.** Functions such as grocery stores, drug stores, barber shops, variety and clothing stores, and department stores are located here. The pressure for the various functions to cluster arose because customers tended to shop from store to store during a given shopping trip.

**Highway-oriented ribbons.** These are composed of service stations, restaurants, and motels, and they serve demands of customers originating from highway travel.

**Urban arterial commercial developments.** Most of the functions located on arterials enjoy reasonable access to the urban market; but they functioned most efficiently outside the nucleated business centers because of space requirements and the ways in which consumers use them. The establishments in this group were usually associated with special single-purpose trips. Businesses in this group were furniture and appliance stores, automobile repair shops, radio-TV sales and service establishments, and plumbing shops.

**Specialized functional areas.** These areas were characterized by the presence of several related types of establishments, notably dealerships in new and used cars in "automobile rows," and doctors, dentists, and medical technicians in medical office complexes. Such functional areas are held intact by close linkages provided by comparative shopping, economies in advertising in the case of automobile dealers, and referrals and common use of specialists and special services in the case of medical professionals. Most such functional areas required easy accessibility to that segment of the urban market required for their support.

Even this typology fails to capture the real diversity because conventional classifications of business types break down within the metropolis. One cannot speak simply of an automobile repair garage, but must consider explicitly the range of repair service provided. This range of services increases, as does the specialization of shops in different parts of the range, as city size increases. This is equally true for most kinds of business. Within the metropolis, the complex scales of business establishments and the multiple shades of specialization of each must be recognized at the outset. Here in the city a far more complex overlapping and interpenetration of market areas takes place than in the countryside. This has

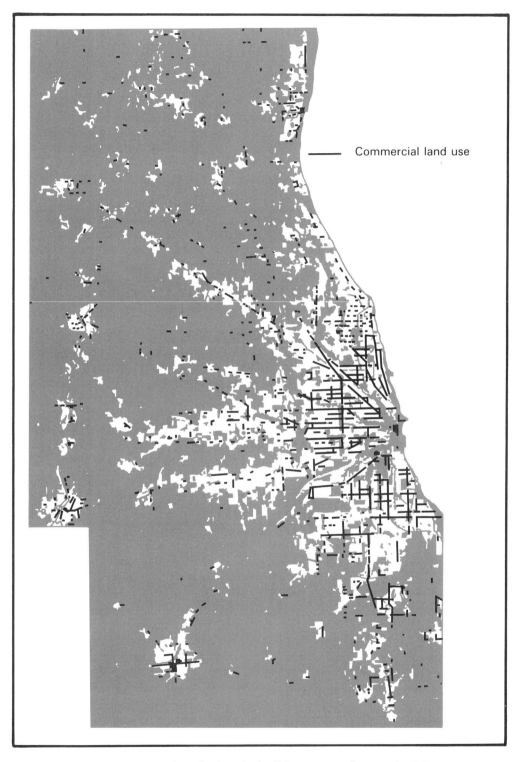

Commercial land use

**Figure 2.15**  Business land use in the Chicago metropolitan area in 1960.

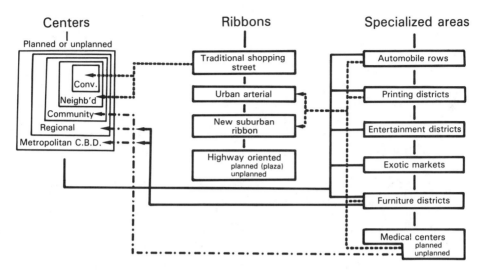

**Figure 2.16**  Typology of business areas within a metropolitan region.

led to the development of somewhat different market analysis models, as will be discussed in Chapter 7.

Chicago's business pattern was typical of American metropolitan areas in 1960. It developed in response to the spread of commuting suburbs across counties in which business was originally provided by a hierarchy of rural market centers and by grist mills which had been built along a string of river towns. Twelve railroads were constructed radiating from Chicago's "Loop," the metropolitan CBD. After the railroads gained access to Loop terminals in the early twentieth century, a fingerlike, rail-commuting suburban development pattern crystallized. The pattern of Chicago was simple: a large central city with 12 radii along which suburbs were strung like beads, their location determined by station locations, out to a distance of 30 miles. Beyond these suburbs was a discontinuous crescent of relatively independent industrial satellites: Waukegan, Elgin, Aurora, Joliet, Chicago Heights, and, in Indiana, steel-making towns such as Gary. The metropolis ended at this crescent in the early part of the century, as it did in 1960. Beyond was open farmland and a central-place hierarchy of cities (county seats), towns, and villages.

Within the satellite crescent each of the railroad axes consisted of a succession of higher-density developments around the railroad stations and lower-density developments along the axes between the stations. Large areas of open space existed between the radii (Figure 2.17). Each of the radii tended to have towns of similar socio-economic status with regard to their residents. Crossing the radii in bands encircling the central city, towns at similar distances from the CBD tended to have similar mixtures of housing types. Those at greater distances were of lower density, with larger lots and fewer apartments. In addition, the kinds of families (in terms of size, ages of family members, and life-style) tended to be similar in the same band. Thus, each small zone of the metropolitan area, comprising towns on a given radial within the same distance band, could be thought of as a "community" of residents with similar income characteristics and lifestyle. The local business center, located by the railroad station, reflected this similarity.

Much of this socio-economic symmetry remains as the underpinning of Chicago's business pattern. As Figures 2.15 and 2.17 indicate, consumer-orientation of business led to a system that crisscrosses the continuously built-up central city, following the section and half-section streets and the spines of the radii. A complete hierarchy of business centers was clearly identifiable in 1960—from street-corner clusters of convenience shops, through neighborhood, community, and regional shopping centers, culminating in the Loop, the metropolitan CBD.

In 1958 the Loop had over 2000 retail stores employing more than 46,000 persons with sales of $700 million. Each of the largest outlying regional shopping centers within the city of Chicago at that time had approximately 250 establishments of more than 70 different kinds employing over 4000 people with sales of almost $90 million. The shopping centers had more than 8000 front feet of space and a ground-floor area of 800,000 square feet. More than 27,000 trips were made to such centers on an average shopping day. The shopping-goods market area of one center within the central city was 15.5 square miles, reaching 350,000 people with an aggregate income exceeding $800 million. Interestingly, its convenience-goods trade area was only 2.1 square miles, reaching 70,000 people with an aggregate income of $90 million. Similarly, community shopping centers had 70 stores of some 36 types, over 100,000 square feet of floor area, 500 employees, and sales of $13 million. They attracted 10,000 trips daily and reached a market area of 40,000 to 50,000 people within the 2 to 3 adjacent square miles.

Suburban centers had similar characteristics. Regional centers performed 80 different functions in 300 establishments, with total center areas of one million square feet (over 500,000 square feet of ground-floor area). Market areas reached 100,000 people. For community centers, comparable data are 40 types of functions and 80 establishments; 400,000 square feet total center area (200,000 square feet of ground-floor area), and 40,000 to 50,000 people reached. The reason why suburban centers had more functions than city centers is that lawyers, accountants, and similar professionals within the city congregated in the Loop. The suburbs, however, at greater distances from the city center, were able to retain the professionals locally.

Minute differences in location within centers make a great deal of difference to sales volumes because of differences in pedestrian traffic. For this reason the retail businesses that cluster in centers compete vigorously to occupy the best possible sites. One result is shown in Figure 2.18. Along Ashland Avenue in Chicago there were two main business intersections in 1960, at 63rd Street and 79th Street. The number of pedestrians dropped off sharply as one moved away from these intersections, so it was essential for retail businesses to have sites as close to the intersections as possible. Competition for these sites led to an increase in their land values. The desirability of sites for business location, as mirrored in

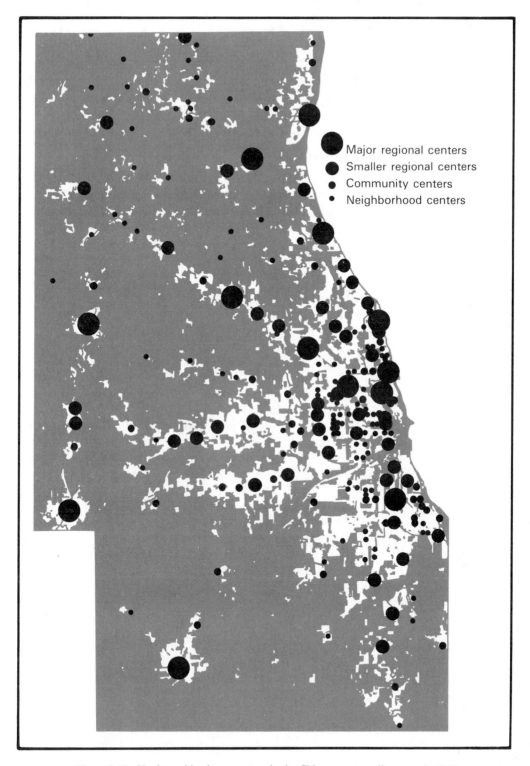

Major regional centers
Smaller regional centers
Community centers
Neighborhood centers

**Figure 2.17** Unplanned business centers in the Chicago metropolitan area in 1960.

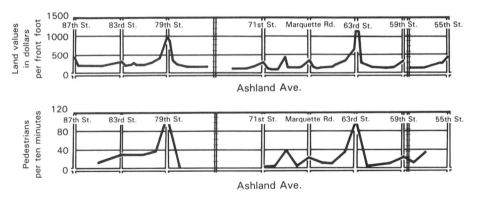

**Figure 2.18**  Relationship of land values and pedestrian counts along Ashland Avenue in Chicago in 1960.

what businesspeople are willing to pay for the land, replicated the traffic pattern of consumers walking along the street.

The land-value profiles for the 63rd and Halsted business center in Chicago in 1960 are shown in Figure 2.19. In this biggest of Chicago's older outlying centers, values at the peak reached $7000 per front foot. At the edge of the intersection area land values dropped to $250 per front foot. (Land values exceeded $40,000 per front foot at State and Madison streets, the central intersection, or "100 percent location," of the Loop.) Lines indicate how the center may be delineated on the basis of land values and separated from surrounding ribbon business uses. With such wide differences in values within centers, businesses sorted themselves out on the basis of need and ability to pay for the most central spot. In 1960 the succession of uses, moving away from the principal intersection of a regional center in Chicago, shows the following: (1) At the core there are stores for apparel accessories, hosiery, candy, shoes, clothes, drugs, jewelry, corsets and lingerie, other miscellaneous clothing, and items found in department stores. (2) In the next zone out from the core were found household appliance stores, bakeries, currency exchanges, motion picture theaters, delicatessens, restaurants, banks, radio and television stores, loan companies, millinery stores, optometrists, gift shops, camera stores, insurance offices, and watch repair stores. (3) At the periphery were found hardware stores, furniture stores, groceries, butchers, liquor stores, sporting goods stores, medical service centers, photographers, real-estate offices, china and glassware shops, drapery stores, music stores, barber and beauty shops, laundromats, and floor covering stores (Garner, 1966).

The distinction is clear. Regional functions of highest threshold were at the core along with those functions whose sales were critically affected by pedestrian volume, for example, candy stores. At the periphery were personal service establishments of the neighborhood level. The intermediate zone contained a mixture of regional- and community-level uses. Rent differences forced large space-

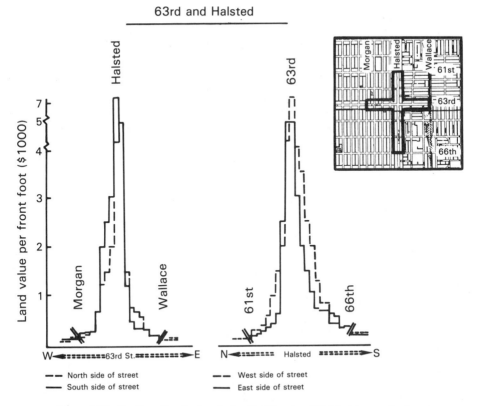

**Figure 2.19**   Profiles of land values in the 63rd Street and Halsted Avenue business center in Chicago in 1960. For other examples see Berry and Tennant (1963).

consumers such as furniture stores to the periphery. In community centers, the core contained community-level functions, with a periphery of those of neighborhood level. Therefore, the rent-paying ability of different businesses appears to be affected predominantly by their order in the hierarchy, and the internal zoning of uses within business centers mirrors the level at which these functions appear in the hierarchy. The highest-level land use (or function) in a center is usually that use needing and able to pay for the most central location within it.

The metropolitan central business district has a distinctive spatial structure (Boyce and Horwood, 1959). In the 1960s, a distinction could be made between the "core" and the "frame" of the CBD. The frame, a concentric zone around the core, included downtown manufacturing and areas devoted to wholesaling and warehousing, although new freeways have led to the decentralization of these services. The core contained the retail district (the most central of all central places in the geography of retailing) clustered around the "100 percent location" of maximum pedestrian densities and land values. Apart from the core were separate office districts devoted to finance, insurance, medical services, and entertainment districts; clusters of hotels; and areas of downtown apartments. Scattered throughout this area were different kinds of more local retail uses. The main retail district attracted consumers from the entire metropolitan area, although it relied to an increasing extent upon the trade of workers in downtown offices and apartments. The entertainment district had its own peculiar assemblage of retail uses and services. Office buildings had restaurants, gift shops, barber and beauty shops, and stores offering a range of clothing and lingerie for office workers. The apartment clusters had neighborhood services, the nature of these varying markedly from expensive high-rise developments to depressed apartment hotels of "skid row." Figure 2.20 maps the functional areas within Chicago's central business district, the Loop, in 1960.

In addition to the hierarchy of outlying business centers, with internal banding of uses, and the internal complexities of the CBD at the top of the hierarchy, the business structure of the metropolis in 1960 included both business ribbons and a variety of specialized functional areas (Figure 2.16). In addition to the kinds of ribbons noted earlier there were: first, strings of highway-oriented establishments; second, arterial developments in which are found uses demanding too much space to be able to afford locations in centers; and third, retail and service uses needing only generally accessible location, not centrality to pedestrians. (In this third type of business, the businessperson is called to the home to perform the service, or the consumer makes a special single-purpose trip to the store for what it offers.) Other kinds of business can also be found. One feature of the old central city was the ethnic diversity of its residential neighborhoods. Each of the traditional neighborhood shopping streets had its own flavor, be it Jewish, Italian, German, Czech, Chinese, Japanese, or Greek.

Specialized functional areas developed because many kinds of uses agglomerated inside the largest cities to facilitate comparison buying, to serve a special market, or to make joint use of specialized facilities. Such clusters included automobile rows, furniture districts, and medical centers. Traditionally, professional offices were found in the CBD or occupying upper floors in outlying business centers. Today, special buildings are constructed for them, often in clusters, providing joint access to laboratories and to services for which they have a common need.

To this diversity of business centers the postwar years brought further complexity. The patterns illustrated in Figures 2.15 through 2.20 developed before the depression of the 1930s and were crystallized by it and the succeeding wartime years. Once the war was over, suburbanization accelerated, a development facilitated by the general ownership of automobiles and promoted by rising incomes and governmental incentives for home ownership. Part of this "sprawl" conformed to the older radial pattern, making use of the railroads. But as new highways were built, suburbs spread into the inner interstices between the fingerlike radii of the railroad lines, creating suburbs of increasing diversity that clouded the earlier socio-economic symmetry of the radii and bands.

At the same time came accelerated technological change in retailing, which

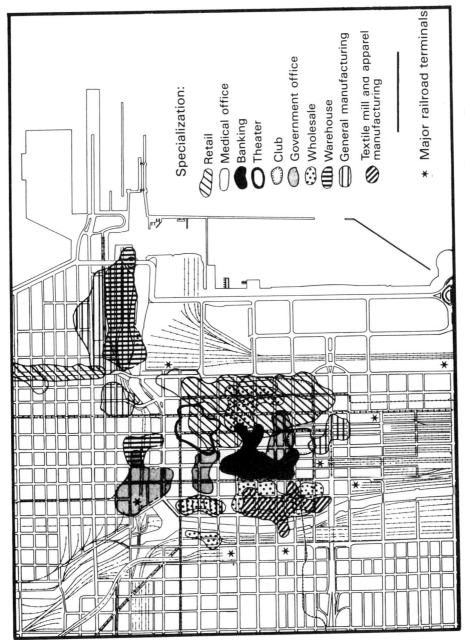

**Figure 2.20** Specialized functional areas within the Loop, Chicago's central business district, in 1960.

Specialization:

Retail

Medical office

Banking

Theater

Club

Government office

Wholesale

Warehouse

General manufacturing

Textile mill and apparel manufacturing

★  Major railroad terminals

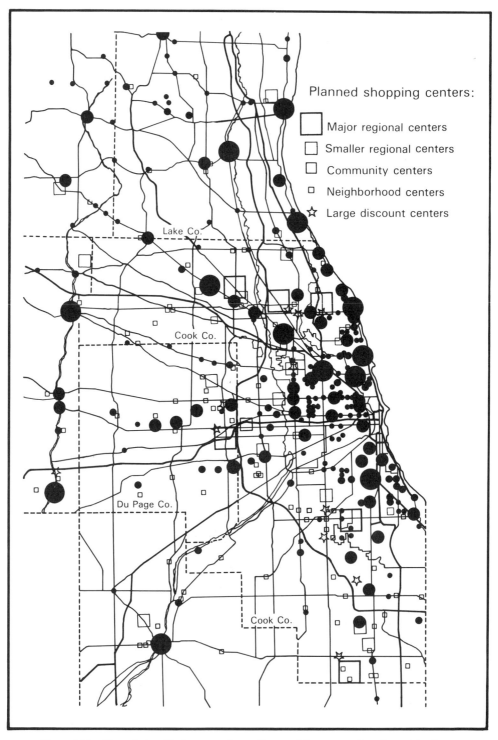

**Figure 2.21** The relationship between the earlier spatial pattern of unplanned business centers and the first wave of planned shopping center locations is shown in this map of the Chicago metropolitan area in 1960. Compare with Figure 2.17.

took into account the increased use of the automobile. The unit of development changed from the single store to the entire planned shopping plaza with parking facilities. Figure 2.21 gives some idea of the results by 1960. The traditional pattern of centers remained, but major planned shopping plazas now were located between and at the outer edges of the prewar built-up area.

Before World War II, the unplanned centers competed only with their nearest neighbors. If they were located in the central city, their market areas overlapped with those of four or six neighbors. At that time densities were so high that several centers could survive within the maximum distances that consumers traveled. Along the radii, competition was with the next center towards the city and the next away from it. Thus, urban consumers, in contrast to those in rural areas, did not make deterministic choices on either side of a trade-area boundary. A variety of alternatives existed, and individual behavior reflected the increased range of choice. This resulted in greater intensity of competition in the postwar period.

After the war there was hierarchy also. In 1960, the new planned centers had the same number of levels as the older, unplanned developments, but they differed in many respects. The prewar unplanned centers were clusters of individually owned and built establishments, located by competition for central sites, and strung along the sides of streets away from a major intersection. In this situation on-street parking and vehicular traffic disturbed pedestrian movements. The postwar planned centers, on the other hand, are complete developments located adjacent to, but not athwart, major highway intersections. Business establishments are located in an island amid surrounding parking lots and carefully arranged along pedestrian walkways and around malls to give maximum exposure of all stores to consumers on foot. Whereas the main attractions of unplanned centers were at the central intersection and other uses dropped off from that point according to the ability of businesses to pay for the space, shopping plaza developers place the major attractions at opposite ends of the walkways, stringing the other uses between the ends. This arrangement is encouraged by the way in which major centers are financed. A developer will persuade prospective major "triple-A" tenants to join in developing a shopping center and in return will give them rent concessions. Since they have triple-A business ratings, the developer is able to borrow money to construct the center. Profits are made out of the smaller establishments attracted by the possibilities of maximum consumer exposure on the walkways connecting the major tenants, whose job, as far as the developer is concerned, is to draw consumers to the center.

## THE "RURAL" TO "URBAN" PHASE SHIFT

Figure 2.10 identifies systematic relations between market areas and population served, levels of the hierarchy, and population densities. The regularity applies at low densities to centers and surrounding rural areas, but at high densities the regularities apply only to business centers within cities. The same ingredients are present at the two extremes, but because of the differences in densities there are two different "states." To use a simile, as with a mineral under pressure there is a "phase shift" when one state changes into another. At what densities and under what conditions does this shift take place?

Burton (1963) has used the concept of the *dispersed city* to identify the beginnings of the phase shift. His idea was simple. Clusters of centers exist with distances between them short enough for consumers to consider several central places within their range of alternative choices for shopping. Such centers perform local functions for their own populations, but they also specialize in the performance of high-level functions for the group. One will become the automobile sales center, another the furniture center, another the medical center, and so forth.

When groups of centers which appear to function as dispersed cities are examined in the United States, it is found that their average levels of density place them exactly between the intensive corn belt and the suburban cases seen in Figure 2.21—exactly where the phase shift is predicted to occur.

Subsequent research has, however, failed to confirm Burton's hypothesis of central-place specialization within regional dispersed-city clusters. More research is needed on the phase-shift problem. Technological change may also be negating older patterns: The contemporary development style is for the developer to use the major shopping mall as the leading edge of metropolitan expansion, creating the central core of future suburban "mini-cities" at major expressway intersections where new expressway-oriented "outlet malls" also may locate. Location patterns and development styles are fluid and dynamic, and basic principles are needed to ascertain what is merely difference in form and what is fundamental change. Such principles are the focus of Chapters 3 and 4. The dynamics themselves should, of course, be a fertile ground for geographical research in the future (Morrill, 1987).

# REFERENCES

BERRY, B. J. L., and R. J. TENNANT (1963) *Chicago Commercial Reference Handbook.* Chicago: University of Chicago.

BOYCE, R. R., and E. M. HORWOOD (1959) *Studies of the Central Business District and Urban Freeway Development.* Seattle, Wash.: University of Washington Press.

BURTON, I. (1963) "A Restatement of the Dispersed City Hypothesis," *Annals of the Association of American Geographers*, 56:285–289.

GARNER, B. J. (1966) *The Internal Structure of Retail Nucleations.* Evanston, Ill.: Northwestern University.

MORRILL, R. L. (1987) " The Structure of Shopping in a Metropolis," *Urban Geography*, 8:97–128.

# 3

# Classical
# Central-Place Theory

Chapters 1 and 2 dealt with regularities in the facts that were plain to see. For an understanding of the spatial structure of retail and service activity, it is necessary to predict these regularities from a theory. Ideally, a theory should embody a minimum of assumptions and postulates, and it should produce the regularities as logical deductions. In central-place theory the focus is on a system of centers or central places, and the regularities relate to their location, size, frequency, economic activity, and the sizes, shapes, and spatial arrangements of their market areas. The bases of central-place theory were laid before World War II by two German scholars: one, a geographer, Walter Christaller (1933), and the other, an economist, August Lösch (1938 and 1941). Certain of their conclusions were anticipated by the American rural sociologist Charles J. Galpin (1915) and various other scholars, including R. Cantillon (1755), J. Reynaud (1841), and L. Lalanne (1863). These scholars stated at least the germ of the idea earlier. Indeed, the antecedents of the theory can be traced back to Al-Muqaddasi who wrote in the tenth century (Hassan, 1972), and they also appear in *The Wealth of Nations* by Adam Smith (1776). In Christaller's work much of the underlying theory was not specified, and it was Lösch who, in an independent derivation, made it explicit. Both theorists agreed on the spatial arrangement of central places required for the supply of a single function to a dispersed population. However, their arguments diverged significantly when they sought to obtain locations for many kinds of functions supplied simultaneously. We examine first the nature of equilibrium in the supply of a single function, as discussed by Lösch (1941, pp. 108–114).

## THE EQUILIBRIUM FOR A SINGLE FUNCTION

Let us assume that identical consumers, distributed continuously at uniform densities over a homogeneous plain, can travel in any direction over this plain at the same cost per mile (such a plain is referred to in the theoretical literature as a "transport surface"). This assumption may seem rather unrealistic, but if it can be shown that most of the regularities that we have observed can emerge on such a plain, the possibility of causation of fundamental patterns by spatial differences in raw materials or significant differences in population distribution can be eliminated. In any event, the model can be refined at a later stage by incorporating more realistic assumptions.

An individual decides to go into business to supply a particular commercial function (a good or a service). Of immediate interest to us are the demand conditions facing this would-be supplier. Let us therefore consider the consumer response if a price $p$ is charged (which is not necessarily the price charged once the supplier is successfully established, but merely one of a number of reference points to gauge demand conditions). This price $p$, termed the "f.o.b. price" or "mill price," represents the price at the supply point or central place. However, it costs a consumer an amount $st$ to visit this supply point to purchase the function (where $s$ is the distance from the consumer's residence to the supply point and $t$ is the transport cost per mile), so that the actual price paid by the consumer is $p + st$. This is sometimes termed the "real price." Figure 3.1 shows the real price increasing with distance from the point of supply.

Every consumer is assumed to have an identical demand curve for the function in question so that as the real price increases, less of it is demanded, as seen in Figure 3.2. The linear demand curve is a simplification and is used purely for the purposes of illustration. The various consumers will have different positions on this individual demand curve (i.e., will demand different quantities) according to their location with respect to the supply point. At a price $p$, a quantity $q_1$ will be demanded. A consumer located at a distance $s$, however, must incur transport costs. It can be seen from Figure 3.1 that the real price is $p + st$, and Figure 3.2

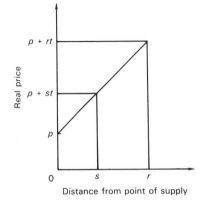

**Figure 3.1**  Spatial price gradient: real price to consumers at different distances (where the f.o.b. price is $p$).

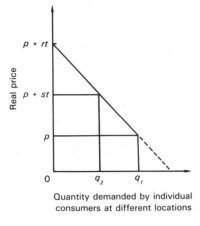

Figure 3.2 showing axes "Real price" (vertical) and "Quantity demanded by individual consumers at different locations" (horizontal), with levels $p + rt$, $p + st$, and $p$ marked, and $q_2$, $q_1$ on the horizontal axis.

**Figure 3.2** Individual demand curve: quantities demanded by individual consumers at different real prices (where the f.o.b. price is $p$).

indicates that at this real price the quantity demanded by the consumer is only $q_2$. At a distance $r$ the real price to a consumer is $p + rt$ (Figure 3.1) but at this price, demand is zero (Figure 3.2). Therefore, the quantity demanded by consumer is a function of price paid at the place of residence, that is

$$q = f(p + st) \qquad (3.1)$$

In other words, quantity demanded falls with distance, a relationship which can be expressed as a "spatial demand curve." In Figure 3.3 curve 1 indicates the manner in which demand varies with distance from the supply point when the f.o.b. price is $p$. Curve 2 shows demand as a function of distance at an f.o.b. price higher than $p$, while curve 3 provides similar information for an f.o.b. price lower than $p$. Generalizing, we can say that the higher the f.o.b. price, the smaller will be the individual quantity demanded at any given distance, and the smaller will be the distance $r$ at which demand becomes zero; of course, the converse also holds true.

Since travel costs per mile are assumed to be identical throughout the plain,

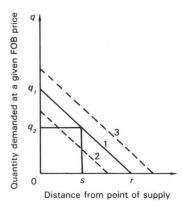

Figure 3.3 showing axes "Quantity demanded at a given FOB price" (vertical) and "Distance from point of supply" (horizontal), with levels $q_1$ and $q_2$ marked, curves labeled 1, 2, 3, and $s$, $r$ on the horizontal axis.

**Figure 3.3** Spatial demand curve: quantities demanded by consumers located at different distances from the point of supply when the f.o.b. price is $p$ (curve 1), higher than $p$ (curve 2), and lower than $p$ (curve 3).

the fall in the quantity demanded occurs at the same rate in all directions. This is illustrated in Figure 3.4 by a "spatial demand cone" centered on the supply point. Such a cone is formed by rotating curve 1 in Figure 3.3 through 360° about the quantity axis $Oq_1$. The floor of the cone (which is a circle of radius $r$) represents the maximum area that can be served from the point of supply at an f.o.b. price of $p$. The aggregate demand $Q$ at this price, which is the total quantity demanded by consumers within this circular area, can be obtained by calculating the volume of the demand cone and then multiplying by population density $S$:

$$Q = S \int_0^{2\pi} \left[ \int_0^r f(p + st)s \, ds \right] d\theta \qquad (3.2)$$

This expression for aggregate demand represents the sum of all individual consumers' demands within the circle of radius $r$, taking into account the decrease in demand with distance described by equation (3.1).

The calculation can be repeated for a variety of different f.o.b. prices $p_i$ (for a price higher than $p$ the cone will be lower, the radius smaller, and the aggregate demand therefore lower than in (3.2); for a price lower than $p$ the opposite will hold). If each calculation of aggregate demand $Q_i$ is plotted against the given f.o.b. price $p_i$, we obtain curve $D$ in Figure 3.5, which shows the various total quantity demanded at different f.o.b. prices. From the supplier's viewpoint, this $D$ curve can also be viewed as an average revenue curve, because it indicates the revenue received per unit of sales at different sales levels. While Lösch (1941, p. 106) indicated the $D$ curve should be concave to the origin, in an earlier work it was shown to be convex to the origin (Lösch, 1938, p. 74), a convention that will be followed in this chapter (Denike and Parr, 1970).

The cost conditions facing the supplier are indicated by curve $C$. This is the

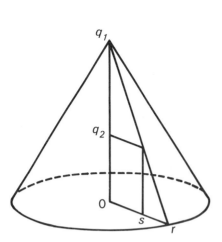

**Figure 3.4**  A spatial demand cone (where f.o.b. price is $p$).

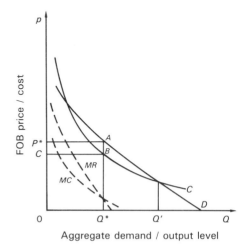

**Figure 3.5**  Demand and cost facing the single initial supplier.

long-run average cost curve, which summarizes the costs per unit of output at different levels of production $Q$. "Costs" include "normal profits," that minimum return to the supplier necessary to stay in that line of business.

As long as the $C$ curve intersects the $D$ curve, revenues exceed costs, profits can be made, and production will be economically feasible. When $C$ is tangential to $D$, normal profits can still be earned so that production is just possible. Lösch (1941, pp. 106–108) indicated that the supplier *could* produce up to an output of $Q'$ (the lower intersection of the $C$ and $D$ curves) and still earn normal profits. It is likely, however, that the supplier will select that output which maximizes profits. This occurs at that level of output where marginal cost is equal to marginal revenue. The marginal cost and marginal revenue curves are shown in Figure 3.5 as $MC$ and $MR$ respectively. At output levels beyond the profit-maximizing level of output $Q^*$, the marginal cost (i.e., the cost of an additional unit of output) would be greater than the marginal revenue (i.e., the additional revenue received for that unit of output/sales). It can be seeen that at an output of $Q^*$, the $D$ curve lies above the $C$ curve, indicating that average revenue is greater than average cost, so that there is an extra profit per unit produced of $AB$. The supplier is thus able to earn an "excess profit" (over and above normal profit) which is given by the area $ABCp^*$. Excess profits reach their maximum value at the output $Q^*$ and steadily diminish with higher (or lower) levels of output and become zero at output $Q'$ where only a normal profit can be earned. If the supplier chose to produce at an output beyond $Q'$, it would be impossible to earn even the normal profit necessary to stay in business.

In order to sell this profit-maximizing output $Q^*$, the supplier will charge a profit-maximizing price $p^*$, which is the f.o.b. price or the price at the point of supply. A consumer located there will exert a demand of $q^*$. However, a consumer located at $s$ will face a real price of $p^* + st$ and will therefore exert a smaller demand. The individual demand of any consumer at distance $s$ in any given direction from the point of supply (point $O$ in Figure 3.4) can be derived by considering a demand cone of height $q^*$ and determining, for this particular consumer's location, the perpendicular distance from the floor of the cone to a point on its surface. Such a demand cone can also be used to derive the market area for the initial supplier. This particular cone would reflect the fact that at price $p^*$ demand falls with distance in all directions until consumers located at distance $r^*$ exert no demand. Thus the floor of the cone represents the market area of the initial supplier by a circle of radius $r^*$, as diagrammed in Figure 3.6.

We have derived the price, output, and market area for the single initial supplier. The ability of this supplier to earn excess profits will encourage other potential suppliers to enter the same line of activity. Here we make the important assumption that "free entry" prevails, that is, there are no cultural, institutional, or governmental barriers to entry. It would be unwise for a second supplier to locate at the site of the initial supplier, because aggregate quantity demanded at any price from each supplier then would be only one-half of that originally received by the initial supplier. The resulting revenue curve $D$ would not intersect with

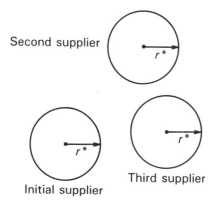

Second supplier

Initial supplier

Third supplier

**Figure 3.6**  Market-area structure for initial supplier and for second and third suppliers in the absence of effective competition.

the cost curve $C$ in Figure 3.5, with the consequence that both suppliers would fail to earn even normal profits. Rather than engage in this unprofitable form of competition, the second supplier should locate to ensure that the new market area does not impinge on the market area of the initial supplier, thus minimizing competition. A third supplier should follow a similar locational strategy. With further entry of other suppliers, the initial supplier will eventually encounter competition at the market-area boundaries since some of the more distant consumers will find themselves located more closely to other suppliers from whom they will purchase the function. In this way, the initial market area is cut back with the result that the revenue curve $D$ for the initial supplier in Figure 3.5 will be shifted to the left. This is because at any given price the aggregate quantity demanded will be reduced as a result of market-area intrusion. Eventually, after more entry, the $D$ curve will be shifted to the left until it is tangential with the $C$ curve. This is shown in Figure 3.7 where the $D_2$ curve represents the new demand conditions. The $D_1$ curve, representing the earlier demand conditions facing the initial supplier who was not encountering competition, is no longer relevant. For the initial supplier

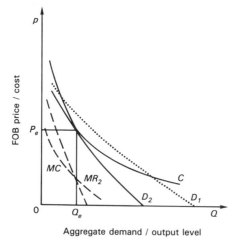

**Figure 3.7**  Demand and cost conditions for each supplier at equilibrium.

and all subsequent suppliers, the profit-maximizing output now becomes $Q_e$ (the output at which marginal cost equals marginal revenue under the new demand conditions). The price charged by each supplier is $p_e$. At this level of output average cost equals average revenue. Excess profits are no longer possible, and each supplier is forced to a competitive minimum and earns only normal profits. Because of this, there is no inducement to further entry (indeed, it is not possible); the system of supply will then settle down into equilibrium. Of course, the shift in the demand curve from $D_1$ to $D_2$ in Figure 3.7 is a highly simplified one. There is a variety of mechanisms by which this shift actually occurs—many paths by which the initial situation is transformed to the final equilibrium.

The equilibrium has a spatial expression. If we assume for the moment that all consumers are served, the problem becomes one of finding the most appropriate market-area shape. It will be recalled that we have assumed free entry of suppliers into the market. The corollary is that at equilibrium, after the process of free entry has run its full course, the number of suppliers (each earning normal profits) must be at a maximum. We therefore need to know what configuration of supply points yields the maximum density of suppliers. Mulligan (1981) has shown that at equilibrium the density of firms is necessarily greater with hexagonal market areas than with square market areas—and still greater than with triangular market areas. Phrased another way, at equilibrium the minimum market area required for economically feasible production will be smaller with a hexagonal shape than with a square or triangular shape. With hexagonal market areas, the number of suppliers just earning normal profits is maximized.

This is related to the fact, demonstrated by Lösch (1941, pp. 111–112), that with a linear individual demand curve of the type shown in Figure 3.2 the demand per unit area is greater for a hexagon than for a square or a triangle of the same area. Such a property exists because the hexagon is a more compact polygon (i.e., closer to the circle than the square or triangle), resulting in demand falling off slightly less rapidly towards the edges of a hexagon than it does with a square or triangle (Beckmann, 1968). Thus in a competitive equilibrium with free entry, each supplier has a hexagonal market area of radius of $r_e$ (Figure 3.8). This configuration is also consistent with the rational locational behavior of suppliers. Each supplier wishes to avoid the others as much as possible so as to serve the greatest number of consumers. With triangular spacing (as opposed to other spatial arrangements) the distance from one supplier to the next is at a maximum.

## CHRISTALLER'S CENTRAL-PLACE SYSTEM

The foregoing discussion of the spatial equilibrium in the supply of the single function follows very closely the treatment presented by Lösch in 1941. Christaller (1933) had earlier provided a less formal analysis in which much of Lösch's argument was implicit. We now turn our attention to a situation in which several functions are supplied with differing market-area sizes that depend on such con-

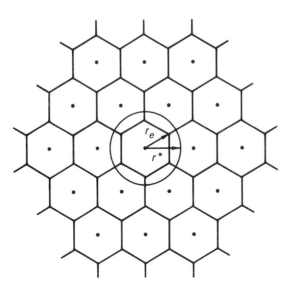

**Figure 3.8** Market-area size structure for suppliers at final equilibrium. (Note: The market area (radius $r^*$) of the single initial supplier is no longer relevant and is included to indicate the diminished market-area extent at equilibrium.)

siderations as demand, transport costs, and economies of scale in production. In considering such a system Christaller imposed the requirement that if a function with a given market-area size was supplied from a particular central place, then that central place would also be the supply point for all functions with similar or smaller market-area sizes. A second requirement put precise limits on the extent of the market areas. In fact, market-area sizes were required to increase from the one level to the next higher level (or decrease from one level to the next lower level) by a constant factor of $K$. These two requirements led to a hierarchical system of central places (or centers) and market areas.

Figure 3.9 represents a particular example of a Christaller central-place system in which $K = 3$, that is, market-area sizes increase from one level to the next by a factor of 3. This involves a market-area structure in which there are three market areas of level $m - 1$ (where $m > 1$) contained within a market area of level $m$: one "whole" level $m - 1$ market area (of the level $m$ center) plus six $\frac{1}{3}$ portions of the level $m - 1$ market areas of the six level $m - 1$ centers surrounding it. One such grouping is shaded in the figure. Also, each center of level $m$ (where $m > 1$) has within its level $m$ market area, two centers of level $m$: the six $\frac{1}{3}$ portions of the six level $m - 1$ centers which surround the level $m$ center.

Within such a hierarchy there are $N$ levels of center and $N$ levels of market area (for the system shown in Figure 3.9 the value of $N$ is 3). The three levels (1, 2, and 3) correspond to the hamlet, village, and town considered in Chapters 1 and 2. In such a system each function supplied makes its first appearance at a particular level $m$ in the hierarchy where $m = 1, 2, \ldots, N$ and is thus referred to as a "level $m$ function." This means that the function will not be supplied from centers of levels lower than $m$, although it will be supplied from centers of levels

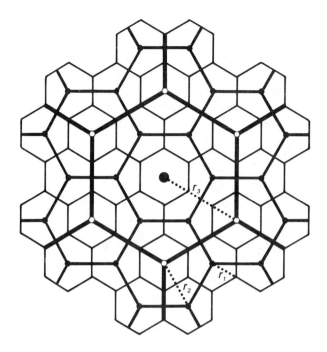

| Center | | Market area |
|---|---|---|
| ● | Level 1 | —— |
| ○ | Level 2 | ▬▬ |
| ⬤ | Level 3 | ▬▬▬ |

**Figure 3.9**  A Christaller $K = 3$ system (the market principle).

higher than $m$. Since there are relatively few levels but a large number of functions, each level has more than one function which is characteristic of that level. These can be grouped together and referred to as the "level $m$ bundle of functions." There will be therefore $N$ levels of bundles, corresponding to the $N$ levels of center and $N$ levels of market area. (Refer back to Table 1.1, Steps of the Hierarchy.) A distinctive feature of this hierarchy, and one which follows from one of Christaller's assumptions, is that it is successively inclusive in terms of centers, market areas, and bundles of functions. It can be seen from Figure 3.9 that a center of level 1 has a level 1 market area to which it supplies the level 1 bundle. A center of level 2, however, has a level 2 market area, to which it supplies the level 2 bundle, as well as a level 1 market area to which the level 1 bundle is supplied. More generally, a center of level $m$ has $m$ market areas and supplies bundles of levels 1 through $m$ to its market areas of levels 1 through $m$ respectively. With the exception of the lowest level, the market areas are not entirely rural, so that a market area of level $m$ contains within it centers of levels 1 through $m - 1$. This successively inclusive hierarchy is a structure which can be observed in many central-place systems, such as that analyzed in Chapters 1 and 2, where the form of the hierarchy was summarized in Table 1.1.

In order to determine the level from which a particular function (as part of a bundle of functions) would be supplied, Christaller introduced the concept of the "range" of a function from the point of supply. The upper limit of this range represents *either* the "ideal range" (the distance at which demand for the function falls to zero) *or* the "real range" (referred to in Chapter 2 as the maximum distance traveled or the distance at which a given market area ends because of competition from a neighboring supplier). The ideal range is equivalent to the distance $r^*$ in Figure 3.6 which indicates the conditions encountered by a supplier in the absence of effective competition. By contrast, the real range represents the distance to the point where a competitive transition occurs (i.e., the market-area boundary). It corresponds to the distance $r_e$ in Figure 3.8. In a hierarchical system, the higher the level of a function, the greater its real range. In Figure 3.9 functions of the level 1 bundle each have a real range of $r_1$, functions of the level 2 bundle, a real range of $r_2$, and functions of the level 3 bundle, a real range of $r_3$. Note that in this theoretical model the real range for any individual function or bundle of functions is identical whatever the level of center from which it is supplied. But as we saw in Chapter 2, the real range of a function in fact tends to increase with the hierarchical level of center from which it is supplied. Thus, in Figure 2.3 the real range (maximum distance traveled) for food was higher for towns than it was for villages and higher for cities than it was for towns. In this respect the theoretical model of Figure 3.9 represents a simplification of reality that must be relaxed in more sophisticated versions, although it will not seriously affect the analysis to follow.

Let us define the real range of the level $m$ bundle as $r_m$ and examine a function $h$ which has an ideal range of $L_h$. In considering the rules by which a function $h$ would be part of a bundle of level $m$, Christaller argued that $L_h$ would have to be greater than $r_m$, otherwise certain consumers (those living beyond $L_h$) would be unserved and there would be opportunities for other suppliers to enter the system. Christaller (1933, pp. 60–62) implicitly adopted the rule that a function would be supplied from centers of the *highest* level $m$ for which the following condition holds:

$$L_h \geq r_m \qquad (3.3)$$

In Figure 3.9, therefore, functions for which the ideal range is greater than or equal to $r_1$ but less than $r_2$ are offered from centers of level 1; functions with ideal ranges greater than or equal to $r_2$ but less than $r_3$ are offered from centers of level 2; and functions with ideal ranges greater than or equal to $r_3$ but less than the real range of the level 4 bundle (this distance is not shown in Figure 3.9) are offered from centers of level 3. This aspect of Christaller's work is in many respects unsatisfactory. The reliance placed on the ideal range as the factor which determines the hierarchical level of a function implies that the number of supply points will be at a minimum (Beavon, 1977, p. 22). In this respect, Christaller's view of the behavior of competitive firms appears to be unrealistic since it runs counter to the notion of free entry, which usually prevails in market economies in some form. Under free entry conditions one would expect the number of supply points to be *maximized*. More importantly, his approach fails to specify a force or mechanism within the system which can encourage this minimization of supply points.

It is desirable, therefore, to adopt another interpretation of the manner in which functions are supplied from different levels of the hierarchy. And to do this we can utilize Christaller's concept of the lower limit of the range, which is called the *threshold range*. This represents the distance to a perimeter which encloses just enough consumers to enable the supplier to engage in commercial production, that is, to earn normal profits. The threshold range is equivalent to the distance $r_e$ in Figure 3.8. Because this refers to a single-function spatial equilibrium in which each producer earns no excess profits, the threshold range of a function coincides with its real range, and the threshold range will not, therefore, be equal in all directions. Note that if we were to consider a single supplier in the absence of competition, the threshold range *would* be equal in all directions. The concept of the threshold range is significant because it reflects the minimum geographic requirements necessary for commercial operation, and it is thus more relevant in determining the levels from which the various functions are supplied. The concept of "threshold" employed in Chapter 2 is very similar to the threshold range. The *threshold* refers to the population served from a center (i.e., the population of the center and its market area) necessary for a function to be commercially supplied, whereas the *threshold range* refers to a distance to a perimeter enclosing such a population. In Figure 2.2 the term *threshold village-level functions* refers to the lowest total population served by a village, indicating that this is the minimum population level for the supply of village-level functions. Similar thresholds are shown for town-level and city-level functions.

We now consider a function $h$ with a threshold range $Z_h$. If, for a particular level $m$, we find that $Z_h$ exceeds $r_m$, the real range for the level $m$ bundle, the function $h$ obviously cannot be offered from centers of level $m$. There would, in effect, be too many supply points and from any single one of them the threshold range could not be attained, with the result that production would not be economically feasible. Under these circumstances, the function must necessarily be offered from fewer centers of a higher level, for example, level $m + 1$ or $m + 2$. In this alternative interpretation of the Christaller system, therefore, a function $h$ is supplied from a center of the *lowest* level $m$ for which the following condition holds:

$$Z_h \leq r_m \qquad (3.4)$$

Figure 3.9 can also be interpreted in these terms, with the real ranges of the bundles of levels 1, 2, and 3 defined (as before) as $r_1$, $r_2$, and $r_3$, respectively. Functions with threshold ranges less than or equal to $r_1$ are offered from centers of level 1. Functions with threshold ranges less than or equal to $r_2$ but greater than $r_1$ are offered from centers of level 2. And functions with threshold ranges less than or equal to $r_3$ but greater than $r_2$ are offered from centers of level 3. The actual threshold range of a function may reflect the fact that consumers engage in multi-purpose trips. This reduces the transport costs associated with any single function, enabling a larger quantity to be consumed and reducing the threshold range for that function. Because of multi-purpose shopping, some functions may be able to locate in lower levels of the hierarchy than if all shopping trips were single purpose.

Only a limited number of sizes of the real range will exist in fact because of the hierarchy of centers. In Figure 3.9 $r_1$, $r_2$, and $r_3$ are discrete. For this reason it is quite possible for the real range to exceed the threshold range for a particular function, making possible excess profits to the supplier of that function. There is another cause for the existence of excess profits, the fact that $z_h$, the threshold range for function $h$, will decline as the hierarchical level $m$ increases. This happens because the higher the level of a center, the greater will be the consuming population within that center and thus the lower the threshold range $z_h$, the distance from the center necessary to secure a sufficient demand for commercial production. This results in the real range exceeding the threshold range by an increasing amount as the level of center increases. As a consequence the extent of excess profits to the supplier of the function within a center also increases with the level of the center. In the single-function equilibrium considered in the previous section, the market-area size for the function is allowed to adjust in such a way that excess profits are completely eliminated—so that the real range coincides with the threshold range and there can only be one supplier at each center. Given the existence of a hierarchy in which numerous functions are supplied such an adjustment is not feasible. Whatever the cause of excess profits, they are likely to be of a hypothetical nature and will tend to be diminished by the competition caused by the entry of more suppliers within the relevant centers, even though the suppliers use a variety of techniques of specialization and product differentiation to attempt to retain some of the excess profits. The retail and service sector nevertheless remains one of the most highly competitive.

Such considerations do not affect the rule, specified in equation (3.4), whereby individual functions are supplied from different levels of the hierarchy. This alternative interpretation of the supply of functions within the hierarchy, which is based on the threshold-range considerations, is more in keeping with the notion of free entry and competitive behavior among firms than Christaller's initial idea. Christaller did consider the influence of the threshold range, but the crucial determinant in his interpretation was the ideal range. It will be appreciated that the manner individual functions are supplied from different levels of the hierarchy might differ according to which of the two interpretations is employed.

## ALTERNATIVE CHRISTALLER SYSTEMS

The $K = 3$ system discussed above is only one variant of the Christaller model. Christaller (1933, pp. 72–80) provided the outlines for others, and, following on from the discussion by Lösch (1941, pp. 130–132), he proposed two additional central-place systems: the $K = 4$ system and the $K = 7$ system (Christaller, 1950). Other Christaller systems have subsequently been suggested. In each case the central-place system can be said to reflect adherence to a particular principle of spatial organization. In all cases the successively inclusive hierarchy is identical to that present in the $K = 3$ system, and the rules by which functions are supplied from different levels of the hierarchy are exactly the same as those outlined in the previous section. These alternative Christaller systems only differ from the $K = 3$ system (Figure 3.9) in terms of the geometrical arrangement of centers and market areas.

Christaller (1933, pp. 60–70) argued that the $K = 3$ system was organized according to the *market principle*. This implied that the spatial structure of the system is only influenced by commercial considerations. In other systems, based on hexagonal market areas, commercial considerations are relevant, although they are constrained by the operation of additional principles of spatial organization. It is worth mentioning that commercial considerations exist in economies based on central planning and state supply as well as within market economies where free entry into production is usually present in some form. The precise nature of commercial considerations will, of course, vary between the two types of economy.

Let us now turn to an examination of hexagonal market-area systems other than the $K = 3$ case. To facilitate comparison among the systems, the distance between two neighboring centers of level 1 is always identical to that in Figure 3.9.

In the $K = 4$ system (Figure 3.10) a center of level $m - 1$ (where $m > 1$) is located midway between two centers of level $m$ rather than equidistant between three centers of level $m$, as in the $K = 3$ system. Thus each level $m$ market area contains the equivalent of four market areas of level $m - 1$, and each level $m$ center dominates the equivalent of three centers of level $m - 1$. Such a locational arrangement of centers reflects adherence to the *transport principle*. This is best understood by considering the pattern of transport routes within the system (Figure 3.11). It can be seen that each center of level $m - 1$ is linked by transport routes to its six neighboring centers of level $m - 1$ or higher. Collectively, these routes represent the level $m - 1$ transport structure. A similar transport structure exists at level $m$, so that each center of level $m$ is linked to each of its six neighboring centers of level $m$ or higher. Since in the $K = 4$ system each center of level $m - 1$ is located midway between two neighboring centers of level $m$ or higher, no additional route mileage is necessary. In both the $K = 3$ and $K = 7$ systems, however, the level $m$ transport structure is such that an additional route mileage *will* be necessary, assuming, of course, that the distance between neighboring centers of level $m - 1$ is identical to the $K = 4$ case. The logic of the $K = 4$ system is that it economizes on route mileage. In the $K = 4$ system, therefore, commercial considerations operate under the constraint of transport efficiency in the locational pattern and frequency of centers. It is not difficult to find examples of central-place systems in which transport routes have exerted such an influence, and an example will be presented later in the chapter.

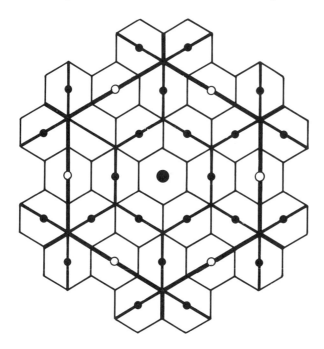

**Figure 3.10**   A Christaller $K = 4$ system (the transport principle).

In the $K = 7$ system (Figure 3.12) each center of level $m - 1$ (where $m > 1$) is located closer to a particular center of level $m$ than to any other level $m$ center so that a center of level $m - 1$ and its level $m - 1$ market area lie almost wholly within the level $m$ market area of a level $m$ center. As a consequence, each level $m$ market area contains the equivalent of seven market areas of level $m - 1$, and each center of level $m$ dominates six centers of level $m - 1$. The basis of this system lies in its administrative rationality, and it is said to adhere to the *administrative principle*. Let us assume that there are $N$ levels of administrative area, corresponding to the $N$ levels of market area. Figure 3.13 shows the administrative structure of the central-place system for three levels. If we now compare Figure 3.12 and Figure 3.13, it becomes apparent that, except for minor discordance at the boundaries, the administrative areas coincide with the market areas at each level. Thus the level $m - 1$ administrative area of a level $m - 1$ or higher center coincides approximately with the level $m - 1$ market area of that center. The important point, however, is that this coincidence occurs in such a way that an administrative area of level $m - 1$, based on a center of

Center          Transport route

●      Level 1    ———

○      Level 2    ▬▬

●      Level 3    ▬▬

**Figure 3.11** The transport structure in a $K = 4$ Christaller system.

level $m - 1$, lies (approximately) within an administrative area of level $m$, based on a center of level $m$. This is the usual rule adopted in the arrangement of different levels of administration. For example, township area boundaries typically do not extend across county boundaries, and county boundaries do not cross state lines. In the $K = 3$ and $K = 4$ systems of Figures 3.9 and 3.10 it can be seen that if administrative areas are made to coincide with market areas, the rule of administrative rationality will be violated, since an administrative area of level $m - 1$ will straddle three different administrative areas of level $m$ in the case of the $K = 3$ system or two such areas in the $K = 4$ system. Alternatively, if administrative areas are arranged in such a way that the rule is not violated, there can be no coincidence of administrative areas and market areas at any level $m$. In the $K = 7$ system, therefore, commercial considerations operate under the constraint of administrative efficiency. In actual central-place systems where administrative

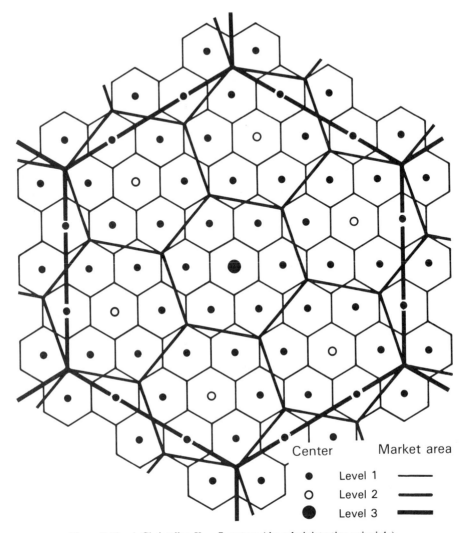

**Figure 3.12**    A Christaller $K = 7$ system (the administrative principle).

organization represents a dominant feature of the urban system, the location of central places emerges so as to follow the administrative principle, although relatively few examples are to be found.

Up to now, we have been concerned with central-place systems in which the market-area shapes were hexagonal. Alternative market area shapes such as the square are possible (Hoover, 1971, pp. 128–129). In the real world, central-place systems based on a square lattice with square market areas are to be observed, reflecting rectangular land surveys or the manner in which the transportation or administrative systems were initially laid out. Three systems based on

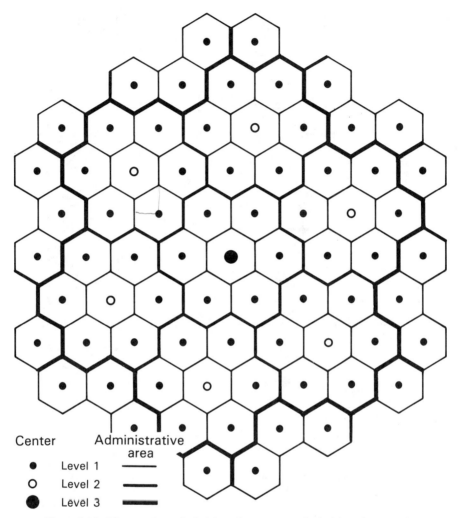

**Figure 3.13**   The structure of administrative centers and administrative areas in a $K = 7$ Christaller system.

square market areas are shown in Figures 3.14, 3.15, and 3.16, where the distance between a center of level 1 and a neighboring center of level 1 or higher is identical for all three systems. As with systems based on hexagonal market areas, the value of $K$ can be viewed as an indication of the prevailing organizational principle. The $K = 2$ system in Figure 3.14 is an example of adherence to the market principle, whereas the $K = 4$ system in Figure 3.15 reflects the influence of the transportation principle. The $K = 9$ system in Figure 3.16 represents a spatial structure based on the administrative principle, but, in contrast to the hexagonal $K = 7$ system (Figure 3.12), the coincidence between market areas and admin-

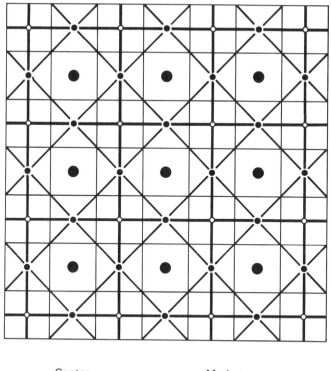

Center                          Market area

●    Level 1                    ―――――

○    Level 2                    ―――――

⬤    Level 3                    ━━━━━

**Figure 3.14** A Christaller $K = 2$ system with square market areas (the market principle).

istrative areas is complete. Moreover, this system also possesses the advantage of transport efficiency (Parr, 1985).

While it may be convenient to regard the value of $K$ in a central-place system (whether based on hexagonal areas or square market areas) as adhering to a particular organizational principle, it is also possible to view the value of $K$ as a reflection of the manner in which the threshold-range characteristics (which depend on the interaction of demand, production costs, and transport costs) vary among the different functions being supplied. It is not clear, however, why these should vary in a manner which leads to the market-area size increasing from one level to the next by a constant factor of $K$. This other view of the $K$ value is perhaps more valid in systems where $K$ varies with $m$, which is, of course, not possible in the Christaller system. These systems will be discussed in Chapter 4.

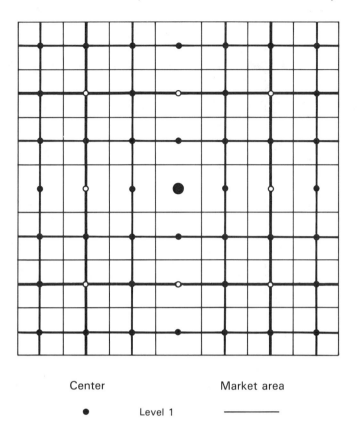

Center                          Market area

●        Level 1        ————

○        Level 2        ————

●        Level 3        ————

**Figure 3.15**    A Christaller $K = 4$ system with square market areas (the transport principle).

## THE SPATIAL STRUCTURE OF THE CHRISTALLER SYSTEM

Each of the Christaller systems shown so far possesses a well-defined spatial structure, the most striking feature of which is the geometrical symmetry of centers and market areas. This stems, in part, from uniform conditions throughout the plain and the behavior of firms under conditions of free entry, factors considered earlier in this chapter. It also depends on the market-area extent or real range for a particular bundle of functions being identical for each supply point, regardless of the hierarchical level of that supply point. In other words, the market area or real range for the level $m$ bundle of functions will not only be identical for all level $m$ centers but will be identical for all centers of levels higher than $m$. We have already noted that this is a simplification of actual conditions, and the question of actual conditions will be considered further in Chapter 4.

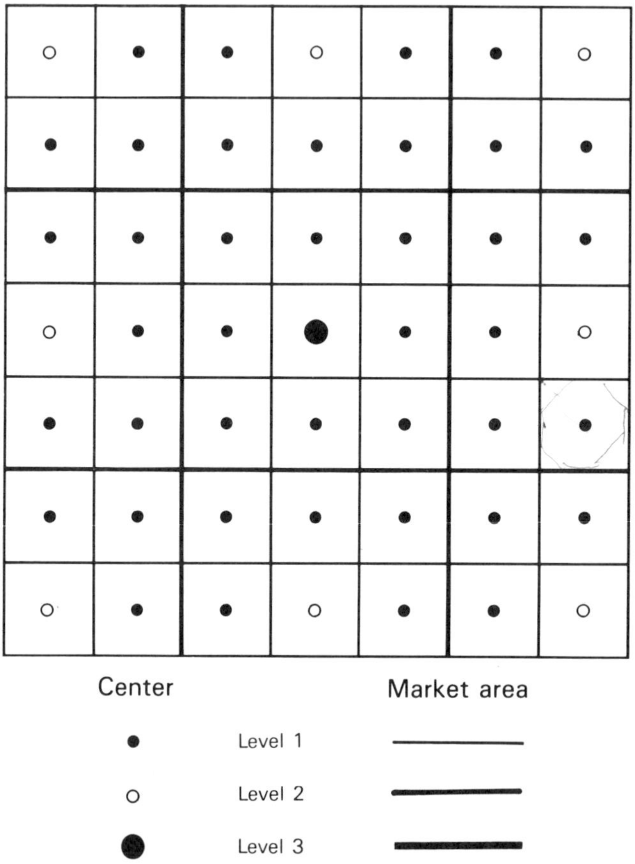

Figure 3.16   A Christaller $K = 9$ system with square market areas (the administrative principle).

The spatial structure of any Christaller system contains a number of properties which can be described in terms of the value of $K$, whether the market-area shape is hexagonal or square. This was defined earlier as the rate at which market-area sizes increase from one level to the next. As we have seen, it is also a "market-area nesting factor," indicating the equivalent number of market areas of level $m - 1$ (where $m > 1$) which are contained within a market area of level $m$. Thus for any system the market-area structure is such that there are $K$, or the equivalent of $K$, market areas of level $m - 1$ contained within a market area of level $m$. Furthermore, within such a system each center of level $m$ (where $m > 1$) dominates (or has within its level $m$ market area) the equivalent of $K - 1$ centers of level $m - 1$.

It is also possible to generalize about the frequency of market areas and centers within the hierarchy, and to generalize about the location or spacing of centers. For example, $F_m$, the frequency of level $m$ market areas in a system composed of $N$ levels, can be expressed as

$$F_m = K^{N-m} \tag{3.5}$$

In a $K = 3$ system this yields a progression of market-area frequencies from the highest level downward as follows: 1, 3, 9, 27, 81, . . . . The formulation of the frequency of centers of level $m$ in a system of $N$ levels is slightly more complicated. The center frequency of the highest level is usually taken as 1, while $f_m$, the frequency of centers of level $m < N$, is given by

$$f_m = K^{N-m} - K^{N-m-1} \qquad (3.6)$$

For a $K = 4$ system, therefore, the progression of center frequencies from the highest level downwards is: 1, 3, 12, 48, 192, . . . . In the case of the spacing of centers $d_m$, the distance between neighboring centers of level $m$ or higher, is given by

$$d_m = d_1(\sqrt{K})^{m-1} \qquad (3.7)$$

where $d_1$ is the distance between neighboring centers of level 1.

## EXAMPLES OF THE CHRISTALLER SYSTEM

Lest these principles seem too abstract or theoretical, it must be emphasized that actual central-place systems are capable of being analyzed in terms of the Christaller model, and we have already noted that the successively inclusive hierarchy of the Christaller model is a feature of many central-place systems in reality. Christaller himself undertook a pioneering study of the central-place systems in prewar southern Germany, and this gave rise to numerous studies of central-place systems (Berry and Pred, 1961). One of the best known is the study done by Skinner (1964). Figure 3.17 depicts a two-level structure of centers and market areas in a portion of Szechuan Province in the People's Republic of China, and Figure 3.18 illustrates how closely this can be described in diagrammatic form by the Christaller $K = 4$ hexagonal market-area system. This theoretical structure, based on the transportation principle, is able to highlight the influence of lines of communications on the location of centers in Figure 3.17. The central-place system of southwest Iowa (shown in Figure 1.2) can also be represented by a theoretical model. In this case, the closest structure is the $K = 4$ system with square market areas shown in Figure 3.15. As with the $K = 4$ system based on hexagonal market areas this system also adheres to the transport principle and thus reflects the influence of lines of communication on the locational pattern of centers. In addition to this diagrammatic approach, it is possible to analyze actual central-place systems by comparing the observed frequency and spacing of centers of the various levels with those of the theoretical model. Such an approach was followed by Rallis for Denmark (1963, p. 153) and by Lösch for Iowa (1941, pp. 434–435). Table 3.1, which summarizes their findings in a slightly different form from that originally presented, indicates just how well the two versions of the Christaller model are able to describe actual conditions. Recently, central-place theory has been applied to the analysis of settlement systems in traditional societies with similar results (Smith, 1974; and Steponaitis, 1978 and 1981).

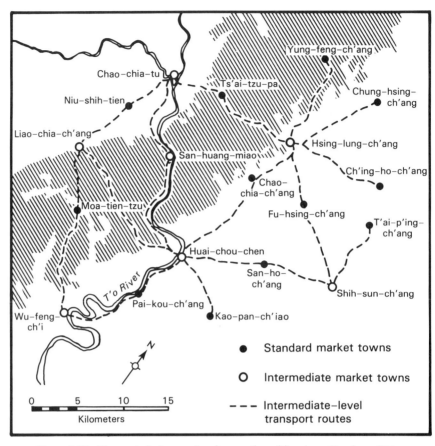

**Figure 3.17** The central-place system in a portion of Szechuan Province, China, before the People's Republic of China was established.

**TABLE 3.1** APPLICATION OF THE CHRISTALLER MODEL TO THE CENTRAL-PLACE SYSTEMS OF DENMARK AND IOWA

| | Denmark | | | | | Iowa | | | |
|---|---|---|---|---|---|---|---|---|---|
| | Frequency | | Spacing (mi) | | | Frequency | | Spacing (mi) | |
| $m$ | Observed | $K = 3$ | Observed | $K = 3$ | $m$ | Observed | $K = 4$ | Observed | $K = 4$ |
| 7 | 1 | 1 | 170.8 | 170.8 | | | | | |
| 6 | 2 | 2 | 87.0 | 98.6 | | | | | |
| 5 | 5 | 6 | 43.5 | 56.9 | 5 | 3 | 3 | 94.0 | 94.0 |
| 4 | 13 | 18 | 32.3 | 32.9 | 4 | 9 | 9 | 49.6 | 47.0 |
| 3 | 43 | 54 | 16.8 | 19.0 | 3 | 39 | 36 | 23.6 | 23.5 |
| 2 | 147 | 162 | 9.9 | 11.0 | 2 | 154 | 144 | 10.3 | 11.8 |
| 1 | 458 | 486 | 5.6 | 6.3 | 1 | 615 | 576 | 5.6 | 5.9 |

*Note:* For each case the frequencies and spacings for the Christaller ($K = 3$ or $K = 4$) system were determined first by setting the theoretical values equal to the observed values for the highest level $N$, and then deriving the frequencies and spacing for levels $m < N$ from the form of equations (3.6) and (3.7), respectively.

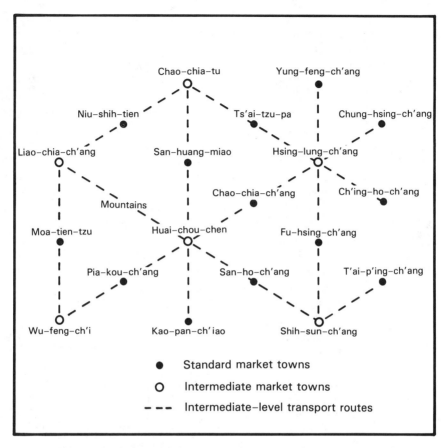

**Figure 3.18**   The central-place system of Figure 3.17 shown in diagrammatic form as a Christaller $K = 4$ system.

## LÖSCH'S CENTRAL-PLACE SYSTEM

In extending the analysis of the single-function equilibrium (see pages 50–56) to deal with the supply of many functions, Lösch derived a system of central places that was quite distinct from that of Christaller. This was largely due to the different assumptions involved. In the multi-function case, Lösch employed a discontinuous, though still uniform, distribution of population located in farmsteads or nucleated rural settlements. In the single-function case a continuous distribution was used. Following the analysis of the single-function case, Lösch first considered the lowest-order or level 1 function. This was assumed to have an equilibrium market-area size such that it served three basic settlements: the one at which the supply point was located plus the equivalent of two others (Figure 3.19). The lowest-order function would be offered from certain basic settlements, which would also be central places, and there would be formed a net of these smallest-sized hexagonal market areas covering the plain. The equilibrium market-area size for the next-higher-order (or level 2) function is then derived. This would serve four basic settlements: the one at which the supply point was located plus the equivalent of three others. A net of these slightly larger hexagonal market areas would extend over the plain. Lösch continued this process by deriving increasingly larger equilibrium market-area sizes for increasingly higher-order functions. Figure 3.19 shows the four smallest market areas. If the smallest market-area size was 3 units of area because the equivalent of three uniformly spaced basic settlements were being served, then the sequence of equilibrium market-area sizes (in terms of the same units of area, starting from the smallest) would be as follows: 3, 4, 7, 9, 12, 13, 16, 19, . . . (Lösch, 1941; Dacey, 1964; Beavon and Mabin, 1975). If the supply and demand characteristics of a particular function required, for example, eight basic settlements for commercial production, the market-area size would be 9 units. This would necessarily involve a measure of excess profits in the supply of that function which could not be competed away through further entry since the next smaller feasible market-area size (seven basic settlements) would be insufficiently large for commercial production (Lösch, 1941, p. 120). Lösch constructed what he called a "complete system" of market areas in which each feasible market-area size would have an associated function, although two or more functions could have market areas of identical size. The most crucial aspect of Lösch's approach was that the net of market areas for each function was derived independently, without reference to the supply of other functions, that is, each function was considered in isolation (Parr, 1973). Given our previous discussion of multi-purpose shopping, this assumption was unrealistic, but it was required for the integration of the various market-area nets into an overall pattern. This was accomplished by imposing two other conditions. The first was that each net of market areas had one point in common (as they do in Figure 3.19). The second was that the various market-area nets had to be related to each other in such a way that the total number of supply points would be at a minimum. This would be an advantage in terms of the efficiency of the transport network.

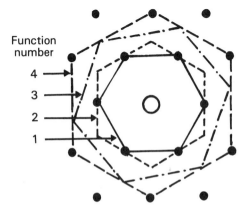

Function number

4

3

2

1

**Figure 3.19**   The four smallest market area sizes in the Lösch system.

The final structure was a system of centers based on a common supply point, which Lösch called the *metropolis*, from which radiated six "center-rich" sectors and six "center-poor" sectors. A simple Lösch system, based on the four smallest market-area sizes of Figure 3.19 is shown in Figure 3.20. The center Z represents the metropolis, and the six center-rich sectors are indicated by shaded triangles. The market-area nets extend indefinitely and in a repetitive manner, so that the center Z (the metropolis) is surrounded, at a considerable distance, by six other Z centers of comparable functional complexity. The boundary of the single-center Z-based system can thus be derived by taking perpendicular bisectors between the center Z and each of the surrounding centers (the bold lines in Figure 3.20). The centers of the system are differentiated according to their functional specialization. For example, center A supplies only function 1, while center X supplies functions 1, 2, and 4.

As with the Christaller system, a hierarchy emerges but it is a good deal more complex. While there are N functions (or bundles of functions) and N market-area sizes, there are more than N levels of the hierarchy! Moreover, the hierarchy is not successively inclusive, as can be seen from Table 3.2 which refers to the functional complexity of centers in Figure 3.20. For example, center S supplies functions 1 and 4, but not functions 2 and 3. One may contrast the functional hierarchy of Table 3.2 with that of Table 1.1, representing the comparable functional hierarchy of the Christaller system. It should be noted that the hierarchy of centers in Figure 3.20 is based simply on functional complexity, that is, on the possession of functions (Parr, 1973).

As noted, a weakness arises in the Lösch system as a result of each market area having been derived independently of the others. Therefore, in a multi-function system the possibility of multi-purpose trips is not taken into account, nor is the possibility that a center may exert an additional demand because, as a supply point for one or more functions, it will have a production-based population. Furthermore, the demands of other centers in a given center's market areas are not considered (Parr, 1973). Despite these weaknesses, the Lösch model does contain features that are identifiable in actual central-place systems. Lösch himself presented evidence of the existence of a sector structure around the metropolis-based regions of Indianapolis and Toledo (1941, p. 125). A more detailed investigation of the former area by Nicholls (1970) revealed that much of the nineteenth-century development of urban centers was consistent with the Lösch model.

**TABLE 3.2** A HIERARCHY OF FUNCTIONAL COMPLEXITY IN THE LÖSCH SYSTEM

| Functions supplied | Level of center | | | | | | | | | | |
|---|---|---|---|---|---|---|---|---|---|---|---|
| | A | G | M | P | R | S | V | W | X | Y | Z |
| 1 | x | | | x | x | x | | x | x | x | x |
| 2 | | x | | x | | | x | x | x | | x |
| 3 | | | x | | x | | x | x | | x | x |
| 4 | | | | | | x | | | x | x | x |

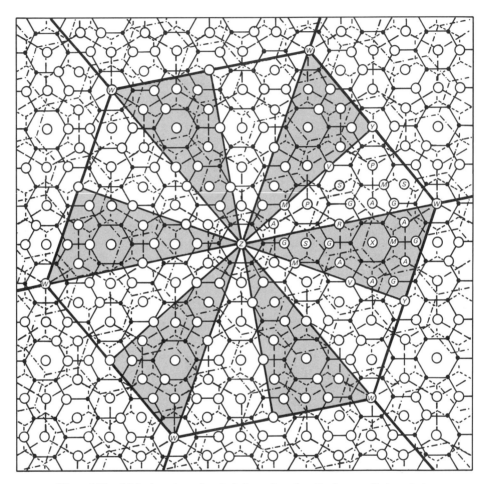

**Figure 3.20**  A Lösch system of central places, based on the four smallest market-area sizes. The "center-rich sector" is the triangle $ZYW$ containing center $X$ and has the equivalent of 13 central places, while the "center-poor sector" is represented by the triangle $ZYW$ containing center $P$ and has the equivalent of 11 central places.

## CHRISTALLER AND LÖSCH COMPARED

Both Christaller and Lösch agree that the triangular arrangement of central places and hexagonal market areas represents an equilibrium for a single function under the assumptions of free entry and uniform densities on a homogeneous plain with equal access in all directions. Lösch provided the more explicit analysis, however. In his solution, the location of individual firms is as advantageous as possible, excess profits disappear, market areas are as small as possible, every consumer is served, and the boundaries of market areas are points of consumer indifference. Interlocking nets of markets for different functions were produced in two completely different ways by the two theoreticians, however. Christaller imposed much more severe limitations on market-area sizes than Lösch, and this gave rise to significant differences between the two systems in terms of market-area structure and the nature of the functional hierarchy of centers.

Because of its greater complexity the Lösch model does not lend itself to empirical testing as readily as the Christaller model. Nevertheless, in their different ways, each model contains certain features of actual central-place systems. In the Christaller case, the well-defined successively inclusive hierarchy is characteristic of numerous central-place systems, particularly in the lower half of the hierarchy. Moreover, there is considerable scope for multi-purpose trips (not only for functions within a bundle of a given level, but also for bundles of different levels), even though the implications for market-area structure were not fully explored. In the Lösch case, it is possible for a small center (of low functional complexity) to serve a large center (of high functional complexity), and the structure contains the pattern of alternating center-rich and center-poor sectors. These features, neither of which is present in the Christaller system, also can be identified in actual central-place systems. It has been suggested that Christaller's approach appears most relevant for understanding the spatial structure of retail and service business (involving consumer travel), whereas Lösch's framework offers a background for analyzing the spatial distribution of market-oriented manufacturing (von Böventer, 1963).

The models of Christaller and Lösch suffer from another weakness. They are concerned with central-place systems as they exist at equilibrium. No attempt is made to focus on the processes of adjustment and change which (as discussed in Chapter 1) influenced the attainment of this equilibrium. It is true that Christaller and Lösch constructed their respective systems in a sequential or function-by-function manner, but this was done for presentational purposes and did not really cast light on the historical emergence of the system. For this reason, both models contain a number of logical weaknesses which might have been avoided had the question of evolutionary adjustment of the hierarchy been made more explicit. A related weakness concerns the fact that the models are static in conception and say little about how the systems behave if major changes in underlying conditions occur. Christaller (1933) did devote a substantial portion of his book to "dynamic processes," but these were not treated in a systematic way within the context of his initial model. These weaknesses notwithstanding, the works of Christaller and Lösch remain as important landmarks in economic geography and regional economics. They provide an indispensable foundation for further work in the analysis of central-place systems, which is reviewed in Chapter 4.

## REFERENCES

BEAVON, K. S. O. (1977) *Central Place Theory: A Reinterpretation*. London: Longman.

BEAVON, K. S. O., and A. S. MABIN (1975) "The Lösch System of Market Areas: Derivation and Extension," *Geographical Analysis*, 7:131–151.

BECKMANN, M. J. (1968) *Location Theory*, New York: Random House.

BERRY, B. J. L., and A. PRED (1961) *Central Place Studies: A Bibliography of Theory and Applications*, Philadelphia: Regional Science Research Institute.

VON BÖVENTER, E. (1963) "Toward a Unified Theory of Spatial Economic Structure," *Papers of the Regional Science Association*, 10:163–187.

CANTILLON, R. (1755) *Essai sur la nature du Commerce en Général*. Edited with an English translation and other material by Henry Higgs, C.B. Reissued for The Royal Economic Society by Frank Cass, London, 1959.

CHRISTALLER, W. (1933) *Die zentralen Orte in Süddeutschland*. Jena, Germany: Fischer. English translation by C. Baskin: *The Central Places of Southern Germany*. Englewood Cliffs, N.J.: Prentice-Hall, Inc., 1966. (All text citations refer to the English translation.)

CHRISTALLER, W. (1950) "Das Grundgerüst der räumlichen Ordnung in Europa," *Frankfurter Geographische Hefte*, 24:1–96.

DACEY, M. F. (1964) "A Note on Some Number Properties of a Hexagonal Plane Lattice," *Journal of Regional Science*, 5:63–67.

DENIKE, K. G., and J. B. PARR (1970) "Production in Space, Spatial Competition, and Restricted Entry," *Journal of Regional Science*, 10:49–63.

GALPIN, C. J. (1915) *The Social Anatomy of an Agricultural Community*, Research Bulletin 34, Agricultural Experiment Station of University of Wisconsin, Madison, Wisc.

HOOVER, E. M. (1970) *An Introduction to Regional Economics*. New York: Knopf.

HASSAN, R. (1972) "Islam and Urbanization in the Medieval Middle East," *Ekistics*, 33:108.

LALANNE, L. (1863) "Essai d'une théorie des réseaux de chemin de fer, fondée sur l'observation des faits et sur les lois primordiales qui président au groupement des populations," *Comptes Rendus Hebdomadaires des Séances de l'Académie des Sciences*, 57:206–210.

LÖSCH, A. (1938) "The Nature of Economic Regions," *Southern Economic Journal*, 5:71–78.

LÖSCH, A. (1941) *Die räumliche Ordnung der Wirtschaft*. Jena, Germany: Fischer. English translation of the second German edition (1944) by W. H. Woglom and W. F. Stolper: *The Economics of Location*. New Haven, Conn.: Yale University Press, 1954. (All text citations refer to the English translation.)

MULLIGAN, G. F. (1981) "Lösch's Single-Good Equilibrium," *Annals of the Association of American Geographers*, 71:84–94.

NICHOLLS, J. A. F. (1970) "Transportation Development and Löschian Market Areas: An Historical Perspective," *Land Economics*, 46:22–31.

PARR, J. B. (1973) "Structure and Size in the Urban System of Lösch," *Economic Geography*, 49:185–212.

PARR, J. B. (1985) "Square Market Areas, Löschian Numbers, and Spatial Organization," *Geographical Analysis*, 17:284–301.

RALLIS, T. (1963) "A Communication: Urban Development in Denmark," *Papers of the Regional Science Association*, 10:153–156.

REYNAUD, J. (1841) "Villes," "Voies de Communication," "Terre," "Vauban," *Encyclopedie Nouvelle*, 8:670–687, 700–712, 417–488, 609–614.

SKINNER, G. W. (1964) "Marketing and Social Structure in Rural China-I," *Journal of Asian Studies*, 24:3–33.

SMITH, A. (1776) *An Inquiry into the Nature and Causes of the Wealth of Nations*. Modern version edited by E. Cannan. New York: Modern Library, 1937.

SMITH, C. (1974) "Economics of Marketing Systems: Models from Economic Geography," *Annual Review of Anthropology*, 3:167–202.

STEPONAITIS, V. P. (1978) "Location Theory and Complex Chiefdoms: A Mississippian Example," in B. D. Smith (ed.), *Mississippian Settlement Patterns*. New York: Academic Press.

STEPONAITIS, V. P. (1981) "Settlement Hierarchies and Political Complexity in Nonmarket Societies: The Formative Period of the Valley of Mexico," *American Anthropologist*, 83:320–365.

# 4

# Modern Central-Place Theories

The works of Christaller and Lösch should be seen as initial attempts to come to grips with the spatial organization of market-oriented economic activity and the urban system to which it gives rise. The translation of these works into other languages had the effect of stimulating interest in central-place theory, resulting in a substantial literature on the subject.

The first research emphasis has been concerned with elaborations and extension of the traditional models, particularly with regard to their nature and properties. For example, the Christaller central-place model has been analyzed in terms of axiomatic statements of the geometrical and mathematical structure inherent in this system (Dacey, 1976; Dacey et al., 1974; Alao et al., 1977). The Lösch model has also been subjected to thorough theoretical scrutiny, and analyses by Webber (1974), Hartwick (1973), Eaton and Lipsey (1976), and Mulligan (1981a) have focused on the stability conditions and on the nature of the single-function equilibrium. In addition, Long (1970) has explored some of the economic implications of the multi-function version of the model, while the construction of this model and the existence of the center-rich and center-poor structure have been discussed by Beavon and Mabin (1975), Beavon (1970), and Marshall (1977; 1978).

A second research emphasis has been concerned with modifications of the traditional models and with the development of alternatives to them, sometimes in order to increase their theoretical generality and sometimes to render them more realistic (Mulligan, 1984b).

In this chapter we deal with both of these research emphases. We begin by looking at theoretical refinements of the traditional models in terms of market-area structure and the size of centers. This is followed by a review of alternative models of the central-place system that have been proposed. Consideration is then given to the introduction of more realistic assumptions into central-place models. Approaches to the question of change in a central-place system are then examined, and there is discussion as to how central-place systems can be related to general-systems theory.

## EQUILIBRIUM MARKET-AREA SHAPES

In the previous chapter we examined the pattern of suppliers within a spatial equilibrium. It was shown that, in the absence of other impositions, spatial equilibrium would involve a triangular spacing of suppliers, with each supplier having a hexagonal market area. In fact, Lösch (1941) *assumed* that the equilibrium market-area shape would be hexagonal, an assumption that may not have been warranted. Let us examine the situation by considering a triangular lattice of supply points, so that each supplier is surrounded by six other identical suppliers. For the purposes of the argument it suffices to consider only three suppliers (A, B, and C). These are shown in Figure 4.1, which illustrates alternative equilibrium market-area structures.

It is obvious that the hexagonal market-area shape will only exist if the consumer at $d$ (located at the maximum distance from each of the three suppliers A, B, and C) is able to exert a positive demand, that is, if the resulting real price (f.o.b. plus the transport cost incurred) at $d$ permits a positive demand. If this condition is satisfied, the relevant parts of the suppliers' market areas are given by the perpendicular bisectors ($ds$, $dt$, and $dv$) of pairs of competing producers, resulting in each supplier within the system having a hexagonal market area.

Now let us consider a situation in which the real price facing a consumer is relatively high because of high transport costs. Let us further assume that for supplier A the last consumer (in the direction of $d$) to exert a demand is located at $e_1$, so that consumers located beyond the arc $se_1v$ exert no demand at all from supplier A. In terms of Figure 3.2, this would mean that the real price facing them (the equilibrium f.o.b. price plus the appropriate transport cost) is higher than $p + rt$. Now if such a situation holds for consumers at $e_1$ served by supplier A, it will also hold for comparably located consumers at $e_2$ and $e_3$ which are served by suppliers B and C respectively. Under these conditions, therefore, the relevant parts of the market-area boundaries for the three suppliers A, B, and C will not be given by the perpendicular bisectors but by the three arcs $se_1v$, $ve_2t$, and $te_3s$. Since every supplier is surrounded by six other suppliers, the equilibrium market area for each supplier will be in the shape of a circle. In this way certain consumers (those located within the areas bounded by three arcs $se_1v$, $ve_2t$, and $te_3s$) are excluded from the market. Further entry of suppliers (to serve the excluded consumers) is ruled out because the system is already assumed to have reached

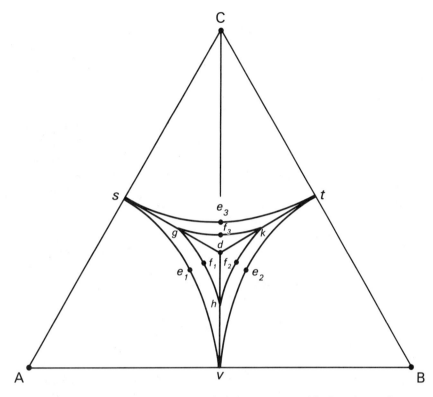

**Figure 4.1**  Alternative equilibrium market-area structures with triangular spacing of suppliers.

equilibrium with each supplier able to earn only normal profits, an indication that the process of free entry has reached its limit. As we saw in Chapter 3, Lösch regarded the circular market area as a temporary phase in the passage to equilibrium, with the process of entry ensuring that the outer limits of the circular market area would be eroded, so that a hexagonal market-area structure would emerge. However, under the rather unusual circumstances considered above, this is not possible. If this situation were viewed in terms of Figure 3.5, the $D_1$ curve would be tangent to the $C$ curve, indicating the existence of an equilibrium with no subsequent erosion of the market area. Expressed in terms of ranges, the ideal range coincides with the threshold range; and, as a consequence, consumers located in the interstices of the tangentially circular market areas inevitably remain unserved.

There is also an equilibrium market-area shape that is intermediate between the hexagon and the circle. Let us consider again the equilibrium situation of Figure 4.1, but in this case with a slightly lower (though still relatively high) equilibrium f.o.b. price. Let us assume that for supplier A the last consumer (in the direction of $d$) to exert a demand is the consumer at $f_1$. (Consumers located at $f_2$ and $f_3$ represent the comparable consumers for suppliers B and C, respectively.) In this situation there is no effective demand from supplier A beyond the arc $gf_1h$. However, consumers located beyond the line $hv$ (in the direction of B) and beyond the line $sg$ (in the direction of C) are obviously able to exert an effective demand from suppliers B and C, respectively. Thus in certain directions from supplier A, demand falls to zero before the competition of another supplier is encountered, but in other directions the opposite is the case. Under these conditions, therefore, the relevant part of the market-area boundary for supplier A consists of the line $sg$, the arc $gf_1h$, and the line $hv$. For the system as a whole, each supplier has a hexagonal market area with each corner excluded by an arc. This implies that the ideal range forms the market-area boundary in certain directions, with the real range forming the boundary in other directions. As with the previous case, which involved circular market areas, certain consumers (those located within the area bounded by three arcs, $gf_1h$, $hf_2k$, and $kf_3g$) remain unserved, and because equilibrium conditions are assumed to obtain, no further entry is possible (Denike and Parr, 1970).

We have seen that with suppliers located in the pattern of a triangular lattice the possible market-area shapes are the hexagon, the circle, and the rounded hexagon. It will be recalled from Chapter 3 that suppliers also may be located in the pattern of a square lattice. This will usually give rise to square market areas, and similar considerations to those discussed above may also apply in this setting. The square market-area shape will only exist if consumers at the corners of each market area are able to exert a demand. If this is not the case, the market area will be in the shape of a circle (each circle tangent with four others) or a square, with each corner excluded by an arc. Both the circle and the square with each corner excluded imply the exclusion from the market of certain consumers.

No matter what the prevailing market-area shape, the question of exclusion complicates the structure of the central-place model. Usually, a bundle of functions of level $m$ is assumed to be supplied from centers of level $m$ or higher throughout their respective market areas. In the light of the preceding discussion, however, it may be better to regard each function of the bundle as having its own market area. Some functions may have market areas which extend in all directions to their competitors' market areas, while some other functions may have truncated market areas which are not adjacent or are only partly adjacent to their competitors' market areas. This phenomenon of exclusion is something of a paradox: The central-place system is in equilibrium, yet certain consumers are unserved, and no further entry is possible. It represents a dramatic manifestation of the "friction of distance" or "the tyranny of space" when transport costs are high. Real prices rise rapidly with distance, and people located in peripheral areas may be unable to exercise positive demand. Some adjustments to these conditions are discussed in Chapter 5, which deals with periodic marketing systems.

The question of exclusion of consumers is not one of purely theoretical interest. The phenomenon can be observed in the real world, and it raises serious policy questions about the provision of service. In developing countries, it is not at all uncommon for the population of large tracts of territory to be excluded from the opportunity of consuming certain goods or services, and this is simply because of the large distances or high transport costs involved and the resulting high real prices. This helps to explain the sometimes significant differences between rural and urban populations in terms of their consumptions of goods and services, and consequently the differences in their living standards. The problem of exclusion may also occur within the metropolitan areas of developed nations. The time, expense, and general inconvenience involved in traveling long distances often discourage low-income groups from consuming certain services, which may even be offered free at the point of supply. The problem typically arises when the service in question is supplied from relatively few, large-scale public facilities, for example, when members of low-income groups have to get medical services from a public hospital (Parr and Denike, 1970). Whatever the setting, should the government decide as a matter of policy that all consumers must be served, it would be necessary for governmental intervention to occur in the form of a subsidy to suppliers, or to consumers, or to the transport sector, or to some combination of these three.

## SIZE OF CENTERS IN A CENTRAL-PLACE SYSTEM

Neither Christaller nor Lösch adequately pursued the question of center size in their respective central-place systems, tending to treat center size in terms of the number of functions supplied. Christaller (1933, p. 67), it is true, did indicate "typical" center populations for various levels of the hierarchy, but these were based simply on observed conditions in prewar southern Germany. However, a good deal of effort has been devoted to the development of models of center populations within a central-place system.

### The Beckmann Model

The first serious attempt to tackle the question of center size was undertaken by Beckmann (1958). This formulation was revised by Beckmann (1968) and Parr (1970). Using the hierarchical central-place framework of the Christaller system, Beckmann argued that the total population $U_m$ served by a level $m$ center would consist of the population of the center itself, $u_m$, and the population of that center's market area, $a_m$ (strictly speaking, the center's largest, or level $m$, market area). In other words $U_m = u_m + a_m$. The crucial assumption of the Beckmann model is that the population of a center of any level $m$ will always be a constant proportion $v$ of the total population served by the center. That is, $u_m = vU_m$. Consequently,

$$U_m = \frac{a_m}{1 - v} \tag{4.1}$$

and

$$u_m = v(u_m + a_m) = \frac{va_m}{1 - v} \tag{4.2}$$

For the lowest level of the hierarchy (i.e., where $m = 1$) the population of a center can be expressed as

$$u_1 = \frac{va_1}{1 - v} \tag{4.3}$$

where $a_1$ represents the population of the smallest market area, which is usually assumed to be entirely rural.

The formulation of the population of a center of higher levels is more complicated. Referring back to the $K = 3$ system depicted in Figure 3.9, the population of the level $m$ market area of a level $m$ center can be seen to consist of the total populations served by the equivalent of two or, more generally, $K - 1$ centers of the next lower level (i.e., level $m - 1$), as well as the population of the level $m$ center's level $m - 1$ market area. In other words,

$$a_m = (K - 1)U_{m-1} + a_{m-1} \tag{4.4}$$

It follows from equation (4.1) that

$$U_{m-1} = \frac{a_{m-1}}{1 - v} \tag{4.1a}$$

Substituting (4.1a) in equation (4.4), we have

$$a_m = (K - 1)\frac{a_{m-1}}{1 - v} + a_{m-1} \tag{4.4a}$$

and then substituting equation (4.4a) in equation (4.2), we finally obtain

$$u_m = \frac{v}{1 - v}\left[(K - 1)\frac{a_{m-1}}{1 - v} + a_{m-1}\right] = \frac{va_{m-1}}{1 - v}\left(\frac{K - v}{1 - v}\right) \tag{4.5}$$

Expressed in terms of the smallest market area $a_1$, the term $u_m$, the population of a center of level $m$, can be written as

$$u_m = \frac{va_1}{1 - v}\left(\frac{K - v}{1 - v}\right)^{m-1} \tag{4.6}$$

The first part of the right-hand side of the equation can be recognized as the population of the level 1 center, as defined in equation (4.3), whereas the term in parentheses represents a progression factor, indicating the increase in center size from one level of the hierarchy to the next. For example, if the progression factor is 5, then level 2 centers are 5 times the size of the level 1 centers. Similarly, level 3 centers are 25 times the size, and level 4 centers are 125 times the size, and so on. This exponential increase in center populations has been observed empirically. We saw in Chapter 2, for example, that the increase in the number of business types with hierarchical level can be expressed as $\eta\rho^{m-1}$. Other characteristics of the central-place system which appear to vary exponentially with hierarchical level include total employment, the number of establishments, traffic generated, and other aspects, as was discussed in Chapter 2.

### The Modified Beckmann Model

While the Beckmann model represents a reasonable approximation to actual center populations, it does contain the rather rigid assumption that $v$ must be constant with $m$—an assumption for which there is no empirical or theoretical justification. To overcome this problem, a modification of the Beckmann model is possible which allows $v$ to vary with $m$, so that $v$ is replaced with $v_m$ (Parr, 1970, pp. 225–226). The population of a center of level 1 can be expressed as

$$u_1 = \frac{v_1 a_1}{1 - v_1} \tag{4.7}$$

which is, of course, identical to the Beckmann model, but for $m > 1$, the formulation becomes

$$u_m = \frac{v_m a_m}{1 - v_m} = \frac{v_m}{1 - v_m}\left[ K^{m-1}a_1 + \sum_{i=1}^{m-1} u_{m-i}(K^i - K^{i-1}) \right] \tag{4.8}$$

with the term in brackets representing the population of the rural area as well as the various lower-level centers within the level $m$ market area of the level $m$ center.

### The Dacey Model

The previous two models of center population are based on an essentially spatial relationship, the proportion of center population to total population served, rather than on a functional or economic one. A model of a more economic slant has been proposed by Dacey (1966) for the Christaller system. This model has two distinctive features. First, it takes explicit account of the fact that a given center supplies different bundles of functions to its different market areas. For example, a center of level $m$ provides the level 1 bundle to its level 1 market area, the level 2 bundle to its level 2 market, and so on, up to the level $m$ bundle which is supplied to its level $m$ market area. Second, the model distinguishes between the external markets of a center and its internal market, and in this sense it resembles an export-base model. The most crucial element in the model is the term $k_m$ which can be defined as the population of a center engaged in supplying the level $m$ bundle as a proportion of the population served. There will be a $k$ value for each bundle supplied. For level 1, involving the supply of bundle 1 to $a_1$, the population of a level 1 center can be expressed as

$$u_1 = k_1 a_1 + (k_1 a_1)k_1 + (k_1 a_1)k_1^2 + \cdots \tag{4.9}$$

where $a_1$ represents the population of the level 1 market area. The term $k_1 a_1$ can be seen as the "export" component of the center's population; that is, it is that part of the center's population which is serving consumers located outside the center. However, this export-providing population will also need to be served, giving an additional internal-market population of $(k_1 a_1)k_1$, which itself will need to be served, giving a further internal-market population of $(k_1 a_1)k_1^2$, and so forth. The terms beyond $k_1 a_1$ represent the various rounds of expenditure within the center and collectively these comprise the "local" component of the center's population, that is, that part of the center's population which serves consumers located within the center. Equation (4.9) can be simplified to

$$u_1 = \frac{k_1 a_1}{1 - k_1} \tag{4.10}$$

For levels of the hierarchy where $m > 1$, the formulation is more complicated. The export component of a center's population, $X_m$, can be expressed as

$$X_m = k_1 a_1 + k_2 a_2 + \cdots = \sum_{i=1}^{m} k_i a_i \tag{4.11}$$

reflecting the fact that each bundle is supplied to a separate market area. The population of a level $m$ center is therefore

$$u_m = X_m + X_m \sum_{i=1}^{m} k_i + X_m \left( \sum_{i=1}^{m} k_i \right)^2 + \cdots = \frac{X_m}{1 - \sum\limits_{i=1}^{m} k_i} \tag{4.12}$$

and if (4.11) is substituted for $X_m$ in (4.12), this can be expressed as

$$u_m = \frac{\sum\limits_{i=1}^{m} k_i a_i}{1 - \sum\limits_{i=1}^{m} k_i} \quad \text{with} \left( \sum_{i=1}^{m} k_i < 1 \right) \tag{4.13}$$

where the term

$$\frac{1}{1 - \sum\limits_{i=1}^{m} k_i} \tag{4.14}$$

represents the *export multiplier,* and the inequality expression in parentheses ensures that center populations remain finite. In specifying this model of center population, Dacey elaborated upon the numerator so as to indicate the composition of the various market areas, which obviously depends on the spatial structure of the system as represented by $K$. He also introduced two special cases relating to the $\{k_i\}$ values ($i = 1, 2, \ldots, m, \ldots, N$), which in the general model of the equation (4.12) were unspecified. In one case $k_m$ was constant with $m$, and in the other case $k_m$ was part of a power series in which $k_m = k_1^m$. A third special case could be added in which $k_m = k_1 m$. In all cases the elements of $\{k_i\}$ must sum to less than unity.

   It will be recognized that the Dacey model requires center populations to be derived recursively, that is, the level 1 center population must be calculated before the level 2 center population can be calculated and this must be known before the level 3 center population can be determined, and so on. For a more general model (of which the Christaller structure is a particular case) Beckmann and McPherson (1970) have proposed a formulation where this problem of recursive determination does not arise, although the explicit export-base character of the formulation disappears (Parr, Denike, and Mulligan, 1975).

An advantage of the Dacey model is that it can be modified to include the effect of non–central-place functions within a center, such as mining or certain types of manufacturing. The population based on these "specialized function" activities is added to the numerator of the equation (4.13) and the total center population is derived in the usual way (Parr, 1970; Marshall, 1975). One shortcoming of the model, however, is its implicit assumption that the levels of consumption for a bundle of functions in a particular market area of a center are identical to those within the center. This is not consistent with the analysis of spatial demand in Chapter 3, where it was seen that demand decreased with distance from the point of supply due to the influence of transport costs. The model can, however, be modified so as to incorporate this factor. This involves using two sets of $\{k_i\}$ values. The elements of one set are applied to the respective market-area populations, and each element takes into account that demand falls with distance from the center. The other set is applied collectively to the export component of the center's population.

Clearly, there exists a wide variety of population models (especially when the special cases are included), and attempts have been made by Dacey (1970) and Parr (1970) to draw these together in a common form and language. These models generally refer to central-place structures based on the Christaller system but they can readily be applied to the Lösch system (Parr, 1973) and, indeed, to other central-place systems which will be discussed later in this chapter.

### Other Approaches to Center Size

Despite the obvious importance of population as an indication of center size in a central-place system, it is only one of several measures. In analyses of trade patterns with a central-place system, size has been considered in terms of output levels (Hartwick, 1974) as well as in terms of the value of exports and imports (Alao et al., 1977). A further model considered the income flows among hierarchical levels, from which the total income of a center of level $m$ can be derived (Mulligan, 1981b). These other approaches to center size, which assume the same spatial structure and pattern of functional specialization as the population models, not only provide alternative perspectives on center size, but they can, themselves, form the basis for more sophisticated models of center population.

Once the sizes of centers have been determined, by whatever means, it is then possible to extend the central-place model to incorporate additional economic and social processes. For example, passenger traffic among centers and the structure of commodity flows could both be introduced into the system. In a similar vein, a number of authors have examined the question of innovation diffusion in a central-place system, using different assumptions about the size of centers. Hudson (1969), for example, has considered the process of diffusion within a central-place system in which there would be a "filtering down" process of diffusion within the hierarchy. He states:

> . . . the sudden appearance of an innovation at widely separated centers without the existence of intervening adapters is consistent with central place theory. . . . The earliest centers are those most likely to be first exposed, and they are those having the greatest value of interaction: the largest centers. Very small centers are the last to be exposed since they must wait until higher order places in their area. . . . (Hudson, 1969, p. 46)

In addition to this hierarchical diffusion, there would also be the more familiar contagion or neighborhood effect, particularly at the lower levels of the hierarchy. Hudson's analysis was extended by Alves (1974) and Beaumont and Keys (1980). An alternative model of diffusion has been proposed by Pederson (1970) in which differentiated rates of distance decay (of information flows) and differential per capita acceptance rates would influence the final pattern of adoption. Pederson (1970) contended that hierarchical diffusion would be fostered if the distance-decay rate was slow, while contagious diffusion would be associated with a high rate of distance decay.

## ALTERNATIVES TO THE CHRISTALLER AND LÖSCH SYSTEMS

The central-place systems of Christaller and Lösch, while of major theoretical significance, have not proven themselves to be especially useful in the analysis of particular characteristics such as the size, spacing, and frequency of centers in central-place systems. The Lösch system, for example, is complex, and although it does cast light on a number of important features of the urban system, it tends to be difficult to apply. The Christaller system, for its part, is less complex than the Lösch system, but unfortunately it contains an in-built rigidity, the requirement of a constant value for $K$. As a result very few of Christaller's diagrams bear any resemblance to the real world. Except for the important feature of the hierarchical structure, many actual systems cannot be described in terms of a Christaller system.

### The Woldenberg System

One modification of the Christaller system was proposed by Woldenberg (1968), following on from an earlier suggestion by Christaller (1950). Woldenberg's approach involved the existence of "mixed hierarchies." Woldenberg's argument was that in a real-world system all three of Christaller's organizing principles

**TABLE 4.1**  APPLICATION OF THE WOLDENBERG MODEL TO CENTRAL-PLACE SYSTEMS

| Ijebu Province, Nigeria | | | South Bothnia, Finland | | | Christaller | | |
|---|---|---|---|---|---|---|---|---|
| *m* | *O* | *T* | *m* | *O* | *T* | *m* | *K* = 3 | *K* = 4 |
| | | | 6 | 1 | 1 | 6 | 1 | 1 |
| 5 | 1 | 1 | 5 | 2 | 2 | 5 | 2 | 3 |
| 4 | 2 | 2 | 4 | 6 | 7 | 4 | 6 | 12 |
| 3 | 10 | 7 | 3 | 25 | 27 | 3 | 18 | 48 |
| 2 | 25 | 27 | 2 | 115 | 110 | 2 | 54 | 192 |
| 1 | 36 | 35 | 1 | 362 | 371 | 1 | 162 | 768 |

$m$ = hierarchical level; $O$ = observed frequency; $T$ = theoretical frequency.

($K = 3$, $K = 4$, and $K = 7$) would be present, coexisting to some degree. For the $K = 3$ system the frequencies of market-area sizes, from the largest to the smallest, are 1, 3, 9, 27, 81, 243, 729, . . . ; for the $K = 4$ system they are 1, 4, 16, 64, 256, 1024, . . . ; and for the $K = 7$ system they are 1, 7, 49, 343, 2401, . . . . These numbers can be grouped together to form hierarchical levels, and the convergent mean, based on the arithmetic and geometric means, is determined for each level. One such grouping yields the following market-area frequencies: 1, 3.48, 10.33, 37.18, 147.19, 517.86, and so forth. From this series, the center frequencies (rounded off) can be derived: 1, 2, 7, 27, 110, 371. However, different groupings of market-area (and thus "center") frequencies are possible, and this permits a greater flexibility than is possible with the Christaller model, a factor of obvious importance when the model is being used to describe actual central-place systems. Columns 2 and 5 of Table 4.1 indicate the observed center frequencies for Ijebu Province, Nigeria, and South Bothnia, Finland, while columns 3 and 6 indicate the theoretical frequencies derived from two different market-area groupings. For both regions the model provides superior results to those of the $K = 3$ and $K = 4$ versions of the Christaller system (columns 8 and 9). The appeal of Woldenberg's model lies in the fact that, unlike the Christaller model, it acknowledges the simultaneous existence of more than one organizing principle. One drawback of the model, however, is that it is difficult to represent spatially, although attempts have been made to overcome this (Woldenberg, 1968, pp. 572–574).

### The General Hierarchical System

Whereas the Woldenberg model considered the mixing of $K$ values *within* a particular level, we now turn to a model in which there is a mixing of $K$ values *among* levels. As already stated, the value of $K$ in the Christaller system cannot vary among levels within the system. There exists a more general system, however, in which $K$ is not necessarily constant with $m$. The successively inclusive hierarchy of the Christaller system is retained in this system but not the constant $K$

requirement. This system is referred to as the General Hierarchical System or GH system (Parr, 1978). The Christaller system represents a special case of the GH system in which the values of $K$ are constant with $m$. Figure 4.2 indicates a non-Christaller version of the GH system with hexagonal market areas, but square market areas are also possible (Parr, 1985).

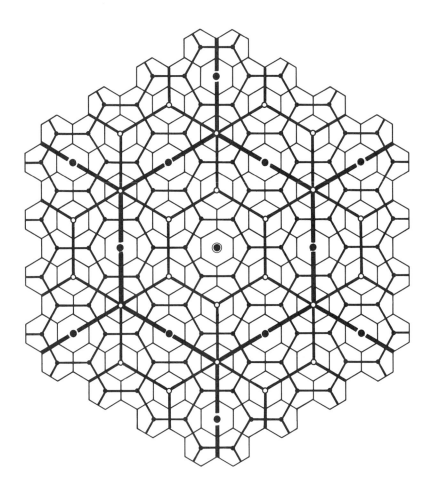

| Center | | Market area |
|:---:|:---:|:---:|
| • | Level 1 | ———— |
| ○ | Level 2 | ——— |
| ● | Level 3 | ━━━ |
| ◉ | Level 4 | ▬▬▬ |

**Figure 4.2**   GH model of a central-place system ($K_1 = 3$; $K_2 = 3$; $K_3 = 4$).

While in the Christaller system a particular structure can be described by the unsubscripted parameter $K$ (e.g., $K = 3$ or $K = 4$), this is not possible in the GH system where the term $K_{m-1}$ has to be used. This indicates the equivalent number of market areas of level $m - 1$ (where $m > 1$) that are contained within a market area of level $m$, that is, the rate of increase of market-area size from level $m - 1$ to level $m$. Each level $m$ (where $m > 1$) has an associated $K$ value, which is referred to as $K_{m-1}$. For example, for $m = 5$ the associated $K$ value is $K_{m-1}$ or $K_4$. Thus, if there are $N$ levels of the hierarchy, there will be $N - 1$ values for $K$. A particular system can therefore be specified by defining the set $\{K_i\}$ where $i = 1, 2, \ldots, N - 1$. In the four-level system depicted in Figure 4.2, we have $K_1 = 3$, $K_2 = 3$, and $K_3 = 4$. The real virtue of the GH system, however, rests with its plausibility. Instead of insisting, as Christaller does, that a particular organizational principle be present at all levels, the GH model allows different organizational principles to operate at different levels. And if instead of interpreting the elements of set $\{K_i\}$ in terms of organizational principles, these are viewed as reflecting the manner in which the threshold-range characteristics (involving demand, production costs, and transport costs) vary among the different functions being supplied, the GH system again seems more credible than the Christaller system since the GH system does not require a variation in demand and supply characteristics such that market-area size increases by a constant factor of $K$.

Using the set $\{K_i\}$, it is possible to derive expressions for market-area frequency and center spacing in the GH system (whether the market-area shapes are hexagonal or square). Since the Christaller system exists as a special case of the GH system, these expressions are also valid for the Christaller system. The frequency of market areas of the highest level ($m = N$) is usually taken as 1, but $F_m$, the frequency for market areas of levels $m < N$, is given by

$$F_m = \prod_{i=m}^{N-1} K_i \tag{4.15}$$

where $K_i$ is the number of market areas of level $i$ contained within a market area of level $i + 1$. In the case of frequency of centers, the frequency at level $N$ can be taken as 1, while the frequency of centers of level $N - 1$ is $K_{N-1} - 1$. For $m < N - 1$ the value of $f_m$, the frequency of centers of level $m$, is given by

$$f_m = \prod_{i=m}^{N-1} K_i - \prod_{i=m+1}^{N-1} K_i \tag{4.16}$$

The distance $d_m$ between neighboring centers of level $m$ is given by

$$d_m = d_1 \prod_{i=1}^{m-1} \sqrt{K_i} \tag{4.17}$$

where $d_1$ is the distance between neighboring centers of level 1. With respect to center size, the Christaller models of center population presented in the previous section can be adapted to derive center populations in the GH system, the most useful being the Dacey model (Beckmann and McPherson, 1970; Parr, Denike, and Mulligan, 1975).

The GH system lends itself to the analysis of a much wider range of central-place structures than is possible with the Christaller system. With the aid of equation (4.16), it is possible to construct a model which closely describes actual conditions in terms of center frequencies. Columns 2 and 5 of Table 4.2 indicate the observed center frequencies for the Philippines and the Owen Sound area of Ontario, Canada, while columns 3 and 7 indicate the best-fitting theoretical frequencies, derived from the highest level downward. In both cases there is a high degree of correspondence, certainly higher than that which can be obtained with the $K = 3$ and $K = 4$ versions of the Christaller system, which are indicated in columns 10 and 11.

**TABLE 4.2**  APPLICATION OF THE GH MODEL TO CENTRAL-PLACE SYSTEMS

| Philippines | | | | Owen Sound, Ontario | | | | Christaller | | |
|---|---|---|---|---|---|---|---|---|---|---|
| $m$ | $O$ | $T$ | $\{K_i\}$ | $m$ | $O$ | $T$ | $\{K_i\}$ | $m$ | $K = 3$ | $K = 4$ |
| 4 | 1 | 1 | — | 4 | 1 | 1 | — | 4 | 1 | 1 |
| 3 | 4 | 3 | $K_3 = 4$ | 3 | 6 | 6 | $K_3 = 7$ | 3 | 2 | 3 |
| 2 | 67 | 60 | $K_2 = 16$ | 2 | 12 | 14 | $K_2 = 3$ | 2 | 6 | 12 |
| 1 | 126 | 128 | $K_1 = 4$ | 1 | 60 | 63 | $K_1 = 4$ | 1 | 18 | 48 |

*Note: m* = hierarchical level; $O$ = observed frequency; $T$ = theoretical frequency; $\{K_i\}$ = the set of nesting factors on which the theoretical frequencies are based.

### The Tinbergen System

A further model of the central-place system, developed by Tinbergen (1960), can be distinguished from the previous ones by the structure of its supply pattern. There exists a hierarchy of centers and a hierarchy of bundles (1, 2, . . . , $m$, . . . , $N$), and the centers have a functional structure such that the successively inclusive hierarchy exists, as in the Christaller system. In the Tinbergen system, however, although the level $m$ center supplies bundles 1 through $m$, it is only the bundle of level $m$ that is exported from the level $m$ center to the level $m$ market area, bundles of levels 1 through $m - 1$ being retained for consumption within the center. Thus, unlike the situation prevailing in the Christaller and GH systems, a central place of a given level does not act as an export point for all lower level bundles. This constraint in the Tinbergen system requires that any center of level $m$ will have only one market area, namely, the level $m$ market area. As a result, a distinctive pattern of market areas emerges. In one variant of the model, $K_{m-1}$ is constant with $m$, so that market areas increase from one level to another by a factor of $K$. Figure 4.3 indicates a $K = 3$ system involving hexagonal market

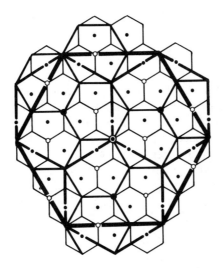

Center        Market area

•     Level 1     ———

○     Level 2     ———

●     Level 3     ———

◉     Level 4     ▬▬

**Figure 4.3** A Tinbergen central-place system with hexagonal market areas ($K = 3$).

areas, though not a triangular lattice of centers, and Mulligan (1982) has derived a $K = 4$ system based on square market areas, although the lattice of centers is not square. In both cases the locational pattern of centers differs from that of the Christaller system, shown in Figure 3.9 for hexagonal market areas, and Figure 3.15 for square market areas. Most important is the fact that a center of level $m$ has within its level $m$ market area $K$ centers of level $m - 1$, rather than $K - 1$ centers as in the Christaller system. In a second variant of the Tinbergen model, $K_{m-1}$ varies with $m$.

Regardless of market-area shape and whether $K_{m-1}$ is constant with $m$, the frequency of market areas of any level $m$ is given by the same expression for market-area frequency as in the GH system, that is, equation (4.14). However, the nature of the Tinbergen system is such that $F_m$, the frequency of market areas of level $m$ (where $m < N$), coincides with $f_m$, the frequency of centers of level $m$. For $m = N$, we have $F_m = f_m = 1$, but for $m < N$,

$$F_m = f_m = \prod_{i=m}^{N-1} K_i \tag{4.18}$$

where, as before, each $K_i$ value represents the equivalent number of market areas of level $i$ that are contained within a market area of level $i + 1$. The distance $d_m$

between any two neighboring centers of level $m$ is given by

$$d_m = d_1 \prod_{i=1}^{N-1} \sqrt{K_i} \tag{4.19}$$

where $d_1$ is the distance between two neighboring centers of level 1.

In the original Tinbergen model, center size was expressed in terms of income, but the center population models discussed above can readily be applied. Of most interest in this connection is the Dacey model (Mulligan, 1982). If $k$ is defined as earlier in the chapter, then the population of level 1 center is identical to the Dacey result of equation (4.10), but here the similarity ceases. The population of any level $m$ is not given by equation (4.13), but by

$$u_m = k_m a_m + k_m a_m \sum_{i=1}^{m} k_i + k_m a_m \left( \sum_{i=1}^{m} k_i \right)^2 + \cdots = \frac{k_m a_m}{1 - \sum_{i=1}^{m} k_i} \tag{4.20}$$

The term $a_m$, the market-area population of a level $m$ center, can be elaborated and will be dependent on the spatial structure of the model, that is, the value of $K$, if $K_{m-1}$ is constant with $m$ or the values of $\{K_i\}$, if $K_{m-1}$ varies with $m$.

## TOWARDS MORE REALISTIC THEORETICAL MODELS

So far we have been considering extensions and modifications to traditional central-place theory which involved the removal or the easing of certain spatial rigidities. In most cases, however, these extensions have been very much in the tradition of the models of Christaller and Lösch, and they have generally adhered to the basic assumptions of the earlier models. There is another strand of work which has attempted to inject more realism into central-place models by modifying some of these assumptions. In some cases these modifications can be readily incorporated into the traditional models or their derivatives, whereas, in other cases, it is necessary for the models to be drastically reformulated.

### Relaxing the Underlying Assumptions

The assumptions introduced in Chapter 3 may have appeared rather severe, but these assumptions were employed to assist in the construction of the models. In most cases the nature of the models was not dependent on these assumptions. One such assumption was the uniform plain populated by consumers with similar demand preferences. Clearly, this assumption can be dispensed with, as Rushton (1972) has shown. He considered the effect of variations in the density of the underlying rural population. Figures 4.4a and 4.4b indicate two cases where rural population density varies systematically over the plain. From the earlier analysis it is obvious that such variations will cause market-area sizes, as well as the

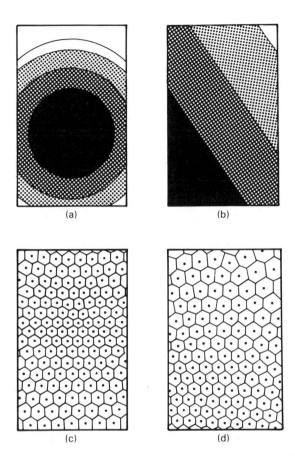

(a)                              (b)

(c)                              (d)

**Figure 4.4**  The effect of varying population density patterns *a* and *b* on market area sizes *c* and *d* for a single function.

spacing of centers, to vary within a given level of the hierarchy. The parts of a region with low population density will tend to have lower levels of demand and therefore larger market areas to compensate for this, and as a consequence, more widely spaced centers. This tendency is indicated in Figures 4.4c and 4.4d and reflects the empirical findings of Chapter 2. Only a single level of the hierarchy is depicted, but higher and lower levels could be added, with a comparable variation of structure within each level. A related analysis by Beavon (1977, pp. 127–128) considered the effects of variation in the income of consumers on market-area size. This would tend to cause those parts of a region with low incomes to have reduced levels of demand and thus relatively large market areas and widely spaced centers.

A further underlying assumption that can be abandoned is the conventional linear demand curve and the spatial demand cones, which were outlined in Chapter 3. Baumol and Ide (1956) have provided a model with different demand conditions that sets the solution for a single function within the context of a bundle of functions and involves the following definitions:

$P(T)$ = the probability that a consumer will find the function required to make the trip a success in the center which offers $T$ functions

$st$ = the costs of traveling $s$ miles to the center at $t$ cents per mile

$M\sqrt{T}$ = the difficulty of shopping, emerging out of size and congestion, defined as costs proportional to the square root of the size of center (where $T$ refers to population or total sales or some other index of size)

$c$ = the opportunity costs of alternative activities foregone, including other shopping opportunities

The consumer, it is argued, will not shop at a center unless

$$f(t, s) = eP(T) - l(st + M\sqrt{T} + c) \tag{4.21}$$

is positive. In this equation $f(t, s)$ indicates the proportion of consumers willing to shop at the center. The constant $e$ represents the subjective weighting functions assigned by the consumer to the expectation of success. (The constant $e$ will also be affected by price levels since the probability of success is the probability of obtaining the function at a price.) The constant $l$ represents feelings concerning costs involved. Solving for $r_{max}$, the maximum distance consumers are willing to travel to shop, yields

$$r_{max} = [eP(T)/lt] - (M\sqrt{T} + c)l/t \tag{4.22}$$

The term $r_{max}$ is similar to (though slightly different from) the real range, as used in Chapter 3. Increased variety is important to consumers up to a point. The minimum number of items needed to induce a consumer to a center must increase with distance $s$ from the center, but the optimal variety is independent of distance.

Let us assume that the center's sales of the function in question depend directly upon the number of individuals who can be induced to shop there. At any distance $s$, the function $f(T, s)$ gives the proportion of consumers who will shop there. Then, with a uniform plain of population density $S$, the aggregate demand will be

$$Q = S \int_0^{2\pi} \left[ \int_0^{r_{max}} \{[eP(T) - l(M\sqrt{T} + c)] - lts\}s \, ds \right] d\theta$$

$$= 2\pi S r_{max}^2 \left[ \frac{eP(T) - l(M\sqrt{T} + c)}{2} - lt \frac{r_{max}}{3} \right] \tag{4.23}$$

but

$$r_{max} = \frac{eP(T) - l(M\sqrt{T} + c)}{lt}$$

therefore substituting,

$$Q = \tfrac{1}{3}(lt\pi S r_{max}^3) \tag{4.24}$$

If it is assumed that population densities are not uniform, but vary inversely with distance from a point of maximum concentration $S$ at the center (a common occurrence within urban areas), then the results become

$$Q = S \int_0^{2\pi} \left\{ \int_0^{r_{max}} [eP(T) - l(M\sqrt{T} + c) - lts] \, ds \right\} d\theta$$

$$= 2\pi S \left\{ [eP(T) - l(M\sqrt{T} + c)]s - \frac{lts^2}{2} \right\}_0^{r_{max}}$$

$$= lt\pi S r_{max}^2 \qquad (4.25)$$

In both cases aggregate demand is a function of maximum distance $r_{max}$ that consumers are willing to travel. On the uniform plain it varies as the cube of distance; whereas, if population densities decrease inversely with distance from the center, it varies with the square of the distance. A related model has been proposed by Lange (1978) in which shopping behavior is considered with the context of competing centers.

### Models with Alternative Consumer Behavior Patterns

Models of the type just discussed are able to cast light on the tendency for the market-area size for a given function to increase steadily with the hierarchical level of the center. This phenomenon, which was implicit in Figures 1.12 through 1.19 and quite obvious in Figure 2.3, has received a good deal of attention in the literature. In the traditional models, it will be recalled, the market-area size for a given function (i.e., the real range) is constant regardless of the level of center from which it is supplied. However, we know reality to be otherwise, and it is important to isolate the factors that cause this. One influence at work here is the possibility of multi-purpose shopping, involving functions of different hierarchical levels. Multi-purpose shopping trips involving two or more functions within a bundle were possible in the Christaller system, but there was no consideration of multi-purpose shopping involving functions or bundles of different levels. Suppose that a consumer purchases one or more level 2 functions in a level 2 center. In doing so, the consumer will also probably take advantage of this opportunity and purchase one or more level 1 functions, these also being supplied from level 2 centers. The incentive for this behavior on the part of the consumer is based on transport costs (the costs of visiting the level 2 center) which can be spread across level 1 *and* level 2 functions, thus lowering the real price of the level 1 functions, and so permitting a greater amount of each function to be consumed. However, this additional demand for level 1 functions at level 2 centers, which in the absence of multi-purpose shopping would be supplied from level 1 centers, is limited by the fact that the frequency of trips for level 2 functions is lower than the frequency of trips for level 1 functions.

The effect of this additional demand for level 1 functions at level 2 centers is to cause the f.o.b. price for level 1 functions at level 2 centers to be lower than at level 1 centers. This is due to greater scope for economies of scale in supply. Another factor encouraging lower f.o.b. prices in level 2 centers for level 1 functions would be the relatively larger consuming population located *within* level 2 centers. Again the greater scope for economies of scale in supply would exist. It is this factor of lower f.o.b. prices in level 2 centers that influences the structure of level 1 market areas. It leads to the level 1 market areas being larger for level 2 centers than for level 1 centers.

The mechanism by which this occurs can be understood by reference to Figure 4.5 which is a linear or one-dimensional version of a two-level Christaller $K = 2$ system. The horizontal axis represents distance and the vertical axis represents the real price paid by consumers for a level 1 function at various locations, that is, at various distances from particular points of supply. The price levels $p_1$ and $p_2$ represent the f.o.b. prices at level 1 centers and level 2 centers, respectively. The "funnel-like" shape above the price line at each center indicates the manner in which real prices increase with distance from a center. It is assumed that the transport costs are comparable from centers of both levels, since we are only concerned here with trips involving the purchase of a level 1 function. Where these lines intersect, the real price is identical and the consumer will be indifferent between the two centers, so that this location represents a point on the market-area boundary. It can be seen that because the f.o.b. price for the level 1 function is lower in level 2 centers than in level 1 centers, the level 1 market areas of the level 2 centers will be of greater extent than those of level 1 centers.

The same tendencies are likely to be at work at higher levels of the hierarchy for level 1 market areas. For example, centers of level 3 will probably be able to offer level 1 functions even more cheaply (at lower f.o.b. prices) than level 2

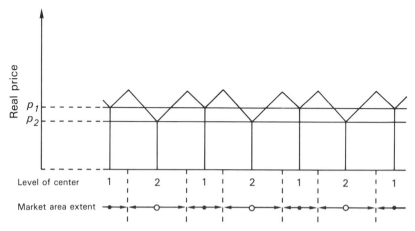

**Figure 4.5** The effect of different levels of f.o.b. prices on market-area size for a level 1 function.

centers. Consequently, the level 1 market area of level 3 centers will be larger than those of level 2 centers, which in turn will be larger than those of level 1. Moreover, as a result of similar forces, such a pattern of market areas will exist with higher-level functions, so that level 3 centers will have larger level 2 market areas than those of the level 2 centers, and level 4 centers will have larger level 3 market areas than those of the level 3 centers.

There exists one further factor encouraging market-area enlargement. This concerns the practice of comparison shopping. For a bundle of functions at a given level, the range of stock and possibilities for selection, as well as the opportunities for specialization in the supply of a bundle, all tend to improve as the level of center increases.

Up to a point, therefore, consumers are prepared to incur the greater costs of transport by traveling to a more distant center in order to gain the advantages of lower prices and greater choice. For example, a consumer may be prepared to drive 12 miles to a level 2 center solely to purchase level 1 functions, and the consumer may neglect the opportunities available at a level 1 center only 9 miles away. This general tendency for market areas (real ranges) of a particular bundle of functions to increase with the hierarchical level is illustrated in Figure 4.6 which diagrams a more realistic pattern of market areas in a five-level Christaller $K = 3$ system (Saey, 1973). The market-area structure may be contrasted with that existing in the traditional Christaller $K = 3$ system of Figure 3.9, although it now becomes difficult to employ $K$ in the characterization of this more realistic structure.

Considerations of the kind discussed above prompted Rushton (1969) to suggest that the analysis of consumer behavior ought to occupy a more prominent

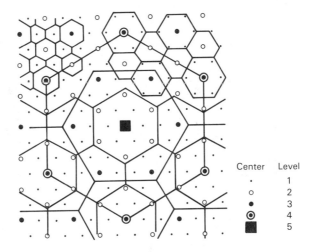

| Center | Level |
|--------|-------|
| . | 1 |
| o | 2 |
| ● | 3 |
| ◉ | 4 |
| ■ | 5 |

**Figure 4.6**   Market-area enlargement in a five-level hierarchy.

position in central-place theory. He argued that any model of a central-place system should be based on a realistic postulate of consumer behavior. In the traditional models, the consumers of a particular function are always assumed to travel to the closest central place at which that function is available, regardless of the size of that center. This is a *distance-minimizing* principle, and it represents a crucial behavioral postulate on which the traditional models are built. As we have seen, however, a consumer might be prepared to travel to a more distant center for the function in question. Rushton therefore proposed an alternative behavioral postulate by which consumers trade-off between distance and place utility.

The implications of the two postulates are indicated by sets of indifference curves in Figures 4.7a and 4.7b. Each indifference curve in this context indicates a set of combinations of "size of center" and "distance to center" which a consumer will find equally satisfactory. The indifference curve thus summarizes the conflicting objectives of a consumer when shopping for a particular function: the desire to minimize the inconvenience of travel and the desire to visit as large a center as possible, in order to take advantage of low prices and comparison shopping. There will exist a family of indifference curves, but any indifference curve to the left of another would be preferred to it because the left-hand one would always involve less travel to gain access to a center of a given size. Figure 4.7a indicates a family of indifference curves for a Christaller system, each "curve"

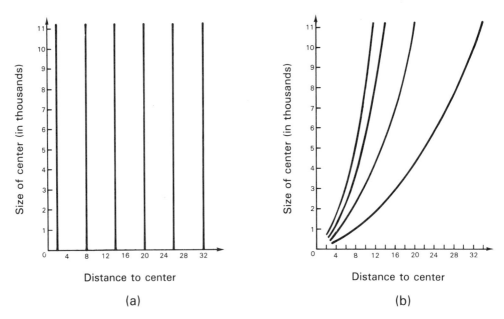

**Figure 4.7** (a) Trade-off functions between distance and center size for the distance-minimizing postulate of traditional central-place models. (b) Trade-off functions between distance and center size for an alternative behavioral postulate.

being in the form of a vertical straight line, reflecting the fact that consumers are always assumed to visit the closest center supplying a particular function, regardless of its size. Figure 4.7b (which is reminiscent of Figure 2.3) indicates a family of indifference curves based on observed patterns of consumer behavior, reflecting the tendency for consumers to forego the inconvenience of longer trips in favor of the advantages derived from shopping at larger centers. Rushton (1971) later considered the effect of this alternative behavioral postulate, and he demonstrated that the pattern by which functions were supplied from centers of different hierarchical levels would not be the same as in traditional models, although the hierarchical structure would still exist.

### Center Populations and the Distribution of Center Size

The introduction of these more realistic modes of behavior in central-place models will inevitably require a modification in the approach to center populations. For example, the models of center population discussed earlier, which are based on market-area populations, will obviously need to be adjusted in the light of the realistic market-area structure of Figure 4.6. In the case of Rushton's (1971) analysis, the implications for center population were clearly recognized, and he was able to demonstrate that the structure of center populations would differ from the Christaller model. These results were confirmed in a study by Mulligan (1984a) on the influence of multi-purpose shopping behavior on center populations. By specifying a simple linear production function and certain rules governing purchases, the population structure of centers in a central-place system with multi-purpose shopping was shown to differ significantly from that which would emerge with single-purpose shopping. Not only would centers of the same level have unequal populations, which would not occur with single-purpose trips, but also the manner in which population was distributed among the different levels would exhibit a more concentrated pattern than would be the case with single-purpose shopping.

While it is possible to make certain modifications to the models of center populations, a fundamentally different approach to the question of center population within a central-place system has been suggested by Beckmann (1958, 1968). As we saw earlier in the chapter, he started with a Christaller system in which the population of all centers of each level would be identical. If such a population distribution were plotted on logarithmically scaled axes of rank and size, the graph would have a step-like character, as indicated by Figure 4.8a. This is a $K = 3$ Christaller system in which center populations correspond to a particular case of the general version of the Dacey model, equation (4.13). Beckmann then suggested that each level of the hierarchy might be subjected to random influences. These would reflect the expected distortions of the central-place model, such as local variability based on departures from the homogeneity conditions with respect to population density, income, tastes, and particular patterns of consumer behavior, and the presence of non–central-place elements within the urban system such as

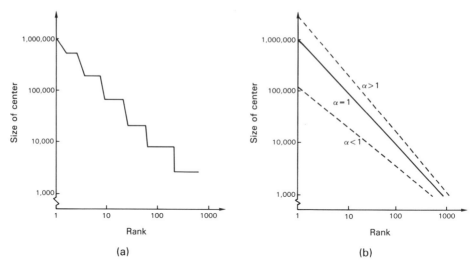

**Figure 4.8**   (a) A $K = 3$ central-place system plotted on axes of rank and size. (b) Three cases of a rank-size distribution.

populations based on resource exploitation and certain types of manufacturing activity.

Beckmann argued that the introduction of these random influences would yield a distribution of center sizes in which the decline of size with rank would be much smoother than in a step-like distribution and would approximate the solid negatively sloping straight line of Figure 4.8b. Under other circumstances the line might be steeper or less steep that this solid line. Such patterns of center sizes are said to conform to the "rank-size distribution" and can be expressed as follows:

$$u_R = u_1/R^\alpha \qquad (4.26)$$

where $u_R$ is the population of a center of rank $R$, and $u_1$ and $\alpha$ are constants, $u_1$ representing the population of the center of rank 1 (the largest center), and representing $\alpha$ the slope. When $\alpha = 1$ there exists the special case in which $u_R$, the population of a center of rank $R$, is exactly one-$R$th the population of the largest center $u_1$. The rank-size distribution of equation (4.26) represents a fairly accurate summary of actual conditions, at least down to a certain minimum size, and for most urban systems (regional and national) $\alpha$ lies within the range 0.8 to 1.2. Since many of the characteristics of centers are highly correlated with population, the rank-size relationship can be applied to such variables as sales, number of establishments, levels of traffic generation, and so on. The relationship between hierarchical models and the rank-size distribution has been discussed by Beguin (1979), Carrol (1982), Mulligan (1979), and Parr (1970). An additional explanation of rank-size regularity, based on the outcome of a growth process, was proposed by Simon (1955, 1968) and extended by Vining (1974, 1977).

## CHANGE IN THE CENTRAL-PLACE SYSTEM

It was mentioned at the close of Chapter 3 that a major deficiency of traditional models of the central-place system considered so far lies in their static conception. This weakness stems largely from the fact that in attempting to deal with considerations of spatial organization in the formulation of the traditional models, it was deemed convenient to disregard to question of time. Unfortunately, this had the effect of rendering the models somewhat unrealistic since it was impossible to appreciate fully the processes that were involved in forming the system and how these may have varied over time. Recall the profound shifts in pattern portrayed in Chapter 1. But, as we shall see, it *is* possible to introduce time, or more generally the element of change, into these traditional models, and in the interests of simplicity this will be done without considering the refinements of the previous section.

Change in a central-place system is inevitable, if only because the economic and social environment within which the system exists becomes modified over time. Such modifications affect the demand, supply, and transportation conditions under which particular functions are supplied within the hierarchy and thus cause the system to change. There appear to be three major categories of change within a central-place system: changes relating to the long-term emergence of the hierarchy itself; changes in the hierarchical level from which a particular function is supplied; and changes in the structure or form of the hierarchy. In discussing these three categories of change, the theoretical approaches that have to be employed to deal with them will be reviewed. Consideration will then be given to additional approaches to change within a central-place system.

### Long-Term Emergence of the Hierarchy

The first change involves the level-by-level development of the hierarchy itself. This results from a wide range of other changes in the economic and social environment, and they usually occur over a relatively long period of time. Various forms of development are possible. For example, a system might develop from the bottom upward as successively higher levels are added. Alternatively, a system might develop from the top downward as lower levels are filled in between major points of focus. The formation of successive levels of the hierarchy may also occur in a nonconsecutive sequence. The actual sequence will, of course, depend on initial conditions, as well as on the nature of the background changes. A number of approaches exist which permit this kind of development to be incorporated into the existing models. One such approach traces the development of a central-place system, starting with a plain populated by dispersed, self-sufficient farmers (Parr, 1978). As technical improvements occur and as cash incomes increase, an initial level of the hierarchy emerges. Subsequently, there is scope for the emergence of additional higher levels of the hierarchy. This model involves development from the bottom upwards, and it would be most likely to occur in older-settled nations such as those of Europe. Vance (1970) had earlier introduced a model that involved development from the top downwards. This model of urban-system development is more in keeping with the patterns experienced in new lands such as the United States, Canada, Australia, and Argentina. Vance referred to this as a *Mercantile Model,* and as the term implies, the role of international trade is crucial in the initial establishment of the system. As development occurs, the initial points of trade focus maintain their dominance and eventually emerge as regional or national metropolitan centers, although this process is complicated by the factor of uncertainty (Webber, 1972).

A rather different approach to the development of a central-place hierarchy was outlined by Huff (1976). This involved a theoretical model which examined long-term changes in the population of centers of different levels of the hierarchy, and it was prompted by a dissatisfaction with the existing static models of center population. These static models, it was argued, lacked a generative or redistributive process which would produce a given distribution of center size. Huff assumes that migration occurs within a central-place system of the Christaller type, according to the following migration rules: First, a constant proportion of the population of a center or a rural area moves during each time interval. Second, migrants from a center only go to centers that are directly dominated by the given center, or they go to centers which directly dominate the given center, so that between pairs of centers a two-way migration exists. And third, certain migrants move only within the center in which they are located. Having specified the rules for migration, a transition matrix is then introduced which specifies the migration process over any time interval.

Huff assumes that, at an initial period, all central places have a population of 10 and that each of their rural areas has a population of 1000. At the early stages of development, centers grow at the expense of surrounding rural areas, and within a relatively short period of time there is a succession of hierarchical differentiation of centers starting with level 2. Soon, higher-level centers attract migrants from centers which they directly dominate. Growth at the lower level due to the attraction of rural migrants leads to even greater rates of growth for higher-level centers. Obviously, growth at all levels of the hierarchy cannot continue indefinitely, and because the flow of migrants from the rural areas is decreasing, the level 1 centers reach a maximum level and then actually exhibit a decline. Subsequently, the higher-level centers in succession attain stationary populations, and center populations eventually converge to an equilibrium. This equilibrium size distribution does not conform to the center populations of the conventional central-place model in that centers of the same level do not have identical populations. However, if certain constraints are added to this general model, then the equilibrium distributions will correspond to either of the two models considered by Dacey (1970). Alternative constraints produce conformity with the Dacey (1966) model, as outlined in equation (4.13). While the Huff model makes particular assumptions about the nature of migration without specifying the economic and social forces upon which they rely, and while it is based on a closed system (there being no interregional migration), it is nevertheless able to illustrate the emergence of a central-place hierarchy based on processes of population redistribution.

### Changes in the Distribution of Functions among Levels

A second category of change occurs within a system that is already established. This occurs when there is a change in the level from which an individual function is supplied, although the fundamental structure of the hierarchy remains unaffected. For example, a function which is initially characteristic of level 3 of the hierarchy may be faced with a reduced demand, resulting perhaps from a decline in population density or from changing tastes. As a result the threshold range increases and because this has to be less than the real range [equation (3.4)], the supply of the function now takes place from the relatively fewer centers of level 4 of the hierarchy, that is, the function becomes characteristic of level 4 or part of the level 4 bundle. This is an example of upward transference, involving the consolidation of supply points for the function in question. Downward transference involving an expansion of the number of supply points is also possible. For example, a function may be initially characteristic of level 4, but because of an increase in demand (due to changing patterns of consumption, for example) the threshold range decreases and the function can now be supplied from the larger number of level 3 centers. Therefore, the function becomes characteristic of level 3 or part of the level 3 bundle. Empirical analyses of this "hierarchical transference of functions" have been undertaken by Stabler and Williams (1973b) for Saskatchwan, and by Greer-Wootten and Sarbit (1982) for Manitoba.

One approach to incorporating this second category of change into the existing models is to make use of the demand and cost analysis of Chapter 3 (Parr and Denike, 1970). This can be illustrated by an example in which a function is initially characteristic of level 2, that is, it is supplied from centers of level 2 or higher. The curve $D_2$ in Figure 4.9 represents the demand curve facing a single supplier in a level 2 center. The curve $C$ represents the average cost curve, and summarizes the nature of production and marketing technology. The fact that the curves $D_2$ and $C$ intersect indicates that commercial production is possible, but it is possible only from centers of level 2 or higher. The curve $D_1$ represents the demand curve that would face a single producer if the function were to be supplied from centers of level 1, but, because the curve $D_1$ lies below the curve $C$ at all levels of output, commercial production is not possible from centers of this level. However, if there was radical change in production and marketing technology favoring small-scale production, the supply situation would be altered, as indicated by the new average cost curve $C'$. Because the curve $D_1$ intersects the curve

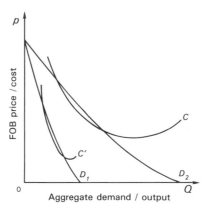

**Figure 4.9** The transference of a function from level 2 to level 1.

$C'$ commercial supply from level 1 centers now becomes feasible, so that the function is characteristic of level 1. The function will continue to be supplied, using the new technology, from centers of level 2 or higher, but only in the centers' capacity as level 1 centers. That is, the function will only be supplied from all centers to their respective level 1 market areas.

A different approach to analyzing the transference of functions among levels has been proposed by Mulligan (1980), following from the work of Beckmann and Schramm (1972). This approach was concerned with evaluating the effect of transference of functions on center populations at different levels of the hierarchy. Using the Dacey model of center population in the context of a GH system, attention was focused on a change in the value of $k_m$, which, it will be recalled, is the population engaged in supplying bundle $m$ as a proportion of the population served. The value of $k_m$ will increase if there is an addition of a new function in bundle $m$, that is, if the function becomes characteristic of level $m$. Conversely, the value of $k_m$ will decline if there is a removal of a function from bundle $m$, that is, if the function becomes characteristic of a level higher or lower than $m$. Naturally, a change in the value of $k_m$ may also reflect other modifications in the economic environment, such as a change in demand for functions of the level $m$ bundle or changes in the degree of labor intensity in the supply of those functions.

Let us consider the effect of a change in $k_m$ on $u_m$, the population of a center of level $m$. If $k_m$ is assumed to be differentiable in a sufficiently small neighborhood of its equilibrium value, then the change in $u_m$ relative to the change in $k_m$ can be expressed as

$$\frac{du_m}{dk_m} = a_1 \left( \prod_{i=1}^{m-1} K_i / I_m^2 \right) \tag{4.27}$$

where

$$I_m = 1 - \sum_{i=1}^{m} k_i \tag{4.28}$$

However, bundle $m$ will also be supplied from each higher level of the hierarchy since we are assuming the existence of a successively inclusive hierarchy. Consequently,

$$\frac{du_m}{dk_i} < \frac{du_n}{dk_i} \qquad (1 \le i \le m < n \le N) \tag{4.29}$$

This implies that a given, absolute change in $k_i$ will create a greater change of population in larger centers than in smaller centers. From equation (4.13) it is apparent that the export component of the population associated with supplying bundle $i$ will be the same for all centers of level $m$ and above. However, equation (4.14) indicates that the higher the level of center, the greater will be the value of the export multiplier, by virtue of the larger number of bundles being supplied. As a consequence, a given change in $k_i$ will precipitate a greater change in total population in a center, the higher the level of that center. In other words, the impact of the change in $k_i$ on the population of a center of level $m$ will be an increasing function of $m$.

The impact of a change in $k_i$ can also be examined from the perspective of a given level of the hierarchy. It is known that a center of level $m$ supplies bundles 1 through $m$, so that there will be $m$ values for $k_i$ where $i = 1, 2, \ldots, m$. However, the impact of a given absolute change in $k_i$ will not be identical for all $i$ bundles within a center of level $m$. Mulligan derives the expression

$$\frac{du_m}{dk_i} < \frac{du_m}{dk_j} \qquad (1 \le i < j \le m) \tag{4.30}$$

where the subscripts $i$ and $j$ refer to bundles supplied by a center of level $m$. This expression states that for a center of a given level, the higher the level of the bundle being effected by a given change, the greater the change in the population of that center. A change in $k_j$ for a level $j$ bundle will have a larger effect on center population than a comparable change in $k_i$ for a level $i$ bundle. This is because the level $j$ bundle is supplied to the level $j$ market area which has a larger population than the level $i$ market area to which the level $i$ bundle is supplied. A given absolute change in $k_m$ thus causes a larger change in the export component of a center's population the greater the value of $m$. And since the export-multiplier within the center will be the same in all cases, the impact on total population will be greater the higher the level of the bundle.

### Changes in the Structure of the Hierarchy

A third category of change involves a change in the basic structure of the hierarchy, either in terms of the number of levels present or the number of centers belonging to a single level. The forces that precipitate this structural change in the hierarchy are similar to those that influence the transference of individual functions within the hierarchy. In this third category of change, however, a sufficiently large number of individual functions are affected that the structure of the hierarchy undergoes modification, and it is not difficult to find examples of this in actual central-place systems (Stabler and Williams, 1973b). As with the second category of change, it is possible to analyze structural change in the hierarchy by means of the static analysis. With this third category, however, the focus is on a bundle of functions or a subset of a bundle, rather than on an individual function. From this static framework it is possible to trace the changes in the structure of the hierarchy and in particular the changed hierarchical status of certain centers. Three basic types of structural change can be identified. In order to facilitate comparison, attention will be focused in each case on the level 2 bundle of functions, and the initial structure will always conform to a Christaller $K = 4$ system. The initial structure could also correspond to the Lösch model or to any other market-area-based model considered earlier. The processes of structural change are assumed to occur in such a way that the successively inclusive hierarchy is preserved. This requirement is imposed partly because a theoretical rationale for such a structure exists (Parr, 1978), partly because of the empirical evidence for its widespread existence, and partly on grounds of practicality, that is, without such a requirement the range of possibilities would be enormous.

The Type I change involves the *formation of a new level* of the hierarchy. The situation before the change is indicated in Figure 4.10a, a Christaller $K = 4$ system. We assume that as a result of increased demand there is a decrease in the threshold ranges for *certain* of the level 2 functions. These functions now can be supplied from a larger number of centers, although not as many as would be the case if the function were to be supplied from centers of level 1. In response to this change, a new level of the hierarchy, level 2*, comes into existence with certain level 1 centers being upgraded in status to level 2*. This is shown in Figure 4.10b. Centers of this new level, in addition to supplying bundle 1, also supply a new bundle 2* which consists of those former level 2 functions that can now be supplied from a larger number of centers. Whereas before the change, the structure could be characterized as a Christaller $K = 4$ configuration, we now have a $K_2 = 4$, $K_{2*} = 2$, $K_1 = 2$ configuration. The successively inclusive hierarchy remains, but the system no longer corresponds to a Christaller system since $K$ is not constant with $m$ and market-area shape now varies among levels. It will be appreciated that the more versatile GH model can be used to describe the new system that has emerged.

The Type II change involves a *modification in the extent of a level* of the hierarchy. As before, the initial situation is shown in Figure 4.10a. Let us assume that the equilibrium is now disturbed by a change in marketing technology, leading to a decreased threshold range of *each* level 2 function. As a consequence, supply is possible from a larger number of centers, each having a smaller market area. The situation after the change is shown in Figure 4.10c, and it can be seen that the number of level 2 centers has expanded. Certain centers of level 1 have become upgraded to level 2 status, so that each of the increased number of level 2 centers now has a smaller market area. The hierarchical structure remains intact, but level 2 has become more extensive. The structure, which before the change corresponded to a Christaller $K = 4$ configuration, now becomes a $K_2 = 8$, $K_1 = 2$ configuration, clearly not a Christaller system.

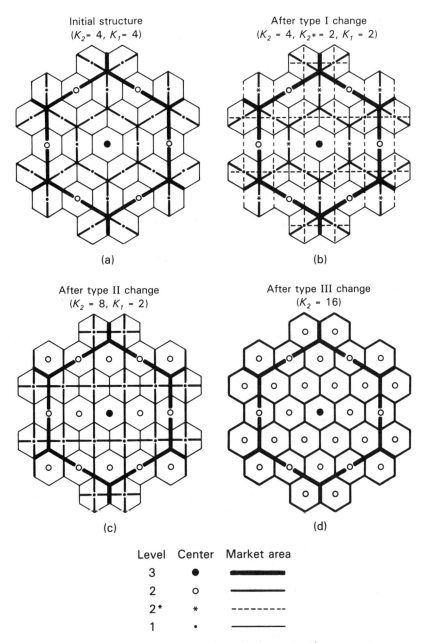

Initial structure
($K_2 = 4, K_1 = 4$)

(a)

After type I change
($K_2 = 4, K_{2*} = 2, K_1 = 2$)

(b)

After type II change
($K_2 = 8, K_1 = 2$)

(c)

After type III change
($K_2 = 16$)

(d)

| Level | Center | Market area |
|---|---|---|
| 3 | ● | ▬▬▬▬ |
| 2 | ○ | ——— |
| 2* | * | - - - - - - |
| 1 | • | ——— |

**Figure 4.10** Types of hierarchical structure change.

The Type III change involves the *disappearance of a level* of the hierarchy. Again, the initial situation is shown in Figure 4.10a. Assume now that because of significantly increased demand based on higher levels of income, each of the level 2 functions has a decreased threshold range. This decrease in the threshold range is sufficiently great that the level 2 function can now be supplied from every level 1 center. As a result, level 1 centers become functionally indistinguishable from centers of level 2. Centers of level 1 are thus upgraded in status to level 2; as a consequence, level 1 disappears, as can be seen in Figure 4.10d. The former level 1 bundle of functions is now combined with the former level 2 bundle to form a larger level 2 bundle. This is supplied from the expanded number of level 2 centers, each having a smaller market area corresponding to the former level 1 market area. The structure changes from a Christaller $K = 4$ configuration to a less complex $K_2 = 16$ configuration.

The three types of structural change have each involved a measure of decentralization in the provision of the level 2 bundle of functions. This decentralization was least intense with the Type I change, where only a subset of the level 2 bundle was affected. The decentralization was more intense with the Type II change and most intense with the Type III change. It is quite possible for a system to pass through a sequence of increasing decentralization, as outlined in Figure 4.10. It is also possible, under a different set of conditions, for the three types of structural change to involve the centralization of supply. This would be based on the downgrading rather than upgrading of particular centers. Under these circumstances the Type I changes would be the least pronounced form of centralization and the Type III change the most pronounced (Parr, 1981). Whether the changes involve decentralization or centralization of supply, the center populations of the relevant hierarchical levels will obviously be affected, and it would be possible to model these developments in terms of the various approaches to center size considered earlier. The kind of analysis described above can also be applied to actual central-place systems to characterize the frequency of centers at various hierarchical levels (Parr, 1980 and 1981), and from this it is possible to generate hypotheses as to how particular processes of structural change may have led to the emergence of systems in their present form.

The analysis of structural change within a hierarchy emphasizes that change takes place under the constraint of a preexisting spatial structure, and this is true of the other two categories of change as well. The system cannot be redesigned, but it must adjust to the changed conditions as best it can. For this reason the process of changing hierarchical structure should be viewed as involving the changing *allocation of a bundle* among levels or among centers within a level, rather than the changing *location of the centers* at particular points in space.

### Further Approaches to Change in a Central-Place System

The foregoing discussions of change within central-place models have generally assumed that the system initially exists in equilibrium, and that it is then exposed to a set of changed conditions to which it adjusts and finally reaches a new equilibrium. This represents an essentially comparative-static approach that makes no attempt to specify the adjustment paths from one equilibrium to another. There has emerged, however, a different approach to the treatment of change within a central-place system, and this approach emphasizes the evolutionary nature of the system. It focuses on the specific processes by which a system adjusts, and it tends as a result to dispense with many of the assumptions and much of the hierarchical structure of the traditional models or their derivatives.

One of the earlier models of this type was proposed by White (1974). This model was concerned with ". . . the aggregate development of the system as it depends on its internal structural features, initial conditions, and autonomous trends in such background conditions as population or transport technology." The model is based on three major assumptions: first, that the locations of central places are given and fixed; second, that the cost and revenue functions for each potential activity are known; and third, that the growth or decline of each activity is a function of the current profit or loss. The model deals with centers ($g = 1$, $2, \ldots, G$); activities or functions ($h = 1, 2, \ldots, H$); and times ($\tau = 0, 1, \ldots$). In this way the evolution of a central-place system can be described by a set of $G \times H$ first-order difference equations of the following type:

$$Z_{gh}^{\tau+1} = Z_{gh}^{\tau} + \gamma_{gh}[\phi_{gh}(Z_{11}^{\tau}, \ldots, Z_{gh}^{\tau}, \ldots, Z_{GH}^{\tau}, \tau)] \qquad (4.31)$$

where $Z_{gh}^{\tau} \geq 0$ is the size of activity or function $h$ at center $g$ at time $\tau$; $\phi_{gh}$ is the profit function; and $\gamma_{gh}$ is the growth function. The analysis first considers the equilibrium conditions for the simple case of a single function at a single center. It then turns to the case of a two-center, one-function system, indicating the relationship between center growth and the competition for markets and the manner in which the system adjusts to shocks.

White (1977) extended this approach with a simulation model that demonstrated that the interaction parameter, the exponent modifying distance, was critical in determining the structure of the system. For low values of the interaction parameter, the centrality of a center within the system is the primary determinant of center size. By contrast, for high values of the interaction parameter, distance to neighboring centers is the sole determinant of center size. The introduction of substantial fixed costs and economies of scale in production also has important implications for the spatial structure, with certain centers being eliminated and the location patterns modified. For low values of the interaction parameter the centers tend to be few and centrally located, whereas for high values the centers tend to be small and dispersed in an even pattern and of generally similar size. The significant feature of the analysis is that the results were independent of the initial sizes of the centers and their locations. White (1978) subsequently carried the analysis further by examining the size distribution of centers within a two-sector, central-place system. It was found that where the interaction, cost, and population parameters have their most realistic values, the resulting size distribution of centers tends towards rank-size regularity, which as we have seen is a feature that can be observed in actual central-place systems.

White's approach was continued in a somewhat different manner by Allen and Sanglier (1979). In their central-place model, however, centers were permitted to appear and not simply to disappear. A crucial assumption was that population and employment would interact with each other. The change in the population $u$ of a center $g$ during time interval $z$ was expressed as follows:

$$\frac{du_g}{dz} = Bu_g[u_{max} + \sum_{h=1}^{H} V_{gh} - u_g] - Wu_g \tag{4.32}$$

where $B$ is related to the birth rate, $W$ to the death rate, and $u_{max}$ represents the maximum population that can be sustained by a center. The summation term represents the additional carrying capacity of $g$ due to $V_{gh}$, the potential employment offered at $g$ by each function $h$. A complementary equation is then introduced which relates potential employment to the spatial distribution of the population. For each function $h$ it is assumed that the employment offered at $g$ is related to the potential employment at $g$, which in turn is proportional to the quantity of function $h$ demanded by the population at beyond $g$. Thus we have

$$\frac{dV_{gh}}{dz} = \beta V_{gh}(Y_{gh} - V_{gh}) \tag{4.33}$$

where $Y_{gh}$ is the potential employment capacity for function $h$ at center $g$, and $\beta$ is a measure of the responsiveness of entrepreneurs in adjusting the size of function $h$ to its perceived potential. The two equations imply a dynamic interaction among centers. Together with other equations dealing with consumer demand and center attractiveness, these form the basis for a computer simulation in which the populations of triangular lattice points are generated. Initially, each point is allocated randomly with a positive feedback mechanism of agglomeration. Centers would have different patterns of evolution and their hierarchical status might change. As with the White (1978) model, the end-state size distribution of centers represents an approximation to the rank-size regularity.

Allen and Sanglier (1981) later elaborated upon this model by considering the effect of "crowding" or diseconomies of agglomeration. They considered that people will commute to employment centers, the extent of which would depend upon the quality of the transportation system. With this added feature, the patterns of growth and decline among centers tend to produce four identifiable phases of urbanization: First, the growth of centers is concentrated at relatively few locations; second, the decentralization of residences occurs as a result of crowding; third, and as a consequence of this, a partial decentralization of functions and central-core decay occurs; and fourth, the onset of intercity competition begins, with growth occurring in a more decentralized pattern.

While these evolutionary models offer a valuable complement to the comparative-static models of change discussed earlier, two other approaches have recently emerged which are worthy of mention. One involves the use of *Control Theory*, which provides a framework for plotting the transition of the spatial structure of a central-place system from one state or equilibrium structure to another. This has yet to be applied to the analysis of change in a central-place system, but it has been considered in the related context of a system of regions (Domanski,

1973). A second approach concerns the application of *Catastrophe Theory,* the term *catastrophe* being used in the French sense of a "sudden change" rather than in the English sense of a "disaster." Catastrophe theory is able to cast light on the manner in which a system may "jump" from one equilibrium state to another, even though the changes in the underlying conditions are smooth. The theory offers a means of modeling discontinuities in such a way that the discontinuity itself becomes incorporated into the overall model of structural change. Many of the changes in central-place systems considered earlier can be viewed in terms of catastrophes or discontinuities, for example, the disappearance of an additional level of the hierarchy, a function becoming characteristic of a different level, or the development of a hierarchy. Unfortunately, the mathematics upon which catastrophe theory is based tend to be very complex, and it has only so far been applied to central-place systems in a restrictive (i.e., nonhierarchical) context (Poston and Wilson, 1977), although a number of studies in related areas have appeared (Amson, 1974; Mees, 1975; Wagstaff, 1978; Wilson, 1981).

## CENTRAL-PLACE SYSTEMS AND GENERAL-SYSTEMS THEORY

This discussion of change in a central-place system inevitably leads to the relationship between central-place systems and General-Systems Theory. A system can be thought of as containing the following: a set of objects (for example, central places); attributes of the objects (such as population, establishments, business types, traffic generated); interrelations among objects (for example, locations of centers, uniform spacing at any given level); interrelations among the attributes (such as logarithmic or semi-logarithmic relationships); and interdependencies between objects and attributes (for example, the central-place hierarchy).

The two kinds of systems often identified by the systems theorist are the closed system and open system. The closed system is entirely self-contained, while the open system exchanges energy (commodities, information, and innovations) with a surrounding environment. A closed system has a given energy supply available to do the work. As work is performed the energy is dissipated and will eventually become randomly distributed throughout the system. Using the terminology of the Second Law of Thermodynamics, the system will then have reached a condition of maximum entropy (von Bertalanffy, 1956). If a central-place system were closed and had run down to a state of maximum entropy, population and other attributes of centers would be completely unrelated to level of centers in the hierarchy. In fact, any trace of a hierarchy would vanish. Several attempts have been made to analyze a central-place system using the concept of entropy (Fano, 1969; Medvedkov, 1968; Semple and Golledge, 1970).

With relative constancy in energy inputs and approximate balance of inputs and outputs, the open system settles into an organized equilibrium between the tendency to move toward maximum entropy and the need for organization to perform work. Such an organized equilibrium is called a "steady state." A central-place system is open. Energy inputs come from the demands of consumers, who constitute the "environment" of the system. Demands are balanced by the outputs of the system, the goods and services supplied to consumers. Assuming a uniform plain, the inputs and outputs will have relative constancy over a period of time, and the central-place hierarchy is a form of organization that performs the work involved as efficiently as possible. However, as already argued, there is always some tendency for local variability, so that perfect conformity to the steps of the hierarchy cannot be expected. A steady state balances the need for organization into a hierarchy in order to perform the work efficiently against randomization due to chance local differences. Rank-size regularity is this steady state (this is the essence of the Beckmann argument). Such regularity not only exists at a point in time, but also tends to persist through time.

Any decrease in energy inputs increases the entropy in an open system and causes adjustments changing the form of the steady state. By the same token, increasing energy inputs cause form adjustments leading to further organization or negative entropy. Open systems also contain feedback mechanisms that affect growth even under conditions of constant energy inputs. Positive feedback would tend to decrease the randomizing effects of local variability and increase organization. Negative feedback increases randomizing effects and thus increases entropy. Maruyama (1963, pp. 161–179) discusses positive feedback mechanisms involving circular and cumulative causation. In central-place systems, they are represented by the tendency of consumers to prefer larger centers and bypass the smaller, which permits the larger to grow and constrain the smaller.

One conclusion of the general-system theorists is worthy of note: The steady state in an open system is one that obeys principles of equifinality. What this means is that whatever the initial sizes of the central places, the *same* resulting steady state will be achieved provided the energy flows are the same, that is, there is "equal finality." The steady state results solely from energy flows, independent of the initial size conditions.

## MODERN THEORETICAL DEPARTURES: A CLOSING COMMENT

In this chapter we have tried to explore some of the more recent extensions of (and alternatives to) the models of Christaller and Lösch that were first put forward before World War II. Starting from a common base of the original theoretical structures, these extensions have taken a number of widely different directions. Unfortunately, each extension tends to be partial in the sense that it typically takes the traditional structure as its point of departure and ignores other extensions that have been made. This can be frequently justified in the interests of presentation and exposition. Nevertheless, it means that we are still lacking an overall model that synthesizes the various developments, even though the building blocks for such an overall model are not lacking. It is hoped that in the future a framework of this type will emerge. One final point is worth stressing, and this relates to the relevance of central-place theory. However useful it may eventually prove to be in explaining or casting light on aspects of the urban system, it can never be regarded as a theory of the entire urban system. Central-place theory refers to only one aspect of the overall urban system, albeit an important one, and there are many aspects of the economic and social organization of urban systems that are wholly beyond the scope of central-place theory (Pred, 1977). The refinement of central-place theory should therefore be seen as a contribution to the development of a more general theory of the urban system.

## REFERENCES

ALAO, N., M. F. DACEY, O. DAVIES, K. G. DENIKE, J. HUFF, J. B. PARR, and M. J. WEBBER (1977) *Christaller Central Place Structures: An Introductory Statement,* Northwestern University Studies in Geography, No. 22, Evanston, Ill.: Northwestern University.

ALLEN, P. M., and M. SANGLIER (1979) "A Dynamic Model of Growth in a Central Place System," *Geographical Analysis,* 11:256–272.

ALLEN, P. M., and M. SANGLIER (1981) "A Dynamic Model of a Central Place System II," *Geographical Analysis,* 13:149–164.

ALVES, W. R. (1974) "Comments on Hudson's 'Diffusion in a Central Place System,'" *Geographical Analysis,* 6:303–308.

AMSON, J. C. (1974) "Equilibrium and Catastrophic Modes of Urban Growth," in E. L. Cripps (ed.), *Space Time Concepts in Urban and Regional Models,* London Papers in Regional Science, Vol. 4. London: Pion.

BAUMOL, W. J., and E. A. IDE (1956) "Variety in Retailing," *Management Science,* 3:93–101.

BEAUMONT, J. R., and P. KEYS (1980) "A Theoretical Basis for Diffusion in a Central Place System," *Geographical Analysis,* 12:269–273.

BEAVON, K. S. O. (1977) *Central Place Theory: A Reinterpretation.* London: Longman.

BEAVON, K. S. O. (1978) "A Comment on the Construction of the Löschian Landscape," *Geographical Analysis,* 10:77–82.

BEAVON, K. S. O., and A. S. MABIN (1975) "The Lösch System of Market Areas: Derivation and Extension," *Geographical Analysis,* 7:131–151.

BECKMANN, M. J. (1958) "City Hierarchies and the Distribution of City Size," *Economic Development and Cultural Change,* 6:243–248.

BECKMANN, M. J. (1968) *Location Theory.* New York: Random House.

BECKMANN, M. J., and J. C. MCPHERSON (1970) "City Size Distribution in a Central Place Hierarchy," *Journal of Regional Science,* 10:25–33.

BECKMANN, M. J., and G. SCHRAMM (1972) "The Impact of Scientific and Technical Change on the Location of Economic Activities," *Regional and Urban Economics,* 2:159–174.

BEGUIN, H. (1979) "Urban Hierarchy and the Rank-Size Distribution," *Geographical Analysis,* 11:149–164.

VON BERTALANFFY, L. (1956) "General Systems Theory," *General Systems,* 1:1–10.

CARROL, G. R. (1982) "National City Size Distributions: What Do We Know after 67 Years of Research?" *Progress in Human Geography,* 6:1–43.

CHRISTALLER, W. (1933) *Die zentralen Orte in Süddeutschland.* Jena, Germany: Fischer. English translation by C. Baskin: *The Central Places of Southern Germany.* Englewood Cliffs, N.J.: Prentice-Hall, Inc., 1966. (All text citations refer to the English translation.)

CHRISTALLER, W. (1950) "Das Grundgerüst der räumlichen Ordnung in Europa," *Frankfurter Geographische Hefte,* 24:1–96.

DACEY, M. F. (1966) "Population of Places in a Central Place Hierarchy," *Journal of Regional Science,* 6:27–33.

DACEY, M. F. (1970) Alternate Formulations of Central Place Populations," *Tijdschrift voor Economische en Sociale Geografie,* 61:10–15.

DACEY, M. F. (1976) *An Introduction to the Mathematical Theory of Central Places: Central Place Geometry.* Vol. 1. Evanston, Ill.: Northwestern University.

DACEY, M. F., O. DAVIES, R. FLOWERDEW, J. HUFF, A. KO, and J. PIPKIN (1974) *One-Dimensional Central Place Theory.* Northwestern University Studies in Geography, No. 21. Evanston, Ill.: Northwestern University.

DENIKE, K. G., and J. B. PARR (1970) "Production in Space, Spatial Competition, and Restricted Entry," *Journal of Regional Science,* 10:49–63.

DOMÁNSKI, R. (1973) "A General Model of Optimal Growth in a System of Regions," *Papers of the Regional Science Association,* 31:73–82.

EATON, B. C., and R. G. LIPSEY (1976) "The Non-Uniqueness of Equilibrium in the Löschian Location Model," *American Economic Review,* 66:77–93.

FANO, P. L. (1969) "Organization, City Size Distributions and Central Places," *Papers of the Regional Science Association,* 12:29–38.

GREER-WOOTTEN, B., and L. A. SARBIT (1981) "The Changing Functional Composition of the Central Place Hierarchy," *L'Éspace Géographique,* 10:125–134.

HARTWICK, J. M. (1973) "Lösch's Theorem on Hexagonal Market Areas," *Journal of Regional Science,* 13:213–221.

HARTWICK, J. M. (1974) "Trade in a Central Place System," Discussion Paper No. 168, Department of Economics, Queen's University, Kingston, Ont.

HUDSON, J. C. (1969) "Diffusion in a Central Place System," *Geographical Analysis,* 1:45–58.

HUFF, J. O. (1976) "A Hierarchical Migration Model of Population Redistribution within a Central Place Hierarchy," *Geographical Analysis,* 8:231–254.

LANGE, S. (1978) "The Role of Consumer Behavior in the Distribution of Shopping Centers," in R. Funck and J. B. Parr (eds.), *The Analysis of Regional Structure: Essays in Honour of August Lösch,* Karlsruhe Papers in Regional Science, Vol. 2. London: Pion.

LONG, W. (1971) "Demand in Space: Some Neglected Aspects," *Papers of the Regional Science Association,* 27:45–60.

LÖSCH, A. (1941) *Die räumliche Ordnung der Wirtschraft.* Jena, Germany: Fischer. English translation of the second German edition (1944) by W. H. Woglom and W. F. Stolper: *The Economics of Location.* New Haven, Conn.: Yale University Press, 1954. (All text citations refer to the English translation.)

MARSHALL, J. U. (1975) "A Model of Size and Economic Structure in an Urban Hierarchy," *Environment and Planning A,* 7:637–649.

MARSHALL, J. U. (1977) "The Construction of the Löschian Landscape," *Geographical Analysis*, 9:1–13.

MARSHALL, J. U. (1978) "The Truncated Löschian Landscape: A Reply to Beavon," *Geographical Analysis*, 10:83–86.

MARUYAMA, M. (1963) "The Second Cybernetics: Deviation Amplifying Mutual Causal Processes," *The American Scientist*, 51:164–179.

MEDVEDKOV, Y. V. (1967) "The Concept of Entropy in Settlement Pattern Analysis," *Papers of the Regional Science Association*, 18:165–168.

MEES, A. I. (1975) "The Revival of Cities in Medieval Europe: An Application of Catastrophe Theory," *Regional Science and Urban Economics*, 5:403–425.

MULLIGAN, G. F. (1979) "Additional Properties of a Hierarchical City-Size Model," *Journal of Regional Science*, 19:57–66.

MULLIGAN, G. F. (1980) "The Effects of Multiplier Shifts in a Hierarchical City-Size Model," *Regional Science and Urban Economics*, 10:77–90.

MULLIGAN, G. F. (1981a) "Lösch's Single-Good Equilibrium," *Annals of the Association of American Geographers*, 71:84–94.

MULLIGAN, G. F. (1981b) "A Note on Hierarchical Income Flows," *Environment and Planning A*, 13:747–750.

MULLIGAN, G. F. (1982) "Tinbergen-Type Central Place Systems," *International Regional Science Review*, 7:83–91.

MULLIGAN, G. F. (1984a) "Central Place Populations: Some Implications of Consumer Shopping Behavior," *Annals of the Association of American Geographers*, 74:44–56.

MULLIGAN, G. F. (1984b) "Agglomeration and Central Place Theory: A Review of the Literature," *International Regional Science Review*, 9:1–42.

PARR, J. B. (1970) "Models of City Size in an Urban System," *Papers of the Regional Science Association*, 25:221–253.

PARR, J. B. (1973) "Structure and Size in the Urban System of Lösch," *Economic Geography*, 49:185–212.

PARR, J. B. (1978) "Models of the Urban System: A More General Approach," *Urban Studies*, 15:35–49.

PARR, J. B. (1980) "Frequency Distributions of Central Places in Southern Germany: A Further Analysis," *Economic Geography*, 56:141–154.

PARR, J. B. (1981) "Temporal Change in a Central-Place System," *Environment and Planning A*, 13:97–118.

PARR, J. B., and K. G. DENIKE (1970) "Theoretical Problems in Central Place Analysis," *Economic Geography*, 46:567–586.

PARR, J. B., K. G. DENIKE, and G. F. MULLIGAN (1975) "City Size Models and the Economic Base: A Recent Controversy," *Journal of Regional Science*, 15:1–8.

PEDERSON, P. O. (1970) "Innovation Diffusion within and between National Urban Systems," *Geographical Analysis*, 2:203–254.

POSTON, T., and A. G. WILSON (1977) "Facility Size versus Distance Traveled: Urban Services and the Fold Catastrophe," *Environment and Planning A*, 9:681–686.

PRED, A. (1977) *City-Systems in Advanced Economies*. London: Hutchinson.

RUSHTON, G. (1969) "Analysis of Spatial Behavior by Revealed Space Preference," *Annals of the Association of American Geographers*, 59:391–400.

Rushton, G. (1971) "Postulates of Central Place Theory and the Properties of Central Place Systems," *Geographical Analysis*, 3:140–156 and 416.

Rushton, G. (1972) "Map Transformations of Point Patterns: Central Place Patterns in Areas of Variable Population Density," *Papers of the Regional Science Association*, 28:111–129.

Saey, P. (1973) "Three Fallacies in the Literature on Central Place Theory," *Tijdschrift voor Economische en Sociale Geografie*, 64:181–194.

Semple, R. K., and R. G. Golledge (1970) "An Analysis of Entropy Changes in a Settlement Pattern over Time," *Economic Geography*, 46:157–160.

Simon, H. A. (1955) "On a Class of Skew Distribution Functions," *Biometrika*, 42:425–440.

Simon, H. A. (1968) "On Judging the Plausibility of Theories," in B. Van Rootselaar and J. F. Staal (eds.), *Logic, Methodology and Philosophy of Science*, Vol. 2. Amsterdam: North Holland.

Stabler, J. C., and P. R. Williams (1973a) "The Changing Structure of the Central Place Hierarchy," *Land Economics*, 49:454–458.

Stabler, J. C., and P. R. Williams (1973b) "The Dynamics of a Central Place System," Geographical Papers No. 22, Department of Geography, University of Reading, Reading, U.K.

Tinbergen, J. (1961) "The Spatial Dispersion of Production: A Hypothesis," *Schweizerische Zeitschrift für Volkswirtschaft und Statistik*, 97:412–419.

Vance, J. E. (1970) *The Merchant's World: Geography of Wholesaling*. Englewood Cliffs, N.J.: Prentice-Hall, Inc.

Vining, D. R. (1974) "On the Sources of Instability in the Rank-Size Rule: Some Simple Tests of Gibrat's Law," *Geographical Analysis*, 6:313–329.

Vining, D. R. (1977) "The Rank-Size Rule in the Absence of Growth," *Journal of Urban Economics*, 4:15–29.

Wagstaff, J. M. (1978) "A Possible Interpretation of Settlement Pattern Evolution in Terms of 'Catastrophe Theory,'" *Transactions of the Institute of British Geographers*, New Series 3:165–175.

Webber, M. J. (1972) *The Impact of Uncertainty on Location*. Cambridge, Mass.: Massachusetts Institute of Technology Press.

Webber, M. J. (1974) "Free Entry and the Locational Equilibrium," *Annals of the Association of American Geographers*, 64:17–25.

White, R. W. (1974) "Sketches of a Dynamic Central Place Theory," *Economic Geography*, 50:219–227.

White, R. W. (1977) "Dynamic Central Place Theory: Results of a Simulation Approach," *Geographical Analysis*, 9:226–243.

White, R. W. (1978) "The Simulation of Central Place Dynamics: Two-Sector Systems and the Rank-Size Distribution," *Geographical Analysis*, 10:201–208.

Wilson, A. G. (1981) *Catastrophe Theory and Bifurcation: Applications to Urban and Regional Systems*. London: Croom Helm.

Woldenberg, M. J. (1968) "Energy Flow and Spatial Order: Mixed Hexagonal Hierarchies of Central Places," *Geographical Review*, 58:552–574.

# 5

# Periodic Marketing Systems

Thus far we have dealt with central-place hierarchies in modern market economies. Most of the world's people still live in peasant societies, however, with ways of life that combine market activity with subsistence production. In such societies markets are often periodic rather than permanent (Smith, 1970).

Periodic markets play a vital role in facilitating exchange and trade, particularly in rural reas, and are distinguished from continual or daily markets by their frequency. Meetings of buyers and sellers at these market places do not occur every day. Rather, there is a set schedule of market meetings separated by marketless days or by days on which the level of activity is substantially reduced (Symanski, 1973). Thus, there is a decided rhythm to the number of buyers and sellers present so that the "level of activity intensity" varies systematically throughout the market week (Sada, McNulty, and Adalemo, 1978). Periodic markets arise because the demand for goods sold in the marketplace is small due to low per capita income or low population density. The low level of aggregate demand is insufficient to support permanent shops. Periodic markets, on the other hand, allow supply and demand to be concentrated in space as well as time and thus make trade viable.

Periodic marketing systems are found in many parts of the world. They have always been an integral part of the indigenous economies of Asia, Africa, and Latin America and are one of the basic types of formal exchange mechanisms found in these societies. Periodic markets are found in many countries in Europe and on both sides of the Mediterranean where their persistence reveals vestiges of the peasant markets of the past. Periodic markets are important to the internal trading process, mediating exchange among different groups of local producers on the one hand and itinerant traders and wholesalers on the other. In many areas periodic marketplaces are a basic element in the spatial organization of economic and social life. Periodic market systems have spatial, temporal, institutional, and behavioral attributes which distinguish them from other trading systems, yet they may be studied as systems from the vantage point of central-place theory. These attributes of periodic markets are the focus of this chapter.

The participants in the activities of a market center are present for a number of reasons. Some are there to buy, some to sell, and some to both buy and sell. A useful distinction is that between local marketers and traders. Local marketers come to the market to sell their agricultural surplus and possibly to purchase items of food or cooking and farm utensils. They are both sellers and buyers, but they engage in horizontal exchange. In contrast, traders either buy agricultural produce for resale at other markets or sell urban goods to the local marketers. Their objective is to engage in spatial and temporal arbitrage. Thus, the primary motivation for market participation, be it for local marketers or traders, is economic exchange, although there are other social reasons for attending market centers, too.

The social and political functions of market centers have been well documented. Piault (1971), for example, argues that the Mawri of the Niger visit the market to reaffirm a spatially dispersed social identity. Similarly, the markets of the Tiv in north-central Nigeria constitute a well-formed political and social network (Bohannan and Bohannan, 1968, p. 613). Here marriages are arranged, theatrical performances seen, loans paid, and friendships renewed.

## WHY IS TRADING PERIODIC?

The essential reason for trading to be periodic rather than fixed is that the low spatial concentration of consumer demand does not allow traders to cover the costs of permanent operation. The cost of permanent operation cannot be recovered from the sales to be made within the maximum distance consumers are willing to travel to the market. A large portion of this cost of permanent operation is attributable to "overhead cost"; that is, the fixed cost of setting up a trading operation. In most elementary marketing systems, the major element of these overhead costs is the cost to the trader of the time spent traveling between markets. Periodicity allows a more efficient use of time and reduces the barriers of high overhead costs.

There are three ways in which a person can reduce overhead costs. As a first strategy, overhead costs can be reduced by diversifying activities to make more efficient use of time. Thus, time is allotted to trading as well as other income-producing activities, usually producing the good itself. These types of traders, therefore, can earn only a part of their livelihood from trading itself. Markets dominated by such part-time traders meet periodically so that the participants can efficiently allocate their time between producing and selling. Exchange systems dominated by such part-time marketers are referred to as *part-time marketing systems*. Part-time marketing can be successful only if the reduction in trading effort does not result in a drastic fall in demand. Further, part-time traders must find a profitable use for their nontrading time. In predominantly agricultural systems, the opportunity cost of time has seasonal variations. It is thus not uncommon for farmers to become part-time traders when the demand for agricultural labor is low. Indeed, according to Harriss (1975), a major economic role of periodic markets is the opportunity they provide for marginal agricultural participants to engage in entrepreneurial activities.

As a second strategy, a trader may reduce the burden of high overhead costs by being mobile or itinerant. The trader may visit several market centers in sequence over the market week and thus accumulate the trade of several market areas. Stine (1962) describes this second situation as *mobile (or itinerant) trading*. Periodic markets are essential to itinerant trading since they allow the spatial and temporal concentration of demand. By being itinerant, traders can serve a much larger and more dispersed population than would be possible from a fixed location. The additional revenues earned from visiting several market centers help cover overhead costs.

Mobile or itinerant trading is not only advantageous to traders who sell but also to traders who buy agricultural produce from local producers. These buying traders often visit several periodic market centers to procure their goods since the volume of activity in any one market is insufficient to maintain a permanent operation (Hay, 1977). For both buying traders and selling traders a mobile marketing strategy will be successful only if the additional cost of travel does not exceed the additional revenue generated from being mobile.

A third strategy for reducing overhead costs is to diversify the assortment of goods that are traded. This results in increased average demand and higher revenues over the fixed amount of time. However, constraints on capital availability—a situation characteristic of many small traders—makes this alternative difficult to implement.

Just as there are many types of traders at periodic market centers, so is there also a diversity of economic exchange functions performed by these markets. Eighmy (1972) generalizes these functions into three categories: first, to facilitate local exchange; second, to facilitate interregional trade; and third, to provide urban goods and services to a geographically dispersed rural population (i.e., the central-place function).

Markets in the local exchange system arise because of the inherent need for neighborhood exchange. Even in subsistence agricultural systems there is an elementary division of labor and specialization of production between farmers, craftspeople, and service providers. The role of the periodic market in the local exchange system is to provide a mechanism for balancing the surpluses and deficits of the different producer groups. The market centers of the Tiv in north-central Nigeria are a good example of local exchange markets. For the local population the market centers provide an opportunity to acquire daily cooking and other low-order needs in exchange for minor surplus produce (Bohannan and Bohannan, 1968, pp. 194–219). (See also Tait, 1961, pp. 17–21, on the Konkomba of northern Ghana.) The participants in the local exchange markets are essentially part-time traders since they are producers as well as retailers of their produce and since their focus is on horizontal exchange among local inhabitants.

Facilitating local exchange is not the only function of periodic markets, however. Specialization of production between ecological zones motivates a larger scale exchange of goods between complementary zones of supply and demand. Periodic markets facilitate such interregional trade by serving as channels of export and import in long-distance trade between ecological regions. Periodic markets in Africa, for example, have often been associated with long-distance caravan trade between coastal and interior areas or between forest and desert areas. (For examples see Hodder, 1965; Vansina, 1962.)

In addition to long-distance trade there is also the situation where wholesalers visit several periodic markets in sequence to collect the surplus marketed by local producers (Hay, 1977; Wanmali, 1981). A producer can sell to a wholesaler either at the farm or at the market center. Where transportation infrastructure is poor, wholesalers cannot achieve transportation economies by visiting the farm gate. Hence the producer will choose to market the goods personally at the market center. The result is that many producers "appear as part-time marketers in the local market" regardless of the level of local demand (Hay, 1977, p. 77). These periodic market centers are then the focal points for the export of agricultural surplus from the area. The amount of surplus, however, may be insufficient for the wholesaler to maintain a permanent operation. Periodicity allows the offerings of the local producers in the area to be temporally synchronized with the wholesaler's wants, making the operation economically viable. Wanmali (1981) describes the operation of such markets in eastern India. Wholesale traders visit a number of rural periodic markets to procure local produce from the farmers to resell to urban traders at high-order settlements.

Finally, periodic markets facilitate the distribution of low-order urban goods and services to a dispersed rural population—a task similar to that performed by firms in the central-place systems. Itinerant traders who procure these goods from higher-order urban markets sell them to local consumers at periodic intervals. The central-place function of periodic markets has been documented in a number of studies from different areas in the world. These are discussed later in the chapter.

While it is useful to distinguish between the different functions performed by periodic market centers (see Figure 5.1), it is important to stress that most market centers perform more than one function and have more than one role. Many markets, for example, serve both as bulking centers for the accumulation of agricultural surplus as well as centers from which urban goods are distributed to the rural population. Indeed such dual roles seem to be the rule rather than the exception. The money earned by local producers from selling agricultural

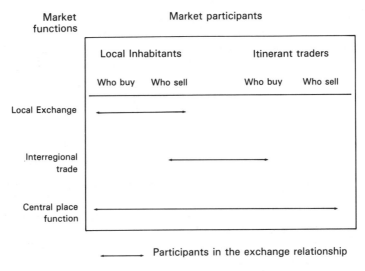

**Figure 5.1**   Exchange relationships in periodic marketing systems.

produce is spent in the purchase of goods and services provided by itinerant traders (Wanmali and Ghosh, 1975). While acknowledging this diversity in the functioning of periodic markets, the following discussion emphasizes the role of these markets in distributing goods and services to rural populations and their similarity to the central-place systems discussed in earlier chapters.

## THE THEORY OF PERIODIC MARKETING

The first attempt at an economic theory of periodic markets was by Stine (1962). Stine, who was concerned with mobile traders, based his theory on the relationship between the minimum (or threshold) range and the maximum (or ideal) range of a good, as developed by Christaller. Stine argued that if the maximum range is greater than the minimum range, then the firm will be fixed at a location. However, if the minimum range exceeds the maximum range, then the firm must become mobile or go out of business. Thus, in areas of low population density or low demand, a product for which people are not willing to travel very far has to be sold by itinerant traders if it is to be sold at all.

According to Stine, the number of market centers a trader has to visit in order to obtain an adequate level of return is governed by the difference between the maximum and minimum ranges of the good. The smaller this difference the fewer moves the trader has to make. The distance of each move, on the other hand, is related to the maximum range.

Whereas Stine addressed only the question of why some traders are mobile while others are fixed, his analysis can be expanded to investigate the broader question of how traders should choose among mobile, part-time, and fixed–full-time marketing strategies. The model presented by Ghosh (1982), for example, predicts the conditions under which a trader will adopt one of these three strategies. Further, the model can also select the optimal travel pattern for a mobile trader. This model draws from the logic of central-place theory discussed in Chapter 3.

### The Trader Model

Assume, as in central-place theory, an unbounded plain with a uniform distribution of consumers. The consumers have identical demand and income characteristics and they can travel with equal ease in all directions. Let $Q_g^\tau$ be the total quantity of good sold by a trader located at site $g$ on day $\tau$. This can be found by using the concept of the "spatial demand cone" discussed in Chapter 3. Now if $\mu$ is the margin (i.e., the selling price of the good minus its unit operating cost), then $\Omega_g^\tau$, the trader's expected net earnings on day $\tau$, is

$$\Omega_g^\tau = \mu Q_g^\tau \tag{5.1}$$

Since the level of earning must cover fixed costs for trading to be viable, the minimum condition for the trader to break even is

$$\Omega_g^\tau - E - E' > 0 \tag{5.2}$$

where $E$ is the overhead cost associated with trading at a center (e.g., site rent, license fee, and so forth) and $E'$ is the trader's cost of time.

The distinguishing feature of periodic market systems is that the demand for products at any place changes with time. This is because some people who buy the product on day $\tau$ may be unwilling to buy the product again until the product is consumed or until their budget is replenished. At the same time, due to low overall demand, the number of new people extected to buy the product on day $\tau + 1$ is low. This leads to temporal variations in demand for the good at any particular site. Thus

$$D_g^\tau < D_g^{\tau+1} \tag{5.3}$$

and consequently

$$Q_g^\tau < Q_g^{\tau+1} \tag{5.4}$$

For the trader to break even at center $g$ on day $\tau + 1$, the expected net earnings must cover the trader's cost of time. For this to be true the following condition must hold:

$$\Omega_g^{\tau+1} - E' > 0 \tag{5.5}$$

If the trader cannot break even at center $g$, an alternative strategy for the trader is to travel to some other center $g^*$. The expected revenue at center $g^*$ is

$\mu Q_{g*}^{\tau+1}$. The expected profit $\pi$ can therefore be expressed as

$$\pi = \Omega_{g*}^{\tau+1} - A - E - E' \tag{5.6}$$

where $A$ is the cost of relocation from $g$ to $g*$. The best center for the trader to move to on day $\tau + 1$ can be found by evaluating this expected profit equation for each possible center and finding the center which maximizes the value of that expression. Let $g*$ be the center which maximizes the expression. The expected net earnings on day $\tau + 1$ from a mobile strategy is then $\Omega_{g*}^{\tau+1}$.

We have then the following conditions:

*First*, if

$$\Omega_g^{\tau+1} - E' < 0 \quad \text{and} \quad \Omega_{g*}^{\tau+1} - A - E - E' > 0 \tag{5.7}$$

the trader cannot profitably continue to be in business either at center $g$ or $g*$. The trader then can adopt a part-time trading strategy if the expected earnings from alternative employment exceed $E'$. Otherwise the trader will go out of business.

*Second*, if

$$\Omega_g^{\tau+1} - E' < 0 \quad \text{and} \quad \Omega_g^{\tau+1} - A - E - E' > 0 \tag{5.8}$$

the trader will be mobile.

*Third*, if

$$\Omega_g^{\tau+1} - E' > 0 \quad \text{and} \quad \Omega_{g*}^{\tau+1} - A - E - E' < 0 \tag{5.9}$$

the trader will be locationally fixed.

*Fourth*, if

$$\Omega_g^{\tau+1} - E' > 0 \quad \text{and} \quad \Omega_{g*}^{\tau+1} - A - E - E' > 0 \tag{5.10}$$

the trader will be mobile when

$$\Omega_g^{\tau+1} - E' < \Omega_{g*}^{\tau+1} - A - E - E'$$

Otherwise, the trader will be fixed.

These four conditions define the strategies available to the trader. Note from equation (5.10) that a trader may sometimes choose to be mobile even when fixed locations are viable. If the additional net earnings achieved by trading at a new location $(\Omega_{g*}^{\tau+1} - \Omega_g^{\tau+1})$ are greater than the sum of relocation cost and the overhead cost $(A + E')$ associated with setting up trading in a new center, then the trader will be mobile even if a locationally fixed strategy is profitable. Thus, due to the temporal variations in demand, the return from a mobile operation may be higher than that from a locationally fixed operation. Similarly, in some cases mobility may allow traders to reduce prices and forestall competition. Stine's hypothesis thus becomes one of many reasons for the existence of periodic markets. In general, the lower a trader's relocation cost and the higher the overhead costs in relation to daily net earnings, the more likely is the trader to be mobile.

This is one reason why one often finds large numbers of periodic traders at a market center that does not have even a single permanent outlet. While the market may be able to support some permanent operations, a mobile strategy is more attractive to traders.

## SPATIAL ORGANIZATION OF PERIODIC MARKETS

A number of studies have suggested that periodic market-center systems should be viewed as part of the hierarchical system of central places, sharing common features of spatial organization. The classic study of periodic markets in prerevolutionary China by Skinner (1964, 1965a, 1965b) may be used an example, although the details of periodic markets vary from one part of the world to another. In his study Skinner identified the following five-level hierarchy of central places: standard market towns, intermediate market towns, central market towns, local cities, and regional centers. Periodic markets are an integral part of the market centers which belong to three lowest levels of the urban hierarchy (Skinner, 1964). The markets associated with each of these centers possess distinctive size, functionality, and periodicity characteristics.

The central market towns, for example, have permanent shops in addition to periodic traders and are located on strategic points on the transport network. These markets have important wholesale functions. They receive imported items and distribute them, along with the merchandise produced in the central market town, to the dispersed rural population of its adjacent hinterland. These goods move from the central market to the standard markets through the intermediate market towns. The central markets also act as the collection point for local produce which is exported to other central markets or to higher-order urban centers. The central market towns are the bases for itinerant traders to replenish their stocks as well as to dispose of purchases made at lower-order centers.

The standard market town, on the other hand, is the lowest level of the hierarchy (with the exception of minor "green vegetable" markets). Each standard market town and its market area function as an economic and social community incorporating, on the average, about 18 villages. These standard market towns, therefore, are similar to low-order central places (see Figure 5.2). Typically one out of every five adults living in the villages went to the standard market town on market day. The upward flow of goods begins with peasants selling their produce to buyers at the standard market town. The buyers, in turn, bulk the produce and carry it to intermediate and central market towns to be sold to larger wholesalers. In exchange, local peasants and craftspeople purchase imported merchandise brought from higher-order centers by itinerant traders.

Skinner's adoption of the central-place model to study markets in prerevolutionary China prompted other authors to use that framework in analyzing markets in other parts of the world. Wanmali (1981), for example, identified a four-level central-place hierarchy in South Bihar, India: regional, subregional,

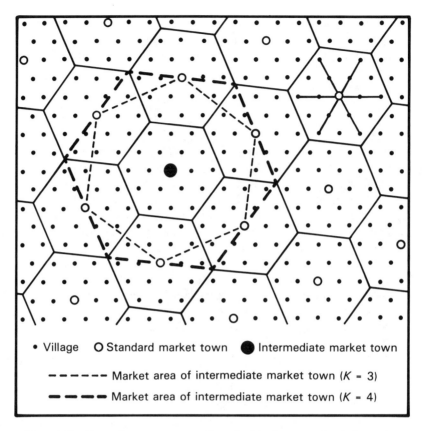

**Figure 5.2**   Alternative arrangements of standard market towns in relation to the intermediate marketing town.

important, and local market centers. As one moves from the low-level local market centers to the regional market centers, the markets attract increasing numbers of people and conduct increasing volumes of business. On market days regional market centers attract as many as 15,000 to 20,000 people as opposed to 4000 to 5000 people attending local market centers. Similarly, regional market centers have a much larger number of traders than markets in lower levels of the hierarchy. One regional market center, for example, attracted 2243 traders on market day as compared to only 29 traders in the smallest local market center in the area. On the average, regional market centers attract about 1200 traders on market day as compared to 250 traders attending local market centers.

As in prerevolutionary China, higher-order market centers, in addition to attracting a larger number of traders and local people, have a number of shops which operate daily. The level of sales at these stores on nonmarket days, however, is substantially less than that on the market day. Another characteristic of the hierarchical organization is that the number of goods and services available in the markets varies considerably. Traders in local market centers deal mainly in low-order goods and services which have low threshold requirements. As one progresses to successively higher levels of market centers, goods and services requiring higher thresholds are found.

A great deal of research on market center exchange and on the role of periodic markets has been conducted in West Africa. Much of this research took place in Nigeria, where Hodder's identification of the functioning of the Akinyele market ring north of Ibadan was one of the early empirical studies of the geography of periodic markets (Hodder, 1961). This research is perhaps best known for Hodder's denial of the relevance of central-place theory in the understanding of these phenomena. However, considerable research during the last 20 years had confirmed the relevance of central-place theory in understanding periodic marketing. The work of Trager (1976) in the Ijesaland area north of Ibadan is quite illustrative of this relevance. Trager identified a five-level network of central places (Figure 5.3). She based her assessment of the order of central places on Marshall's work (1964) and confirmed that the hierarchical level and locational spacing of central places in Ijesaland was greatly influenced by the transport network. Trager's study is also noteworthy for its illustration of the relationship between centrality, transportation, and periodicity. Most of the lower-level market centers are located on the transport network linking higher-order places, either between Ijesa and one of the higher-level market centers or between two high-level market centers. These findings accord with the transport principle of spatial organization discussed in Chapter 3.

A review of these and studies from other parts of the world suggests that periodic market centers possess distinct hierarchical characteristics and can be viewed from the same perspectives as the central-place systems of developed economies. Skinner, for example, argued that the spatial organization of periodic markets in rural prerevolutionary China could be understood in terms of the Christaller $K = 3$ and $K = 4$ sytems. (See Figure 5.2 and also Figures 3.17 and 3.18.) The work of Skinner, as well as that of many succeeding authors, has demonstrated that central-place theory can accommodate markets that meet periodically.

At least three different criteria have been suggested for distinguishing between periodic market centers at different levels of the hierarchy. The first and simplest criterion is the volume of activity at the market center. This can be measured by the number of people present (buyers and sellers), by the number of traders and stalls; and by the amount or value of goods and services exchanged along with the extent of the market area. In using any of these measures, however, the enumeration period must be selected with care since the level of activity at any market varies both with time of day as well as season. Further, the number of traders or the number of occupied stalls are useful surrogates of the level of activity only if traders operated roughly at the same scale. A skewed profile with a few large and many small traders (as is the case in many market centers) would give a misleading impression of the order of market centers if only the *number*

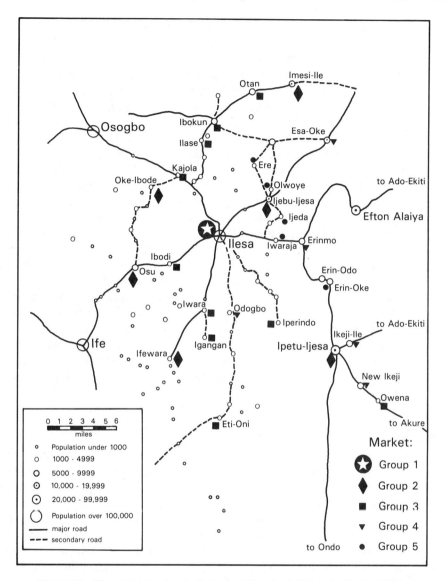

**Figure 5.3** The network of central places in Ijeseland. [From L. Trager (1979) "Market Centers as Small Urban Places in Western Nigeria," in A. Southall (ed.), *Small Urban Centers in Rural Development in Africa,* African Studies Program, University of Wisconsin, Madison, Wis., 138–157.]

of traders were counted. To overcome this problem Bromley (1976) suggests using "trading units" as a standard measure of the daily turnover of a trader. Small traders are counted as one unit, whereas larger traders may count as multiple units.

The second criterion for establishing a hierarchy is the degree to which periodic market centers possess nonperiodic tertiary activities. As noted earlier, in many high-level market centers there is often some daily activity on nonmarket days along with a clearly recognizable peak on the market day. Lower-order market centers, on the other hand, usually do not have such permanent stalls. The ratio of the average activities on nonmarket days to that on the market day can be used to indicate the hierarchical order. Higher-level market centers would be expected to have higher ratios than lower-level ones.

A third criterion for distinguishing among market centers is the variety of trading activities performed. One measure of this is the type of goods and services traded at the market center and their threshold requirements. Wanmali and Ghosh (1975), for example, use this measure to distinguish among markets in southern Bihar, India. Goods and services having high thresholds, such as shoe stores and drug stores, are available only in the few high-level market centers in the area. Lower-level goods and services such as bicycle repair shops and cigarette stalls, on the other hand, are more ubiquitous and available even at the low-level market centers. Similarly, Skinner notes that in prerevolutionary China low-level merchandise consumed by the local population is available in all market centers, whereas consumer goods for the local elite are available at the intermediate market towns. Furthermore, the highest-level consumer goods and industrial supplies can be obtained only at the central market towns. Hodder and Ukwu (1969) note that in Yorubaland the proportion of non–food sellers and traders in European goods can be used to distinguish among market centers at different levels of the hierarchy.

## MARKET-CENTER PERIODICITY

A distinguishing characteristic of periodic marketing systems is the frequency of market meetings. The length of the *market week*, or period of market interval, specifies the frequency of market meetings at any location. Thus, a 2-day market meets every second day (days 1, 3, 5, etc.), while a 7-day market meets regularly on the same day every 7-day week. Market weeks are often described as "natural" or "artificial." The length of a natural market week follows the motions of the heavenly bodies, especially the lunar calendar. The schedule of markets following an artificial cycle, on the other hand, are most commonly regulated by the 7-day calendar week. These market centers meet, say, on every Monday; or, say, on every Tuesday and Friday.

Figure 5.4, which shows the periodicity of market meetings in traditional prerevolutionary China, demonstrates the temporal organization of market centers in a natural cycle. A trader can move among the central market town and two standard market towns in a 10-day cycle divided into units of three. On the first day the trader is at the central market town. The trader then travels to two standard market towns on the next 2 days and then returns to the central market

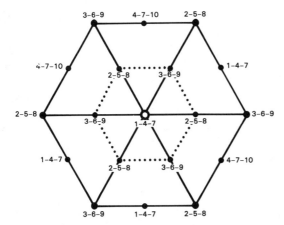

**Figure 5.4** Periodicity of markets in a traditional Chinese 3-per-*hsün* cycle.

town on day four. The sequence of visits is repeated so that the trader is at standard market towns on days five, six, eight, and nine with a visit to the central market town on day seven. The tenth day in the cycle is a rest day on which no business is transacted. On day eleven the trader is at the central market town again, ready to repeat the cycle of the previous 10 days. The movement pattern of the trader corresponds to the lunar decade (*hsün*), beginning on the first, eleventh, and twenty-first day of each month. The markets in the figure thus follow a three cycles-per-*hsün* pattern.

In addition to three cycles-per-*hsün* patterns, which were found in the Szechuan basin and in the plains of southeastern China, Skinner found one cycle-per-*hsün* patterns in the remote areas as well as two and four cycles-per-*hsün* patterns in the more populated areas of northeastern China. Two cycles per-*hsün* patterns were also common in Korea, whereas one cycle-per-*hsün* patterns were found in Japan prior to modernization. Both are presumably related to the diffusion of Chinese culture to the north. On the other hand, in southwestern China the 12-day duodenary cycle was used, periodic marketing systems beginning with one meeting per duodenum, the frequency of meetings doubling in successively higher-order centers.

Natural market weeks are found in other parts of the world too. In Africa, for example, Yoruba markets meet at intervals of four or multiples of 4 days that correspond to the time referents of local religions. Based on ethnographic evidence, Ojo (1966, p. 203) notes the importance of the number four as follows: " . . . a day each was set aside for the four major deities of Yorubaland and their local variants. . . ." Similarly, in Iboland, the number four was recurrent in thought and symbolism, as well as in "the liturgy of priests and the incantations of the doctors" (Hodder and Ukwu, 1969, p. 128).

Many contemporary market weeks owe their origin to the colonial experiences of many countries and the influences of the Christian calendar. This has resulted in the prevalence of "artificial" market weeks which follow the 7-day calendar. Thus 7-day market weeks are common in east Africa, Latin America, and many countries in southeast Asia (Wood, 1978; Bromley and Symanski, 1974; Bromley, 1976; Lockwood, 1965; Burrough, 1978; Yeung, 1978). In many African regions, such as southern Ghana and Madagascar, the 7-day market actually pre-dated the arrival of Europeans and resulted from the diffusion of the 7-day calendar from the Islamic areas of North Africa and the Middle East (Fagerlund and Smith, 1970; Jackson, 1978; Hill and Smith, 1972; Hill, 1966).

Indeed, the continuing influence of religious institutions on the organization of market centers can be seen in the prevalence of small Sunday markets in Mexico and the Andean areas of Latin America (Bromley, 1976; Bromley and Symanski, 1974; Beals, 1976; Gormsen, 1978) as well as that of Friday markets in the Islamic areas of West Africa (Hill and Smith, 1972).

In some areas, such as Java, the 7-day market was simply superimposed on the traditional 5-day market week (Dewey, 1962; Nilsson, 1920). Adelmo (1972, pp. 13–15) describes a somewhat similar situation in the Kainji Lake area in Nigeria where there are both 4-day and 7-day market centers. Each market center meets according to one periodicity schedule or the other, but not both schedules. The 4-day–week markets were pre-Islamic and persist where original local customs prevail.

The length of the market week is clearly associated with the economic as well as the cultural characteristics of a region. From a purely economic viewpoint, the length of the market week should be determined by the density of demand. The greater the level of aggregate demand the higher the frequency with which the markets can viably meet. In the extreme, if the level of demand is high enough markets can meet daily. However, even if daily meetings could be supported, periodicity of market meetings can be advantageous especially if sales can be concentrated in time. A crucial factor influencing periodicity is the amount of goods consumers buy on a visit to the market center. The greater the amount of goods bought on a trip the longer the interval between consumer purchases and consequently the longer the market week. The lack of cash to buy and store large amounts of goods during a single visit and the perishability of products in areas without refrigeration, however, limit the interval between purchases.

## MARKET RINGS

Related to the issue of locational and temporal organization of market centers are the concepts of *market rings* and the *spatio-temporal synchronization* of market centers.

*Market rings* (or *circuits* or *rounds*) imply that adjacent marketplaces can be viewed as a network which is linked together. In Kusai, Ghana, where the markets have a 3-day week, the rural residents think of the three neighboring markets as being connected together. Each of these markets is held on consecutive days; and, when taken together, the three neighboring markets constitute a market

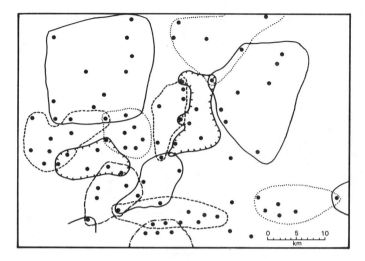

**Figure 5.5**    Periodic markets and interlocking rings in southwestern Nigeria.

ring. Each ring, in turn, is linked to another, so that the entire region is covered by an interconnected network of market rings. This led Hodder (1961, p. 152) to remark that there was a "complete and integrated sequence of markets" in southwestern Yorubaland. With reference to markets in Ghana, Poleman (1961, p. 62) noted that "most farm people think of themselves not as being served by just one market, but as being near the hub of four or more, each of which is held on a different day. These 'circles' generally overlap . . . the countryside is crisscrossed by a sort of chain-mail cycle of circles." Observations of the market-ring patterns in Iboland in Nigeria led Ukwu to remark that the marketing landscape was "a panorama of honeycombs in regular periodic circuit" (Hodder and Ukwu, 1969, p. 156). Figure 5.5 shows an example of the complex pattern of market rings in southwestern Nigeria.

Market rings are best defined from the point of view of the consumer. Such a ring comprises the group of market centers which consumers in an area perceive as belonging to a particular spatio-temporal set. Most consumers do not just visit a single market center, but they consider themselves as being served by a number of neighboring market centers. The market ring is the set of alternative sites a consumer may visit during the course of the market week. In most cases it comprises the set of market centers that is closest to the consumer for each day of the market week.

Figure 5.6 shows the market rings of consumers at three settlements in a hypothetical region having a 5-day market week. Note that each market ring represents the spatial orientation of a particular consumer. In this case it is the set of market centers closest to the consumer on any day of the week. In extreme cases, the market rings of consumers of each of the different settlements may be different. Usually, however, many neighboring settlements will have common

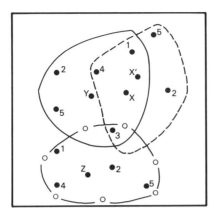

Figure 5.6   Examples of market rings.

market rings, and market rings of neighboring settlements will overlap considerably. In the figure, the market rings of different consumers overlap and they impinge on one another, resulting in an interlocking network of rings. The degree of overlap in market rings may determine the extent and nature of interaction among settlements. Consumers who share common market rings or whose market rings overlap considerably have a high likelihood of meeting at the market center. Consequently, they are likely to exhibit a high degree of social and economic integration.

Bohannan and Bohannan in their description of the Tiv market centers note the high degree of social interaction among settlements which have common market rings. They observe that among the Tiv a dispute between settlements which share a common market is more likely to be settled directly, but beyond the common market there is a tendency to use intermediaries or courts (1968, p. 197). They further argue that settlements that shared the same market ring tend to form a "neighborhood."

Market rings are the empirical expression of consumer travel behavior, constrained by the maximum and minimum range of a good or service. The concept of market rings is especially relevant if consumers can associate days of the market week with particular market centers. The concept of market rings, therefore, is closely related to the level of knowledge possessed by rural inhabitants about the set of market opportunities in an area. Investigations of the rural consumer's cognitive awareness of market locations is crucial for a correct definition of the set of market centers constituting a market ring.

## SPATIO-TEMPORAL SYNCHRONIZATION

The distinctive characteristic of periodic market centers when examined in the context of central-place systems is their hierarchical integration of both spatial and temporal features. Thus, spatio-temporal synchronization is a recurrent theme in the literature on periodic markets. In many studies of periodic marketing, it is asserted that market meetings are arranged in space and time so that the convenience of all participants is served. Thus, in his study of the markets in Yorubaland, Hodder (1961) suggested that synchronization of market meetings within a ring ensured that no settlement was far away from a market center for more than 3 days. Numerous other studies have similarly concluded that the temporal pattern of neighboring markets is so arranged as not to conflict with one another.

The implied relationship between temporal and spatial proximity was formally stated by Fagerlund and Smith (1970, p. 351) as: " . . . proximity in space implies separation in time." Thus, there is an inverse relationship between the distance separating two markets and the time interval between their market meetings. This follows from the argument that a consequence of market periodicity is the partial substitution of temporal for spatial competition. For the consumer in this unique central-place system, spatial choice is conditioned by weighing the cost of waiting a few days for a closer market center (Hodder and Ukwu, 1969). As a consequence, markets meeting simultaneously or separated only by a short period of time, should, on an average, be more widely spaced than markets which are temporally distant. Markets which meet on the same day should be widely spaced so that each is able to attract the threshold level of trade. If two markets which meet on the same day are located close together, they will be competing for the same consumers. One of the markets will eventually emerge as the dominant one, resulting in the disappearance or a drastic reduction in the scope of the other. By contrast, market centers whose market days are widely separated can be located near each other because they do not compete for the same consumer simultaneously.

Fagerlund and Smith (1970) suggested a formal test of this hypothesis by comparing the distances between periodic market centers with the number of days by which their meetings were separated. They argued that markets which were separated temporally would be close spatially. Evidence on this relationship has been presented from a number of market systems located throughout the world. Figure 5.7, for example, shows the relationship between temporal and locational spacing for a number of market systems in Africa. Almost invariably, same-day markets are more widely spaced than markets which are temporally distant. However, the expectation of the *consumer hypothesis* that an inverse relationship between the temporal and locational spacing would hold for all categories of temporal spacing has not been fulfilled. As seen in Figure 5.7 the distances separating markets meeting at 1-day or 2-day intervals are often more than the distances separating markets meeting on adjacent days.

In addition to the consumer hypothesis, Hill and Smith (1972) have also proposed a *trader hypothesis* which argues that the temporal sequence which is

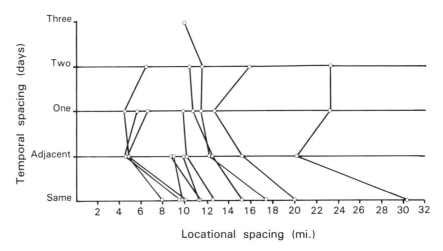

**Figure 5.7**    The relationship between temporal and locational spacing.

optimal for consumers may not be so for the trader. The trader hypothesis states that the itinerant trader will follow the sequence that minimizes the total travel necessary to visit all market centers. This means that markets which are close together in time are also close in space. There is until now, however, little empirical support for the trader hypothesis.

That the observed spatio-temporal pattern of market centers should represent some rational order is a logical expectation. The suggested hypotheses, however, do not adequately represent the situation faced by the consumer and traders in periodic market systems. If the trader visits market centers from a home base, the trader hypothesis does not necessarily represent the optimal travel pattern. Moreover, it is more reasonable to argue that trader's choose the itinerary that maximizes their profit rather than that which merely reduces cost (Ghosh, 1979). A profit maximizing trader must take into consideration the influence of temporal ordering on the profitability of alternative sites, that is, the trader must weigh the profitability of sites against the cost of relocation (Ghosh, 1982). It is not surprising, therefore, that few studies have confirmed either the trader or consumer hypothesis. One has to conclude, therefore, the research on spatio-temporal synchronization is, at this stage, inconclusive. Nevertheless, there is persuasive (if incomplete) evidence that central-place theory provides a coherent framework within which to examine periodic marketing and periodic market centers. Concepts of hierarchy are expressed both temporally and spatially through market weeks and market rings. Thus, while there is considerable temporal diversity, it seems reasonable to view periodic markets as a special kind of central-place system.

# REFERENCES

ADALEMO, I. A. (1972) "The Marketing of Cash Crops in the Kainji Lake Basin," Nigerian Institute of Social and Economic Research Monograph Series 1, Ibadan, Nigeria.

BEALS, R. L. (1976) "The Oaxaca Market Study Project: Origins, Scope, and Preliminary Findings," in S. Cook and M. Diskin (eds.), *Markets in Oaxaca*, Austin, Tex.: University of Texas Press.

BOHANNAN, P., and L. BOHANNAN (1968) *Tiv Economy*. Evanston, Ill.: Northwestern University Press.

BROMLEY, R. J. (1976) "Contemporary Market Periodicity in Highland Ecuador," in C. A. Smith (ed.), *Regional Analysis*, vol. 1, New York: Academic Press.

BROMLEY, R. J., and R. SYMANSKI (1974) "Marketplace Trade in Latin America," *Latin American Research Review*, 9:3–38.

BURROUGH, J. B. (1978) "The *tamus* of Sabah," in R. H. T. Smith (ed.), *Market-place Trade*, Vancouver, B.C.: University of British Columbia, Centre for Transportation Studies.

DEWEY, A. G. (1962) *Peasant Marketing in Java*. Glencoe, Ill.: The Free Press.

EIGHMY, T. H. (1972) "Rural Periodic Markets and the Extension of an Urban System: A Western Nigeria Example," *Economic Geography*, 48:229–315.

FAGERLUND, V. G., and R. H. T. SMITH (1970) "A Preliminary Map of Market Periodicities in Ghana," *Journal of Developing Areas*, 4:333–347.

GHOSH, A. (1979) "A Model of Periodic Marketing and Itinerant Trading," University of Iowa, Iowa City, Iowa. Unpublished Ph.D. Dissertation.

GHOSH, A. (1982) "A Model of Periodic Marketing," *Geographical Analysis*, 14:155–166.

GORMSEN, E. (1978) "Weekly Markets in the Puebla Region of Mexico," in R. H. T. Smith (ed.), *Market-place Trade*, Vancouver, B.C.: University of British Columbia, Centre for Transportation Studies.

HARRISS, B. (1975) "Poverty, Caste, and the Rurality of Transactions: A Speculative Explanation for Periodic Marketing in Northern Tamil Nadu." Paper presented to Indo-British Geographic Seminar, Cambridge, U.K.

HAY, A. M. (1977) "Some Alternatives in the Economic Analysis of Periodic Marketing," *Geographic Analysis*, 9:72–79.

HILL, P. (1966) "Notes on Traditional Market Authority and Market Periodicity in West Africa," *Journal of African History*, 7:295–311.

HILL, P., and R. H. T. SMITH (1972) "The Spatial and Temporal Synchronization of Periodic Markets: Evidence from Four Emirates in Northern Nigeria," *Economic Geography*, 48:345–355.

HODDER, B. W. (1961) "Rural Periodic Day Markets in Part of Yorubaland," *Transactions of the Institute of British Geographers*, 29:149–159.

HODDER, B. W. (1965) "Distribution of Markets in Yorubaland," *Scottish Geographical Magazine*, 81:48–58.

HODDER, B. W., and U. I. UKWU (1969) *Markets in West Africa*. Ibadan, Nigeria: University of Ibadan Press.

JACKSON, R. T. (1978) "Nineteenth Century Market Systems in Ethiopia and Madagascar," in R. H. T. Smith (ed.), *Market-place Trade*, Vancouver, B.C.: University of British Columbia, Centre for Transportation Studies.

LOCKWOOD, W. G. (1965) "The Market Place as a Social Mechanism in Peasant Society," *The Kroeber Anthropological Society Papers*, 32:47–67.

MARSHALL, G. A. (1964) "Women, Trade, and the Yoruba Family." Department of Anthropology, Columbia University, New York. Unpublished Ph.D. dissertation.

NILSSON, M. P. (1920) *Primitive Time-Reckoning: A Study in the Origins and First Development of the Art of Counting Time among the Primitive and Early Culture Peoples.* Lund, Sweden: Gleerup.

OJO, G. J. A. (1966) *Yoruba Culture: A Geographical Analysis.* London: University of Ife and University of London Press.

PIAULT, M. (1971) "Cycles de marchés et 'espaces' socio-politiques," in C. Meillassoux (ed.), *The Development of Indigenous Trade and Markets in West Africa*, London: Oxford University Press for the International African Institute.

POLEMAN, T. T. (1961) "The Food Economies of Urban Middle Africa: The Case of Ghana," *Food Research Institute Studies in Agricultural Economics, Trade and Development*, 2:121–174.

SADA, P. O., M. L. McNULTY, and I. A. ADALEMO (1978) "Periodic Markets in a Metropolitan Environment: The Example of Lagos, Nigeria," in R. H. T. Smith (ed.), *Market-place Trade*, Vancouver, B.C.: University of British Columbia, Centre for Transportation Studies.

SKINNER, G. W. (1964) "Marketing and Social Structure in Rural China-I," *Journal of Asian Studies*, 24:3–43.

SKINNER, G. W. (1965a) "Marketing and Social Structure in Rural China-II," *Journal of Asian Studies*, 24:195–228.

SKINNER, G. W. (1965b) "Marketing and Social Structure in Rural China-III," *Journal of Asian Studies*, 24:363–399.

SMITH, R. H. T. (1970) "A Note on Periodic Markets in West Africa," *African Urban Notes*, 5:29–37.

STINE, J. H. (1962) "Temporal Aspects of Tertiary Production Elements in Korea," in F. R. Pitts (ed.), *Urban Systems and Economic Development.* Eugene, Oreg.: University of Oregon, School of Business Administration.

SYMANSKI, R. (1973) "God, Food, and Consumers in Periodic Market Systems," *Proceedings of the Association of American Geographers*, 262–266.

TAIT, D. (1961) *The Konkomba of Northern Ghana.* London: Oxford University Press for the International African Institute.

TRAGER, L. (1976) "Yoruba Markets and Trade: Analysis of Spatial Structure and Social Organization in the Ijesaland Marketing System." Department of Anthropology, University of Washington. Unpublished Ph.D. dissertation.

VANSINA, J. (1962) "Trade and Markets among the Kuba," in P. Bohannan and G. Dalton (eds.), *Markets in Africa.* Evanston, Ill.: Northwestern University Press.

WANMALI, S. (1977) "Periodic Markets in South Bihar—Spatial and Temporal Characteristics," *Management and Labour Studies*, 3:1–16.

WANMALI, S. (1981) *Periodic Markets and Rural Development in India*. New Delhi, India: B. R. Publishing Corporation.

WANMALI, S., and A. GHOSH (1975) "Pattern of Distribution of Urban Consumer Goods in Rural India," *Management and Labour Studies*, vol. 1, 1:79–94.

WOOD, L. J. (1978) "Rural Markets in Kenya," in R. H. T. Smith (ed.), *Market-place Trade*. Vancouver, B.C.: University of British Columbia, Centre for Transportation Studies.

YEUNG, Y. -M. (1974) "Periodic Markets: Comments on Spatial-Temporal Relationships," *The Professional Geographer*, 26:147–151.

# 6

# Changes
# in Time and Space

Hierarchically organized systems of central places appear ubiquitous in market economies. Centrally directed societies find it essential to arrange their systems of control and systems of service delivery hierarchically too. Certain properties of central-place hierarchies are widespread, regardless of divergent historical traditions and systems of political control. Yet, in spite of the commonalities, a rich variety of marketing, distribution, and exchange systems is to be found across the globe. The previous chapter explored the role of periodic markets in peasant societies, where market activity is combined with subsistence production. This chapter will explore other cases. Cultures in which exchange takes the form of reciprocal gift-giving or redistribution will be examined, the role of fairs in peasant societies will be explored, and the sources of differentiation of market economies will be discussed. Sources of change are examined as well, for example, the emergence of periodic markets in systems of local trade and the establishment of fairs along long-distance trade routes. Also the types of change occurring within market economies will be noted.

## HOUSEHOLDING, RECIPROCITY, AND REDISTRIBUTION

Individuals have a variety of wants, such as food, clothing, shelter, and social prestige. As producers they work to satisfy these wants. Economic systems develop out of the need for some form of organization to ensure that demands are met by the production of the proper kinds and quantities of supplies. In most societies, the formal systems of exchange that emerge are mediated by the market, and hierarchies of central places develop for the transactions to take place.

But there are examples of societies where the mediating role of the market is absent. These may be understood by considering a "Robinson Crusoe" case. Responsible for satisfying his own demands, the character of Robinson Crusoe had to decide what he wanted, extract his raw materials and crops, transport them to his workshops, process them to create desired products, store the products at some convenient place until the need for them arose, and finally distribute them in proper proportions to the spots where they would finally be consumed. His *productive process* (employing the stages of extraction, processing, and distribution, and the attendant operations of transportation and storage) thus led to final satisfaction of his needs in consumption.

Crusoe was a complete *economic system*. He originated the *demands* and created the *supplies*, and so organized his work that his demands and supplies were maintained in equilibrium. But his is a textbook case. In real life people are by nature social animals clustering together in communities of varying sizes. In the past, and still in the less Westernized parts of the world today, some of these communities have maintained a Crusoe-like equilibrium as they have also attempted to be self-sustaining.

In Crusoe's case, the decision as to how much to produce and how to distribute the output was his own. In Crusoe-like economies the decision is *social*; the rules, obligations, traditions, and group decisions of the community determine who shall produce what and how it will be distributed.

Three patterns of social control have been identified: *householding, redistribution*, and *reciprocity*.

### Householding

Householding is a literal translation of the Greek word *oeconomia*, the etymon for our word "economy." A more appropriate rendering of the meaning is "production for one's own use," or, as the economic historian Karl Polanyi stated:

> . . . whether the different entities of the family or the settlement or the manor form the self-sufficient unit, the principle is invariably the same: that of producing and storing for the satisfaction of the wants of the members of the group . . . Production for use as against production for gain is the essence of householding. (Polanyi, 1944)

In its pattern and organization, the householding unit is closest to the Robinson Crusoe case. Instead of the single consumer there are several members of the household; and instead of the single producer there are several, with division of labor based upon age, sex, social standing, and tradition. The function of the distribution system is to gather the output of producers and deposit it at the place or places where members of the household will consume it in the quantities and at the times determined by community and custom. (The producers, by virtue of specialization, have become mutually interdependent.)

The medieval *manor*, the Roman *familia*, and the South Slav *zadruga* were comparable householding economic systems. The basic social and territorial unit of organization in Britain was a grouping of hamlets, known as a *maenor*, under the authority of a lord. This unit was self-sustaining (Jones, 1961). It comprised a series of families who worked cooperatively in cultivating their communal fields, woods, pastures, and ponds. But each family had an established right to the output from certain strips of land, to pasture a certain number of animals, to use a certain amount of wood, and so forth. Equity was maintained by these rights. Large numbers of such independent economic units "honeycombed" feudal society in Europe, which thus was blanketed by a network of cellular "little societies."

### Redistribution

In other societies distribution has been assured through the institution of a strong central authority. In one historical arrangement, produce was delivered to a chieftain, who then parceled it out to members of the social group in ways determined by custom. Many of the ancient empires, such as the New Kingdom of Egypt (1570–1085 B.C.), were founded upon this principle of redistribution. Such redistribution also sought to ameliorate the effects of lean and the fat years. The pattern remains common among the cattle-herding tribes of East Africa. One interesting manifestation was found in the *potlatch* of the *Kwakiutl* tribe of the Pacific Northwest, in which the chief assembled the wealth of the tribe and redistributed it by giving it to others in elaborate ceremonies. The ultimate objective of this ceremony was to make the recipient a social debtor.

Redistributive principles have a contemporary manifestation both in the world's welfare states and in centrally directed socialist countries. In the Soviet Union the central-place system is primarily an administrative hierarchy, and only secondarily a distribution system.

### Reciprocity

The third traditional pattern in reciprocity in the assurance of needed exchange. For example, in the Trobriand Islands of Western Melanesia, inland communities were paired with coastal villages in a pattern of exchanging inland breadfruits for coastal fish. The pairing extended to particular individuals who were responsible for the direct exchange in symmetrical arrangements of remarkable regularity and persistence. Many such exchanges were disguised as reciprocal giving-of-gifts, but the arrangement was no less effective as a method of reciprocity.

Karl Polanyi, whose impressive and massive work of synthesis was responsible for the current understanding of the subordination of primitive economic life to social rules and traditions, described the essence of the three patterns. He argued that all economic systems known up to the end of feudalism in Western

Europe were organized either on the principles of householding, reciprocity, or redistribution, or on some combination of the three. The orderly production and distribution of goods was secured through a great variety of individual motives disciplined by general principles of behavior. Gain was not prominent among these motives. Custom and law, magic and religion cooperated in inducing the individual to comply with the rules of behavior which, eventually, ensured one's functioning in the economic system. Further, Polanyi argues that as long as social organization ran in ruts, no individual economic motives had to come into play; no shirking of personal effort had to be feared; division of labor would automatically be ensured; economic obligations would be duly discharged; and material means for an excellent display of abundance at all public festivals would be ensured. Such were and are the simplest forms of exchange, not in feudal Europe alone, but in all societies in which the marketplace was and is absent (Polanyi, 1944, 1957).

## EMERGENCE OF LOCAL AND LONG-DISTANCE TRADE

Market centers emerged only after goods began to move to consumers in exchange systems transcending the limits of the householding unit or the immediate social group, replacing the management of exchange by reciprocity or redistribution. Two possible sources of the change have been identified. One involved the emergence of periodic markets in systems of local trade, the other involved the establishment of fairs along long-distance trade routes. Both of these should be distinguished from central-place hierarchies in modern societies. Neither local nor long-distance trade disturbed the subsistence base of the householding units in peasant societies. The role of modern central-place hierarchies is, on the other hand, predicated upon division of labor and the absence of household self-sufficiency.

A three-stage sequence is seen in the transition from householding to central-place hierarchy. The first involves socially administered exchange. In the second, barter and, later, money provided the standards of value permitting marketplace transactions in peasant societies. And third, the peasant dualism between subsistence and trade has been replaced in many parts of the world by the specialization of modern economies. Periodic markets and fairs have been replaced by an elaborate array of permanent market centers. The series of revolutions (industrial, commercial, agricultural, and political) involved in what Polanyi calls "The Great Transformation" all led toward increasing specialization and the breakdown of local self-sufficiency. Places and social units began to depend on others for sustenance, thereby widening spheres of mutual dependence. To make sure that demands and supplies were in balance, the distribution system assumed a more fundamental role, and a whole range of market centers emerged to ensure that consumers would be supplied with correct quantities and types of goods and services at the proper time.

Perhaps the earliest long-distance trade was exploration beyond the limits of the local area. Such exploration might involve warlike forays or irregular trading, often for ritual goods associated with the god-king and the temple, which were the focus of society and social controls (Adams, 1966). So long as the resulting exchange of goods was sporadic, market centers did not develop. Only when regular trade connections emerged was there justification for establishment of permanent marketplaces.

One regular form of long-distance exchange was between complementary production zones, for example, between plains dwellers and hill folk, each trading surpluses of their own specialty for those of the other. Market sites would frequently develop along the territorial boundary zone, often on neutral ground. At the appropriate season, often in conjunction with religious festivities that guaranteed the safety of the location, people from surrounding areas would converge upon market sites to barter their surpluses. When relations between the different groups were strained, such market times would constitute a truce.

Market centers also developed at stopping places on the great trade routes of the world, such as the silk routes between China and Europe. Fiords, riverheads, ports, other points of transshipment, and the ends of routes became logical places for exchange to take place.

Most luxuries and trinkets found their way from these exchange points to the peasants at great seasonal festivals. The festivals originated as religious celebrations, but soon developed commercial sidelines, which later became their raison d'être. Only a few of the lighter, more expensive items of dress and personal adornment came from the outside. Spices for the elite, ritual materials required for religious purposes, metal implements, salt, and trinkets used by all classes also came from outside. Often these luxury goods came from tremendous distances.

Local trade emerged on the basis of regular intercourse between peasants, local craftspeople, specialists, town merchants, and middlemen. Local surpluses would be traded for such necessities as salt, iron, or other durables, and merchants would have available some luxuries and trinkets obtained from the great fairs. To fit in with seasonal work on the land, the markets would be held periodically. Links connecting long-distance trade, the great fairs, and local periodic markets were provided by the circuits of town merchants.

Neither local nor long-distance trade appear to have been responsible for the growth of cities. Periodic markets and fairs still meet on ground where there is no permanent settlement. Skinner (1964) noted, for example, that there were two urban hierarchies in China. The first was the system of periodic markets and market centers described in Chapter 5. The second was the administrative hierarchy, where cities were the centers of districts (*hsien*), prefectures (*fu*), or provinces (*sheng*)—a hierarchy which corresponds to the tripartite administrative structure. The two hierarchies occasionally met at the same level in the same cities, although this was not a necessity. Market centers are among the main reasons for cities in modern market economies, however, and although there are other reasons for cities (notably specialization in mining or industrial production), there are never markets without an associated urban center in modern economies. For this reason Christaller formulated central-place theory as a theory of both retail location and urban location.

The earliest cities were associated with growth of an urban community around, and initially dependent upon, a palace or a temple which was located within a citadel or stronghold. Such places, performing political, military, religious, or administrative roles, seldom were integral parts of society; a clear separation existed between the urban and the rural. Such cities drew their requirements from the surrounding countryside, either by force of arms or by some socially determined pattern of redistribution. But very little of this wealth was returned to the country folk. (This was accomplished, for example, by maintaining the Pharaoh's grain warehouses in the New Kingdom of Egypt, or, in medieval Europe, by the lord receiving his feudal due and by the Christian church receiving tithings.)

With the emergence of local and long-distance trade, market sites and trading posts became widespread, but most of these sites were occupied for marketing purposes only periodically. Local trade seldom provided any basis for the growth of cities, even if surpluses obtained at the weekly markets did augment the urban food supply. Although grants of market rights and coinage privileges to owners of strongholds were made as early as the ninth or tenth centuries in Europe, these functions were carried on inside the stronghold and did not lead to growth of urban communities outside its walls. On the other hand, the combination of a stronghold or temple with a great fair on a major trade route often did lead to the emergence of great cities. Pirenne (1936) related the regeneration of urbanism in Europe after the Dark Ages to the rebirth of trade.

A debate now wages between two theories of the origins of periodic markets and fairs. The first, dating back to Adam Smith's *Wealth of Nations* (1776), starts with an agrarian society in which surpluses develop, permitting a basic form of division of labor to emerge from the propensity of individuals to barter the surpluses, and leading to the establishment of a specialist group of artificers (smiths, carpenters, and wheelwrights) located in a village central to the farmers they serve and with whom they exchange. The village becomes the most convenient site for trade between the farmers themselves, too, and the village assumes the status of a periodic market. Specialization then proceeds further and additional surpluses lead to interregional trade, especially in crude manufactures using the region's resources. Since the manufacturers have urban locations, an important element of interregional trade is interurban. Ultimately, a hierarchy of urban centers with marketing functions develops to mediate local, intraregional, interregional, and interurban trade. The sequence starts with a propensity and ability to barter; then it proceeds to activities of local exchange, local division of labor, local markets. Finally the external exchanges and the external markets develop. Barter exists among the most isolated and inaccessible societies; and the wordless exchange of goods made without witness in the furthermost recesses of the jungle, in Asia, America, and Africa, is evidence of an economic need. As confidence grows between individuals exchanging their respective goods, local markets spring up; and in the more advanced cultures wide use may be made of money in the more important markets or regional fairs (Hodder, 1965, paraphrasing a 1953 report of the International Labour Organization).

The alternative view of the origins of markets and fairs stems from the work of Polanyi (1957) and Pirenne (1936) and reverses the sequence, stating that trade and markets can never arise within communities, for trade is external, involving different communities. In this view, markets do not develop out of the demands of purely local or individual commerce, but they are primarily induced by external exchanges of complementary products with an alien population. Markets are, therefore, the result rather than the starting point of long-distance trading. The sequence is seen as the establishment of trade routes first, then fairs established on these routes, and finally local (periodic) markets developing around the original fair as a network of tracks or roads spreads.

Hodder (1965) reviewed evidence for and against the two previously stated views in Africa. In Yorubaland the evidence in support of the second theory seemed overwhelming. The earliest markets were located along the contact zone between forest and savanna, along coastal lagoons and creeks, or along boundaries between different peoples. More important, the larger markets were along the chief trade routes and changed in importance with changes in these routes. One important origin of Yoruba markets was located at the resting place where local populations provided services to passing groups of traders. If such resting places became popular, then a market into which farmers brought their wares for sale sprang up and periodic market days developed. Extra large meetings would be held less frequently when large numbers of traders converged.

On the other hand, the essence of the Adam Smith view is identity between the processes of urban development and growth of market centers in an evolutionary sequence. But in Yorubaland locations of periodic markets and of settlements diverged. Traditional markets in Yorubaland were true central places, foci of communication, not nuclei of settlement. This is to be expected when markets originate in external contacts rather than by natural development within a given social context.

To follow Hodder's survey further (although he emphasized the fragmentary nature of the evidence) the materials available suggested growth of long-distance trading contacts in the majority of West African communities. The same story was repeated for Ethiopia, for the Horn of Africa, and for the Congo. The same occurred in contacts among the Kikuyu, Masai, Kamba, Arab, and Swahili in East Africa; and again further south with the Bantu.

In southern and southeastern Africa, on the other hand, there was no evidence of the existence of periodic markets. The markets found there today are of recent origin, introduced by Europeans or other outside groups, although there is some evidence of barter (Bohannan and Dalton, 1962). Lack of periodic markets is explained by the isolation of the most primitive subsistence societies from the main interregional trade routes. If there were internal exchange, it never gave rise to markets, but exchange remained as reciprocal giftgiving, as, for example, among the Bulu of Cameroun.

Hodder argued that without two additional conditions opportunities presented by long-distance external trading contacts can never be grasped and channeled through market institutions. The first condition is a sufficiently high level of population density. Below about 50 persons per square mile there are not enough people within walking distance of any central point to justify a market or to permit much economic diversification among individuals. The second condition is that only where well-developed and highly organized political units existed could communities profit from trading possibilities. That is, without strong political organization, security of markets could not be ensured. These ideas were reiterated by Adams (1966) in his studies of the ritual bases of urban origins and long-distance trade.

The impressive fund of evidence Hodder assembled in support of the nontraditional view parallels the nontraditional arguments concerning urban origins in America and the role of urban centers in the development of the American market economy. The traditional views were those of Frederick Jackson Turner (1956). See also Gras (1922a, 1922b) and Schlesinger (1949).

Turner argued in the following that the continent was occupied in a series of waves:

> It begins with the Indian and the hunter; it goes on to tell of the disintegration of savagery by the entrance of the trader, the pathfinder of civilization; we read the annals of the pastoral stage in ranch life; the exploitation of the soil by the raising of unrotated crops of corn and wheat in sparsely settled farming communities; the extensive culture of the denser farm settlement; and finally the manufacturing organization with city and factory system.

In this evolutionary scheme, market towns developed as the frontier of commercial agriculture passed beyond lands previously transformed by passage of a frontier of peasant farmers.

Gras's thesis involved the following five stages of economic evolution: collectional economy, cultural nomadic economy, settled village economy, town economy, and metropolitan economy. Market centers developed in the settled village stage, and subsequent stages added to the complexity of the urban hierarchy. In the final stage, the metropolis organizes the market, leads the processes of industrial development and transportation, and molds the pattern of financial organization.

The more recent argument of Wade (1959), in tracing the rise of the Old West, is supportive of the alternative nontraditional theory, however: "The towns were the spearheads of the frontier. Planted far in advance of the line of settlement, they held the West for the approaching population." Wade further cites the insights of Strong (1885, p. 206): "In the Middle States the farms were first taken, then the town sprang up to supply its wants, and at length the railway connected it with the world; but in the West the order is reversed—first the railroad, then the towns, then the farms. Settlement is, consequently, much more rapid, and the city stamps the country, instead of the country stamping the city." Vance (1970) has, as was noted in Chapter 4, formulated the idea of externally imposed from the top down market-center development into a "mercantile model."

Our evidence on the development of market centers in southwestern Iowa supports the views of Wade, the insights of Strong, and the mercantile model of Vance. The nontraditional view of emergence of markets out of external contacts appears to have priority.

## Fairs

Fairs complement periodic markets in peasant economies, but whereas periodic markets are chiefly agencies for satisfying local demand, fairs meet less frequently and reflect regional difference in economic activity. Fairs attract buyers from distant areas by virtue of the fairs' specialization. It is at fairs that regular but infrequent long-distance trade has been consummated. If the Latin roots of the word *market* refer to both the act of exchange and the place where exchange is transacted, the term *fair* derives from roots meaning a celebration or festival.

In the most ambitious attempt at comparative investigation of fairs (limited to fairs of the Old World), Allix (1922) distinguished among four analogous institutions—the general commodity fair, the livestock fair, the country market, and the sample fair. The *commodity fair* represented the sole mechanism of large-scale commerce in a state of civilization with no security for regular exchange and limited means of transportation. In many societies, exchange occurred on neutral ground during a period of truce. Historically, much of the commerce in these societies was *Grenzhandel* or frontier commerce. An example is provided by the *mouggars* held on the fringe of the Sahara. Before the coming of the French to the Sahara, the mouggars were the only times when exchange could take place with an assurance of the safety of life and property. And they served as the intermediaries of commercial life between the Sahara, the Sudan, and Morocco (Fogg, 1932).

Allix felt that the fair arose from caravan transport as well as frontier commerce. In North Africa, the fair grew out of the gatherings for trade at the "ports" of caravans. The caravans eventually found it in their self-interest to arrive at the time of religious festivals, so fairs also had a timing related to religious events.

The *livestock fair* appears superficially to be a derivative of the commodity fair, but in reality it was an independent institution. Perhaps the most ancient type of fair and probably the most persistent, its origins were in the rural countryside. Agriculture, by its nature, imposes intermittent structure upon commercial gatherings, which are periodic for convenience. In a sedentary agricultural population, such commercial gatherings could be held at frequent intervals. In pastoral nomadism, however, the interval had to be related to the progression of the seasons and the movement of the herds, so the gatherings attained particular importance at certain seasons of the year. Fogg argues that the livestock fair generally becomes an *annual fair*, and in many cases it developed out of the possibilities of exchange where a large number of people gathered together in the name of a particular saint. The influence of these fairs may be quite local, as in the many religious festivals of India, or they may have very wide appeal and be attended by thousands.

Allix goes on to point out that in the beginning these rural gatherings were nearly always held in the open country, but with time these locations tended to become fixed centers of habitation. The concentration of agricultural exchange in the form of a *country market* was one of the reasons urban settlements come about. As the town developed it began to acquire its own proper functions, and it ended by absorbing all the country products. Thus arose the city market.

The final major form of fair that Allix recognized was the *sample fair*. By 1897, when the Leipzig fair had declined to a point where its very existence was imperiled, an effort was made to preserve the wholesale trade of the fair and prevent its degeneration into a local retail fair. Since the old system was incompatible with direct bulk sales, the idea of sale with immediate delivery was abandoned. Instead, visitors and buyers were offered only samples of merchandise and orders for more were taken. In this way, merchandise was exchanged from buyer to seller without passing through the fair.

Timing of fairs has been complex. The temporal sequence in fair activity often involved seasonal fluctuation in the number of fairs, with changes in fair specialization reflecting variations in products available in the surrounding producing regions. Because of these seasonal changes, the activity of fairs often showed a spatial sequence related to the growing season and climate. Furthermore, the duration of any single fair was often divided into times when special products or economic activity predominated.

Kniffen (1949, 1951), in his study of the American agricultural fair, found that it was closely akin to the ancient harvest festival and traditionally came in autumn. This association became so deeply impressed upon the American mind that many were unaware that fairs occurred in other seasons. Yet, American colonial market fairs commonly had a spring session, and specialty fairs for livestock, poultry, and citrus fruit occurred at other times, too.

For each general region of the United States, Kniffen found a recognized fair season, progressing from the earliest fair held near the Canadian border to those of the last of the year in the southern states. He mapped all of the accurately known cycle for 1949, noting that organized circuits were restricted to areas where fairs were numerous and where horse-racing was a prominent part of the fair.

The association of each fair with a particular calendar week became strongly established. On the whole, the common duration for a fair was six days, Monday through Saturday. Within this fair week, one day—usually Thursday—was traditionally more important than the others.

In the Central Andes of South America, there remains a marked seasonal distribution of fairs. Most fairs take place at the change of season. No fairs of importance are held in January, February, or March during the peak of the rainy season. This seasonal variation has a religious explanation. To the Peruvians, the seasons of germination and maturity are marked by spiritual recognition. They are times of ceremony, when the entire agricultural community comes together. Here too, however, fairs that originally were primarily of a religious character have grown into more mercantile enterprises. Similar examples can be cited throughout the world.

Periodicity, the most obvious trait of commodity fairs, conceals a more fundamental characteristic—the itinerant nature of traders and their merchandise. The merchant is able to travel from fair to fair only by the combination of dates and rhythms of the various fairs. Thus, the trader at fairs repeats on a larger scale the behavior of the peddler in the periodic market.

Allix demonstrated the intimate connection between the livestock fair and pastoral life. In pastoral nomadism, the fair is a permanent element of both economic and social structure. Since herders are accustomed to meeting other herders at fixed intervals, the exchange of animals, the making of contracts for the engagement of herders, and the sale of pastoral produce become commonplace. The livestock fair thereby became a cattle fair. It represents the sole commercial outlet for the pastoral region itself and the only economic contact of the pastoral region with the exterior economy. In addition, since it is the only chance for the pastoral people to buy products of everyday need, the cattle fair is almost always accompanied by a certain amount of general merchandise and is therefore attended by a host of itinerant retail traders. There is an indissoluble connection between the rhythm of the fairs and that of pastoral nomadism. The tenacity of this connection is illustrated by the abortive attempt during the French Revolution to change the traditional dates of fairs.

Like periodic markets, fairs show an internal grouping of products. This is particularly true for the general commodity fair, with diverse products localized within the fair. (This is revealed in Figure 6.1, which reproduces Fogg's diagram of the structure of a large *suq* in Morocco.) This also usually applies to the livestock fair. Internal division facilitates transactions since consumer movements and confusion are kept at a minimum.

There is a complexity in fair location equal to that of periodic markets. Some factors differ in influence or in kind depending upon the cultures. Other factors remain important throughout most peasant societies.

Fairs were most often held on boundaries in neutral lands where rival tribes could meet to trade. In ancient Italy, for example, one of the most important fairs was held on a boundary which separated Etruscan lands from Sabine lands. In Greece, markets were held on boundaries under the protection of the gods of the Agora. Irish fairs were frequently held in or near cemeteries, while similar fair sites at churchyards can be found in England. English fairs were often held on hilltops—St. Giles Hill Fair, Weyhill Fair, and the fair at St. Ann's Hill are examples. There was a close connection between hilltop fairs and ancient trackways.

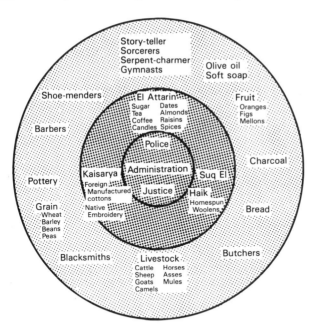

**Figure 6.1**   Plan of a large *suq*.

In northern Morocco, Mikesell (1958) recognized two major types of markets. The local *suq* is the more influential and draws a few hundred people from a radius of 10 to 12 miles. Its primary function is to serve as focus of commerce for a dispersed but sedentary poupulation engaged in subsistence agriculture. The second type is the *suq* which serves as a regional market and draws a larger number of people from a radius of as much as 20 miles. Markets of this type are located at the convergence of major communication lines and on the frontiers of complementary production zones. Each of the markets has four major functions: first, the distribution of local products; second, the exchange of a rural surplus for urban goods; third, the circulation of articles such as pottery and millstones; and fourth, the dissemination for foreign imports. The larger regional *suq* differs from the local *suq* in its greater emphasis upon the last two functions. Siting is on neutral ground (typically a religious shrine) since individual *suqs* or groups of *suqs* are related to particular tribes.

Kniffen points out that in the United States while the chief function of market fairs is commercial, the chief function of the agricultural fair is educational. Different considerations therefore enter into a particular fair's location. The educational American county fair is a quasi-governmental institution, and it is therefore normally situated at the county seat. The state fair is usally held in the capital or largest city. Transportation is an important locational factor. In preautomobile days, some local fairs were accessible only with horse and buggy; those attending larger fairs came chiefly by rail. Today, the automobile is the chief form of transportation. The fairgrounds commonly lie at the edge of the community. Although there have been some cases where fairs are surrounded by an expanding city, few manage to survive the economic competition from the city. The fair must have a good water supply and flat terrain for buildings and the racetrack, and it profits from a grove of trees to shade picnickers and mobile-home living quarters.

In the Central Andes, fairs were located at some equidistant point for the movement of products and people. Several were situated in the Titicaca Basin between the Peruvian valleys and the Argentine pampas; others between the rich valleys of the montana and the coastal ports. Other equating points were on the borders of well-marked natural regions.

In Elizabethan England, distribution of long and recurrent fairs was closely associated with eastern and western ports of entry into England from the sea and with the commercial "boundary" between northeast and southwest. On this boundary traders evidently found an almost continuous market throughout the year. This was the location at which foreign merchants could hope to find a relatively constant demand for continental goods and luxuries. Long and recurrent fairs were also located at well-defined road intersections or near some recognized line of travel. Many of the great fair towns of England lay along the road from London through Leicester to Manchester. Even the variable of road transportation, however, fails to account for a significant number of important fairs and fair clusters. Only when the fair distribution is compared with a map of Roman communications are those "roadless" centers of trade brought into relation with lines of transport. The Roman roads which rationalize the position of important or minor fair sites were still in use during the Elizabethan period.

Allix reiterates the importance of the great highways of communication to the location of fairs. A map viewing a country's fairs at their time of apogee will show them on the great trade routes of the time. Ordinarily, Allix notes, two classes of circumstances favor the location of fairs. First, they may be located in the center of producing regions. The Flemish fairs were essentially the outlet of the 17 cloth-manufacturing towns which, in the Middle Ages, made Flanders the first textile region of the continent. Second, fairs might have a location at places of transit and at crossroads. This is exemplified by the frontier locations of Champagne, Breslau, and the two Frankforts. When these two locational factors can be combined—the producing region plus the crossing of great highways—the conditions are exceptional for making a fortune, as occurred in Lyons and Leipzig.

Allix goes on to examine the importance of settlement to fairs, pointing out that fairs are often held outside towns in the open country. It may be, as at Timbuktu, that the town is an isolated point of fixed habitation around which nomad life is centered. In this case fairs may give rise to fixed centers of population or greatly encourage their growth. When there is a superimposition of fair and town, the institutions are essentially distinct. Allix notes that great fairs have often been long associated with small towns. This was the case at Beaucaire in southern France near the mouth of the Rhone. Similarly, this was true at Briançon, the frontier town of the French Alps on the great road to Italy, and at St. Denis, near Paris. Undoubtedly the towns do derive some benefit from the fair, but less than is commonly thought. The town treasury and inns gain the most, whereas local trade scarcely profits at all. The fair greatly increases the population, but only momentarily. The fair is of a nature entirely different from that of the town, and the fair has only superficial relations with the town. These conclusions were reiterated by Pirenne in his history of Europe.

## CHANGE IN PEASANT MARKETING

Two major sources of change exist within peasant marketing systems. The first change is increasing population densities, and the second change is the increasing household participation in the marketing process that causes both greater specialization and rising incomes. Increasing population initially had the greatest effect, whereas under the pressures of modernization the second is the main source of change today (Belshaw, 1965).

Skinner relates the results of changing population densities in the People's Republic of China. Initially, new markets would be established and existing markets would grow. Next, markets continued to grow in size, but the larger ones would add new dates to their periodic schedules. Finally, markets would stabilize and periodicity would vanish, except perhaps on a diurnal basis. Further increases in population density would, thereafter, be accompanied by increases in the number but decreases in the spacing of permanent market centers. Total volumes of trade would increase, as would the numbers of marketing hours per week. Permanent firms would replace their mobile counterparts, and the degree and scope of economic specialization would widen. There is one common phenomenon in this: the tendency of cycle lengths to decrease with rising population density or, more generally, with rising demand and purchasing capacity. Hodder (1965) notes how some 8-day markets became 4-day markets apparently as a result of the increasing size and importance of surrounding settlements. The halving of the cycle length is a convenient and logical way to increase frequency " . . . for it requires no disruption of the old schedule: new market days are simply added to the old'' (Skinner, 1964, p. 916). In India, a common form of increasing frequency is to open subsidiary markets on nonregular days. A market meeting once a week would have a subsidiary market that meets at the same place during mid-week. With growing demand the subsidiary market grows in importance and finally equals the status of the first, resulting in a semi-weekly market. Increases in frequency may also be a result of the merger of neighboring markets.

The working of this process in India has led Singh (1965) to formulate a *stability theory* of central-place development. He studied central places serving as centers for small rural regions as nuclei of exchange and barter, and as places of entertainment, worship, and social interaction. He shows age of market in the Faizabad district to be related to size of center and tabulates the activity in the weekly cycle (Figure 6.2). In the smallest markets there are one or two meetings per week, and permanent shops are absent from the market site. On market day 75 percent of the sellers are peasant producers, not middlemen. Foodstuffs and

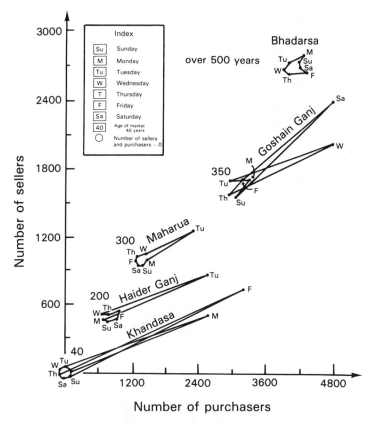

**Figure 6.2**   Age, size, and periodicity of bazaars in the Faizabad area.

handicrafts are the main items traded. Itinerant traders, called *khochiwalas*, walk from one such market to another in a weekly cycle. In larger, older centers the numbers of permanent shops managed by middlemen increase, along with wholesalers and small credit institutions. The final stage is stability.

Skinner also relates the changes that took place in the People's Republic of China as peasant households were linked to growing urban markets for food and handicrafts and to urban sources of exotic goods. In the traditional hierarchy of markets in prerevolutionary China, successively higher levels of center were characterized by greater volumes of trade, more marketing hours per week, higher proportions of permanent to mobile firms, and a greater degree and scope of economic specialization. Traditional change involved extension of the characteristics to lower-level centers as population densities increased. Modernization involved gradual commercialization of the agrarian economy, however, and increases in the marketing done by the household. There was an extension of urban demands into the countryside and a rapid contraction of household self-sufficiency. Marketing systems within the city's trading area became commercialized, and the system of periodic markets was thus transformed into a stable central-place hierarchy.

The interlocked industrial, urban, and agricultural revolutions of the past three centuries can, in this sense, be seen as the reason for the emergence of urban hierarchies out of early systems of fairs and periodic markets. Colonial penetration has been a similar source of change in peasant societies elsewhere, and the commercial transformation of markets established or influenced by colonial administration or economic penetration is a source of further social change in peasant households.

The countries of Western Europe, with a long history of modernization, still retain vestigial traces of earlier fairs and market periodicities in the market days of country towns (Figure 6.3), whereas lands newly settled in the past three centuries in the New World and Southern Hemisphere have purely modern urban hierarchies. Local markets are not permanent elements of the urban hierarchy in the United States, although the system of fairs described by Kniffen does remain.

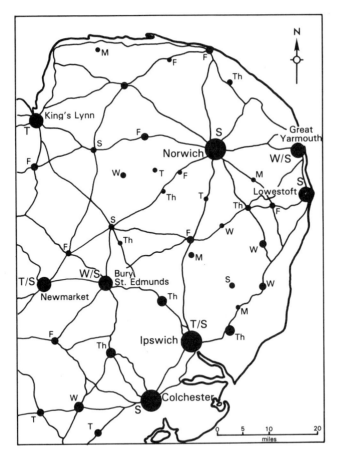

**Figure 6.3** Market days in East Anglia.

Elsewhere, fairs have changed their role. Some of the Central Andes fairs held in the Titicaca Basin towns have been completely abandoned. The pastoral type survived in its original form for the longest period since the animals could be walked to market. Where the railways have penetrated, fairs are of dominant commercial importance.

Allix argued that, as civilization perfects means of exchange and communication and assures the commercial world of increasing security, the conditions which support the commodity fair disappear. Fairs must decline or undergo transformation. International traders cease to frequent fairs and abandon them completely to retail trade. Monetary transactions are carried on more and more by permanent exchanges and clearing houses. Merchandise is shipped only on order, while sales are made on the basis of samples (the sample fair). The system of fairs is superseded by wholesale trade. Large-scale commerce becomes rooted in permanent centers. Between these centers, in all directions and at all seasons, individuals, samples, and goods flow in uninterrupted currents.

The effect of this fixation of commerce, however, is not to diminish the number of fairs. Rather, as their importance declines, their number increases. Little local fairs arise which tend to degenerate into periodic amusements.

In the case of livestock fairs, Allix saw a similar decline. The rhythm of nomadism is no longer vital, so the fair whose *raison d'être* is pastoral nomadism is progressively losing its age-old importance. A more extensive clientele now demands a more regular supply which the system of fairs does not provide. In addition, buyers of pastoral products increasingly tend to travel the mountains at all seasons and purchase directly from producers. The buyers seek to outdo each other and strive to obtain the best of stock some days before the fairs. This decline of stock fairs was slower than that of merchandise fairs, however, and Allix doubted that livestock fairs would disappear entirely. The cattle fair, he believed, must survive as the best way of inspecting all the cattle of a region. In addition, stock raisers can give only a limited portion of their time to buying and selling, and the fairs still give the stock raisers an opportunity for social intercourse and interregional exchange.

## *VARIABILITY AND CHANGE IN URBAN HIERARCHIES*

Once a permanent urban hierarchy is established, it continues to change. According to Skinner's description of change in prerevolutionary China, agrarian modernization took place prior to the spread of modern transportation. Once modern transportation was added, the lowest-level centers (standard markets) began to decline.

Commercialization enabled the peasants to market more often in higher-level centers, even before the coming of better roads, because of the rising demands for imported goods. Better roads induced the villages to market their products in higher-level centers, bypassing the lowest-level centers. Links of higher-level centers to large places because of improved transport also reduced the price and increased the variety of goods available. Increased trade permitted further differentiation and specialization. Decreasing activity in the lower-level centers put them in cumulatively less competitive situations. Schedules were reduced, and finally the lowest-level markets closed.

There was thus a reversal of traditional processes. Traditional change, based largely upon increasing population and greater participation in the market process, led to the addition of centers, the reductions in areas served, and the growth at the lowest levels as functions moved down the hierarchy. Modern change has, however, decreased the number of centers, increased market-area sizes, and forced functions upwards in the hierarchy. Thus, expanding zones around growing cities in prerevolutionary China were undergoing modern changes and concurrent reductions in number of lower-level centers, whereas, beyond the modernization frontier at the same time, traditional processes worked and increases in the number of centers and market schedules occurred.

The principal sources of spatial variation and of change in modern urban hierarchies are, on the demand side, population densities and income differences. On the supply side, the principal sources of spatial variation and of change are the technology of retailing, industrial organization, and, of course, the technology of transportation.

The variability is pronounced across urban hierarchies. One of the last major exercises in comparative marketing analysis, by Hall, Knapp, and Winston (1961), pointed out that while the ratio of stores, including service establishments, to population is remarkably similar in Great Britain, the United States, and Canada, the relative number of stores in luxury trades is greatest in the United States and lowest in Britain. Exactly the converse is true for stores selling necessities. This is in accordance with income differences between the countries. Moreover, store size and sales productivity of labor are greatest in the United States, where earnings of retail employees are highest and there are the greatest pressures to substitute capital for labor.

Similar differences are seen both within and between rich and poor regions in each of the three countries. In poor regions, average sales volumes and the ratio of chains stores to independent stores jump sharply from rural to urban areas. In rich regions the transition from medium-sized to large cities is marked by a relative increase in the number of stores and the proportion of independents and by a decrease in store size. The difference is in the demands for luxury goods in richer regions, which is focused in higher-level central places.

These findings indicate a consistent tendency within each modern economy for chain stores to locate only in places that provide some minimum market size. They also show the fragmentation of tastes that leads to increased numbers of shopping-goods stores in the largest cities of the wealthiest regions, where maximum numbers of customers come together in circumstances that also make for the greatest numbers of entrepreneurs (Thompson, 1965; Duncan, 1952, 1959).

These generalizations can be extended across the whole range of modern economies, yet they are insufficient to account for additional kinds of variety that extend across these economies. For example, where population densities are very low, especially in northern latitudes, the area within the maximum distance consumers are willing to travel to a center is insufficient to support a permanent market. Retailing is therefore conducted by mobile shops that travel from one population cluster to another, accumulating the necessary volume of demand for survival and selling in sufficient bulk so that the customer can wait until the next visit (Helle, 1964). In this way, limitations upon the businesses of insufficient aggregate demand and limitations upon the customer of excessive travel distances needed to purchase goods are overcome in a mutually satisfactory way. In some developing areas, too, peddlers provide retail services to those rural populations so dispersed that market center systems have not emerged. Plattner's study of peddlers based in San Cristobal Llas Casas in southern Mexico illustrates the role of the peddler as an interstitial operator in areas of low population density—areas where distance from a major urban center and the conditions of transport are such that farmers rarely make the trip to a marketplace. Of course, in frontier areas where population density is low and access conditions are poor, neither peddlers nor market center systems exist (Plattner, 1975).

Improvements in transport technology, rising incomes, and the changing technology of retailing have combined to produce continuing shifts in urban hierarchies throughout most of the United States and Canada. In the area of southwestern Iowa discussed in Chapter 1, initial entry of the railroad was instrumental in transforming a peasant economy into a commercial one, and within a relatively few years after the arrival of the railroad the number of central places reached its maximum. Almost immediately complaints were heard of the death of hamlets and villages as a result of the spread of chain stores and the provision of farm-to-market roads. Chains avoided locating in the smallest centers, but better roads enabled farmers to journey to chain stores in the larger centers even before the automobile use became widespread (Landis, 1932). To prevent the centralization of business, the Iowa State Legislature at one time banned the futher construction of highways radiating outwards from Des Moines.

The automobile, along with rising real incomes, accentuated these trends. Two further forces reinforced the changes. Mechanization of agriculture led to declining farm population, affecting demand. In retailing, scale shifts required many functions to be performed in larger centers. This affected the supply of goods (Chittick, 1955). As a result, before 1930 hamlets with populations of 100 or less were declining; thereafter, as centralization of functions in higher levels of the hierarchy progressed, the general decline embraced villages with populations of less than 500. Today, the towns are moribund, and smaller central places continue to decline.

Only certain resilient subcultures have resisted these changes. For example, there is a part of Ontario, Canada, in which both Old Order Mennonites and "modern" Canadians live. The contrast in their shopping habits provides a graphic "before-and-after" picture of the use of central-place systems (Murdie, 1965). The Mennonites use modern methods only to manage their farm businesses. In dress, domestic consumption, and travel they retain the habits of two centuries ago. They wear plain homemade clothes and demand few goods. The horse and buggy is the sole means of transportation. The result is that the set of central places in the area is used in two separate ways. In effect, the two groups have two systems. Where the Mennonites behave like modern Canadians, no real differences in system use are seen. This is seen in Figure 6.4, which shows where the modern Canadians (left) and Mennonites (right) use banks. However, where the traditional beliefs of the Mennonite group operate two types of behavior are evident. Figure 6.5 shows where the modern Canadians purchase clothing (left) and the Mennonites buy their yard goods (right). The difference in transport technology is critical. Modern Canadians demand variety and have the opportunity to react to it, so the maximum distance they travel is related to size of center, as was discussed in Chapters 2 and 4. The Mennonites, on the other hand, are restricted by the use of horse and buggy and buy only a limited variety of yard goods, so that the maximum distance which they travel (or the real range of yard goods) does not vary with the hierarchical level of the center, as can be seen in Figure 6.6.

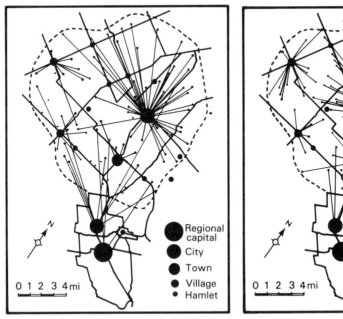

**Figure 6.4**  Banks used by "modern" Canadians (left) and Old Order Mennonites (right) in an area of Ontario.

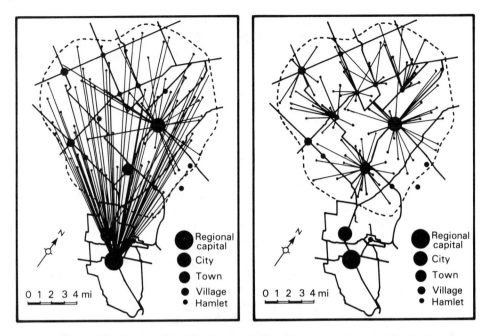

**Figure 6.5** Centers visited by ''modern'' Canadians to purchase clothing (left) and by Old Order Mennonites to obtain yard goods (right).

What happened to North American central-place hierarchies in the half century from the 1920s to the 1970s was a combination of differential growth, selective thinning, and then the transformation of the structure of the retail system as metropolitan areas reached outward to embrace larger territories.

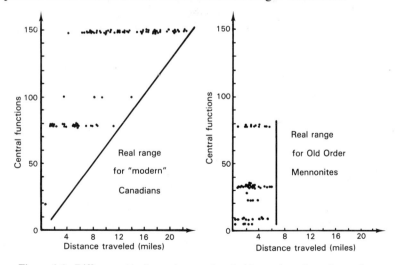

**Figure 6.6** Differences in the real range for clothing and yard-goods purchase.

**TABLE 6.1**  CHANGES IN CENTRAL-PLACE
POPULATION IN IOWA, 1930–1960

| Levels of center | Average annual growth rate (in percent) |
|---|---|
| Hamlet | −2.69 |
| Village | −0.58 |
| Town | −0.15 |
| City (county seat) | +0.44 |
| Regional capital | +0.94 |

Between 1930 and 1960, for example, populations in central places in south-western Iowa changed in the manner recorded in Table 6.1. There was a clear relationship of population change to level of center in the hierarchy. By contrast, the rural farm population of the area fell at a rate of 0.28 percent per annum, whereas the nation's metropolitan areas grew at a rate of 2.8 percent.

These are average rates that combine a thinning of the pattern (by places dropping from one level to another in the hierarchy or ceasing to function altogether) with an increase of the pattern as remaining places expanding their market areas to remain viable. Hodge (1965) recorded such transitions of centers from one level to another in Saskatchewan between 1941 and 1961. (See Table 6.2 and note the drop in status of smaller central places.) No less than 46 percent of all hamlets died in that 20-year period.

Table 6.3 records other relevant data for Saskatchewan. The thinning of centers of town level and lower enabled the remaining centers to increase the sizes of their market areas, and therefore the average space between centers increased. Conversely, larger centers increased in number, and therefore their spacing decreased. In southwestern Iowa, the market areas of lower-level centers increased in size from 1930 to 1960, accompanying the decrease in the numbers

**TABLE 6.2**  CHANGES IN THE PROPORTIONS OF CENTERS OF DIFFERENT LEVELS
IN SASKATCHEWAN, 1941–1961

| Class in 1941 | Died by 1961 | Class in 1961 | | | | | | |
|---|---|---|---|---|---|---|---|---|
| | | Hamlets | Villages | Towns | Smaller seats | County seats | Regional city | Regional capital |
| New centers | 48 | 52 | | | | | | |
| Hamlets | 46 | 52 | 2 | | | | | |
| Villages | 2 | 63 | 27 | 7 | 1 | | | |
| Towns | | 6 | 28 | 39 | 26 | 1 | | |
| Smaller seats | | | 2 | 19 | 63 | 16 | | |
| County seats | | | | | 12 | 73 | 15 | |
| Regional city | | | | | | | 100 | |
| Regional capital | | | | | | | | 100 |

**TABLE 6.3**  CHARACTERISTICS OF CENTERS
IN SASKATCHEWAN, 1961

| Classification | Number in 1961 | Average spacing (in miles) | |
|---|---|---|---|
| | | 1941 | 1961 |
| Hamlet | 404 | 9.1 | 9.6 |
| Village | 150 | 10.3 | 13.5 |
| Town | 100 | 15.4 | 19.8 |
| Small seat | 85 | 25.9 | 22.5 |
| County seat | 29 | 40.4 | 39.5 |
| Regional city | 9 | 119.8 | 67.5 |
| Regional capital | 2 | 144.0 | 144.0 |

of centers (Figure 6.7). The market-area size increases were *exactly* those needed to keep the total populations, served by the remaining low-level centers, approximately constant over the interval (Figure 6.8).

For changes in Saskatchewan between 1961 and 1981 see Stabler (1987). They most closely approximated the Type II change discussed in Chapter 4 as consumer and producer services shifted from the lower to the upper levels of the hierarchy. Since 1960, the major factor transforming North American urban hierarchies has been the spread of metropolitan regions rather than the reshaping of the central-place hierarchy itself, however, with the changes produced by this development extending far into the countryside beyond suburbia into widening

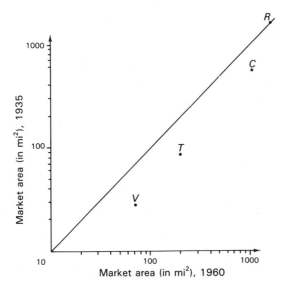

**Figure 6.7**  Market-area size changes in southwestern Iowa, 1935–1960.

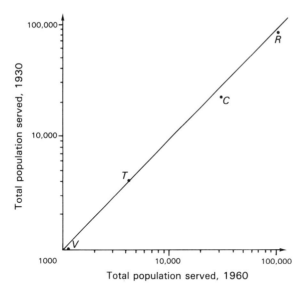

Figure 6.8 Change in the total population served, by level of center, Iowa 1950–1960.

exurban rings. The character and role of central places changes when they are drawn within the pale of metropolitan markets, as we saw in Chapter 2.

Within the metropolitan region, specialization replaces the repetitions of the central-place hierarchy. Some centers continue in their central-place role, but others become resorts or dormitory suburbs. New outlying shopping plazas are constructed, and business ribbons extend along the highways. Some retail complexes grow to the scale of suburban "downtowns" within outlying minicities. In short, the areas brought within expanding metropolitan regions are influenced by new locational forces and forms of interdependence. The classical patterns of the central-place hierarchy breakdown and are replaced by business patterns characteristically internal to cities. Expanding metropolitan regions are responsible for the same "phase shift" in the geography of retailing that was attributed in Chapter 2 to population densities. The two are, of course, not unrelated. Since the North American population is now concentrated in metropolitan regions, this current phase of modernization may be eliminating central-place hierarchies as we know them from the continent. The resulting economic structure is that of a set of interdependent metropolitan regions. Each such region is specialized to a high degree internally instead of being successively subdivided into progressively smaller regions for the retail distribution of goods and services. Locational specialization, rather than the repetitive, nested levels of a central-place hierarchy, appears to be the key to understanding the most modern forms of metropolitan retail geography. In this, the modern system resembles the models of Lösch perhaps, instead of Christaller.

In turn, the shopping centers, business ribbons, and specialized functional areas that comprise the retail geography of metropolitan regions are not unchanging, but undergo continual adjustments in the short run and transformation in the long run.

As the metropolitan population changes and is redistributed, retail facilities expand in areas where population is increasing and contract where population is decreasing. For example, changes in numbers of retail establishments in the Chicago region between 1948 and 1958 shown in Figure 6.9 mirrored the population changes in that metropolitan area during that decade. Declines in the central city involved abandonment of older ribbon frontage, leaving vacant, unwanted structures. On the other hand, new growth at the periphery was accompanied by construction of new planned shopping centers and larger ribbon stores.

Progressive increases in real incomes also played their role, leading to gradual increases in the proportion of stores devoted to specialities and shopping

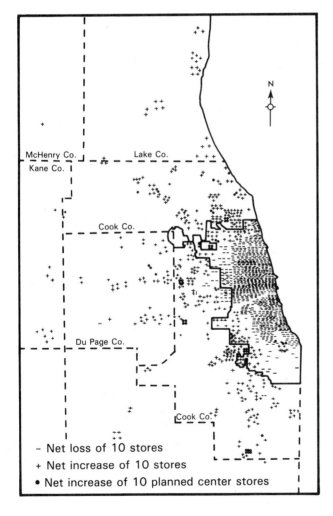

- Net loss of 10 stores
+ Net increase of 10 stores
• Net increase of 10 planned center stores

**Figure 6.9**  Net change in number of retail establishments in the Chicago region, 1948–1958.

goods. The older, unplanned centers and ribbons provided somewhat fewer facilities for higher-income groups than the planned centers, although there were always differences of this kind in the store composition of Chicago centers serving higher- and lower-income segments of the population (Berry, 1963).

Results of the changes in retail technology were not as apparent in the central city of Chicago in 1960 (where most stores had been constructed before the depression of the 1930s) as in the outlying sections of the metropolitan region. There, as was noted in Chapter 2, fingers of prewar development with their older, unplanned centers and ribbons (together with more distant central places drawn within the metropolitan region) were faced with new suburban growth and modern, planned shopping centers in the interstices between the developed fingers as highway improvements pushed the commuting radius further out from the city center. Competition was intense, and the new planned centers, with larger, modern stores, more attractive ground plans, and ample free parking, were the victors. Most of the old retail centers, long since moribund, perished.

Change within the central cities was of another kind, though. The cumulative effects of changing technology and declining population were compounded by profound social change as minority populations urbanized.

The classical picture of the social geography of an American city was one in which central areas provided homes for new immigrants who, as they prospered, moved outwards to wealthier neighborhoods. As the city grew, lower-income neighborhoods, dominated increasingly by minority immigrants, extended outwards from the city center, encroaching upon the higher-income zones. Urban ecologists described these processes as "succession" and the "filtering down" of housing.

What did those changes mean for central-city retailing? Very simply, loss of markets. Black family income has averaged two-thirds that of the white population. Growth of the black population and the flight of the white population to suburbia meant declining retail markets within the inner city. Combining the factors of technological change, population redistribution, income shifts, and social change, it was found that between 1950 and 1960 the following changes occurred in Chicago:

1. Holding constant all variables (save consumer mobility and level of technology), the annual drop in number of retail establishments due to scale changes was 5.87 percent.
2. For every 1 percent change in population there was a 0.98 percent change in the number of retail units.
3. For every 1 percent shift in real income levels, there was a 0.86 percent change in the number of retail stores. Thus, social turnover from a middle-income white population to a low-income black population, which is accompanied by a 30 percent drop in income levels in the decade from initial penetration of an area until it has completely "turned over," implied a de-

cline of retail stores during the decade of at least 2.5 percent per annum. (Berry, 1963)

The process of retail transition during social change thus provided the key to an understanding of the problem of commercial blight that was becoming serious at the time. There were several stages:

1. *The anticipation of neighborhood transition.* During this phase two important things happen. First, normal replacement of businesses that fail or close because the owners retire or die, ceases. Vacancy rates begin to rise. Second, a "maintenance gap" appears. Property owners cease normal repairs or reduce maintenance expenditures because of growing uncertainty about prospective revenues. There are thus the beginnings of dilapidation, especially among the vacant shops, and a generally run-down appearance prevails.

2. *The period of population turnover.* In this phase demands drop precipitously, particularly for more specialized, higher-quality goods. The more flexible stores change their price lines, but smaller, more specialized shops do not have such flexibility and go out of business. Vacancies in centers rise, reaching between one-third and one-half the stores in the worst cases.

3. *The stabilization phase.* The neighborhood then settles down into its lower-income character. There has been a maintenance gap, and now, with lower incomes, it is difficult to restore previously sound buildings. The areas surrounding business centers are seedy and usually continue to deteriorate. Rents in business centers drop, and the more viable establishments from the ribbons move in and fill up the vacant space. Vacancies mount in the ribbons, settling at around 20 percent of all establishments. Vacancies are usually concentrated in the most dilapidated buildings, which, through lack of use, deteriorate even more. Lower-income zones are thus crisscrossed with ribbons of unwanted, blighted commercial property.

At the other extreme, the developing sectors of metropolitan regions since 1960 have seen new retailing forces in response to new markets. Older shopping centers and central business districts have been replaced by large-scale enclosed malls. These have been built on the exurban periphery in zones of inner-city renewal. "Gentrifying" neighborhoods have developed retail complexes attuned to "yuppie" demands. Both shopping centers and malls have become more highly differentiated, depending upon whether they serve high-, middle-, or low-income markets. Major discount chains have risen and fallen. New specialized shopping areas have developed to serve new markets. Modern transportation and rising real incomes have removed the tyranny of distance. People's "life spaces" (the areas in which they travel to work, shop, socialize, or play) have widened immensely. Shopping centers no longer dominate an immediate, exclusive market area; instead, several centers of several types serve the same community-of-interest area. Consumers visit all of these centers at one time or another. Distance no longer provides protection from competition. Centers must compete, and, to achieve some margin of safety, they seek all means to differentiate themselves from their competitors. The only real safety, however, is in the economies introduced by further specialization, and the result of the widening of living spaces is to increase locational specialization.

Such specializations tend, increasingly, to be carefully researched and planned, for the growing scale and concentration of retail development has moved the locus of initiative from the individual business to the large-scale developer and the retail chain, aided by their own or private market-research groups. Continuing transformations in the pattern of retail and service business are being engineered by the marketing specialists whose ideas are dealt with in Chapter 7.

# REFERENCES

ADAMS, R. McC. (1966) *The Evolution of Urban Society*. Chicago: Aldine.

ALLIX, A. (1922) "The Geography of Fairs: Illustrated by Old World Examples," *Geographical Review*, 12:532–569.

BELSHAW, C. S. (1965) *Traditional Exchange and Modern Markets*. Englewood Cliffs, N.J.: Prentice-Hall, Inc.

BERRY, B. J. L. (1963) *Commercial Structure and Commercial Blight*. University of Chicago: Department of Geography Research Paper No. 85.

BOHANNAN, P., and G. DALTON (1962) *Markets in Africa*. Evanston, Ill.: Northwestern University.

CHITTICK, D. (1955) *Growth and Decline of South Dakota Trade Centers, 1901–1951*. Bulletin 448, Agricultural Experiment Station, South Dakota College.

DUNCAN, O. D. (1952) "Urbanization and Retail Sociation," *Social Forces*, 30:267–271.

DUNCAN, O. D. (1959) "Service Industries and the Urban Hierarchy," *Papers and Proceedings of the Regional Science Association*, 5:105–120.

FOGG, W. (1932) "The Suq: A Study in the Human Geography of Morocco," *Geography*, 17:257–258.

GRAS, N. S. B. (1922a) *An Introduction to Economic History*. New York: Harper.

GRAS, N. S. B. (1922b) "The Development of Metropolitan Economy in Europe and America," *American Historical Review*, 27:695–708.

HALL, M., J. KNAPP, and C. WINSTEN (1961) *Distribution in Great Britain and North America*. Oxford: Oxford University.

HELLE, R. (1964) "Retailing in Northern Finland, Particularly by Mobile Shops," *Fennia*, No. 91.

HODDER, B. W. (1965) "Some Comments on the Origins of Traditional Markets in Africa South of the Sahara," *Transactions of the Institute of British Geographers*, 36:97–105.

HODGE, G. (1965) "The Prediction of Trade Centre Viability in the Great Plains." Massachusetts Institute of Technology. Unpublished Ph.D. thesis.

JONES, G. (1961) "Early Territorial Organization in England and Wales," *Geografisker Annaler*, 43:174–181.

KNIFFEN, F. (1949) "The American Agricultural Fair: The Pattern," *Annals of the Association of American Geographers*, 39:264–282.

KNIFFEN, F. (1951) "The American Agricultural Fair: Time and Place," *Annals of the Association of American Geographers*, 40:45–57.

LANDIS, P. H. (1932) *South Dakota Town-Country Trade Relations, 1901–1931.* Bulletin 274, Agricultural Experiment Station, South Dakota State College.

MIKESELL, M. W. (1958) "The Role of Tribal Markets in Morocco," *Geographical Review*, 48:494–511.

MURDIE, R. A. (1965) "Cultural Differences in Consumer Travel," *Economic Geography*, 41:211–233.

PIRENNE, H. (1936) *Economic and Social History of Medieval Europe.* New York: Harcourt.

PLATTNER, S. (1975) "The Economics of Peddling," in *Formal Methods in Economic Anthropology.* Washington, D.C.: American Anthropological Association.

POLANYI, K. (1957) *Trade and Markets in the Early Empires.* Glencoe: Free Press.

POLANYI, K. (1944) *The Great Transformation.* New York: Rinehart.

SCHLESINGER, A. (1949) "The City in American Civilization," in *Paths to the Present*, New York: Macmillan, 210–233.

SINGH, S. M. (1965) The Stability Theory of Rural Central Place Development," *The National Geographic Journal of India*, 11:13–21.

SKINNER, G. W. (1964) "Marketing and Social Structure in Rural China-I," *Journal of Asian Studies*, 24:3–43.

SMITH, A. (1776) *An Inquiry into the Nature and Causes of the Wealth of Nations.* Modern version edited by E. Cannan. New York: Modern Library, 1937.

STABLER, J. C. (1987) "Trade Center Evolution in the Great Plains," *Journal of Regional Science*, 27:225–244.

STRONG, A. (1885) *Our Country: Its Possible Future and Its Present Crisis.* New York: Baker and Taylor.

THOMPSON, W. (1965) *A Preface to Urban Economics.* Baltimore: The Johns Hopkins University Press.

TURNER, F. J. (1956) "The Significance of the Frontier in American History," in G. R. Taylor (ed.), *The Turner Thesis Concerning the Role of the Frontier in American History*, a volume in *Problems in American Civilization.* Boston: D.C. Heath.

VANCE, J. E. (1970) *The Merchant's World: Geography of Wholesaling.* Englewood Cliffs, N.J.: Prentice-Hall, Inc.

WADE, R. C. (1959) *The Urban Frontier.* Cambridge: Harvard University.

# 7

# Retail Location and Marketing Geography

As central-place theory was being developed, two parallel streams of application and modeling emerged. Growing out of the proposal by Reilly (1931) to develop "laws of retail gravitation" there have been various attempts to formulate store-choice models by marketing scientists. Similarly, following the publication of a self-help book on marketing geography by the Alexander Hamilton Institute (Eastman and Klein, 1930), the applied field of marketing geography has emerged, concerned with the practical problems of retail location. While many commonalities exist between store-choice models, store-location criteria, and central-place theory, successful integration of the three has yet to be achieved. The purposes of this chapter therefore are threefold: first, to review the parallel streams of work; second, to give a sense of the nature of business applications; third, to indicate the common elements that might serve to facilitate effective integration with central-place theory.

## STORE-CHOICE MODELS

Which central place or retail store will a customer patronize? Reilly (1931) argued that Newtonian physics provided an answer that would enable market areas to be delineated without surveying individual consumers about their preferences. Later, Converse's "breaking-point equation" indicated the market-area boundary between two centers: $A$ (the larger one) and $B$ (the smaller). If $r_B$ represents the distance from $B$ to the market-area boundary (i.e., the real range for functions supplied from center $B$), and $d_{AB}$ equals the distance between two centers $A$ and $B$, and their sizes are $T_A$ and $T_B$, respectively; then Converse's equation is

$$r_B = \frac{d_{AB}}{1 + \sqrt{T_A/T_B}} \tag{7.1}$$

As an example, let us return to the case of Atlantic and Red Oak in Chapters 1 and 2. We will use the number of different business types in these cities as the measures of size—92 in Atlantic (center $A$) and 90 in Red Oak (Center $B$). The distance from Red Oak to the market-area breaking point becomes

$$r_B = \frac{36}{1 + \sqrt{92/90}} \tag{7.2}$$

or 17.9 miles, that is, less than the midway distance to Atlantic. This is 2 miles south of Griswold by road (Figure 1.10), and it corresponds closely to the actual market-area boundary revealed by both urban and rural residents' responses to questions about their shopping preferences for city-level functions such as clothing (Figures 1.12 and 1.13). The equation could equally well be applied to town-level or village-level market areas.

Reilly's law is very similar to Fetter's "law of market areas" developed earlier by a scholar concerned with the economic theory of location. To paraphrase, Fetter said that boundary line between the territories tributary to two geographically competing markets for like goods is a hyperbolic curve. At each point on the curve the difference between transport costs from two markets is just equal to the difference between the prevailing market prices. On either side of the line formed by the hyperbolic curve, however, the transport cost difference and the market price difference are unequal. The relation of prices in the two markets determines the location of the boundary line, and the lower the price in a market relative to that of a neighboring market, the larger the tributary territory (Fetter, 1924). (This was also discussed by Hyson and Hyson, 1959.)

The apparent predictive success of Reilly's law, and the links to the economic theory of location provided by Fetter's law, stimulated the infant field of marketing science in its earlier years (Converse, 1951; Schwartz, 1963). The predictions also supported the simplest model of store choice, the "nearest-neighbor" model of central-place theory, in which customers patronize the nearest outlet that provides the required good or service, that is, consumers minimize distance (but only in the most elementary case where f.o.b. prices are identical). As Reilly and Fetter both acknowledged, the fact that sizes, prices, and transport costs vary means that the location of the market-area boundary will also vary from the "nearest neighbor" position. (Note that this was discussed in Chapter 4 and illustrated in Figures 4.5 and 4.6.)

Other discrepancies between central-place theory and reality have been noted: first, the distance between competing attractions must *exceed* some minimum threshold before it affects choice (O'Sullivan and Ralston, 1976); the greater the distance to the nearest alternative, the less the impact of distance on consumer choice (Clark and Rushton, 1970); and the greater the population density, the more likely are market areas to overlap and interpenetrate (Berry, 1962). Whereas Reilly's law was useful in modeling a certain class of outcomes, its utility in other cases was strictly limited by the inherent *uncertainty* in consumer behavior.

A different approach, therefore, was taken by spatial choice theorists. These theorists recognized that consumers rate alternatives on the basis of a variety of factors that in combination establish the utility of a store or central place. They also tried to factor in uncertainty—the principle that one can predict the average behavior of large numbers of consumers, but not the choice made by any individual consumer (Craig, Ghosh, and McLafferty, 1984, pp. 14–15). The problem then becomes one of estimating probabilities.

There has been a general acceptance by those theorists of consumer utility functions of the form

$$\Lambda_{ig} = \Gamma_g^{\sigma}(f^{-1}s_{ig}) \tag{7.3}$$

where $\Lambda_{ig}$ is the utility of store $g$ to consumer $i$ and $\Gamma_g$ is some measure of the attractiveness of store $g$. The term $\sigma$ measures the consumer's sensitivity to the store attractiveness factor, and $f^{-1}s_{ig}$ is some inverse function of the distance $s$ of consumer $i$ from store $g$. This inverse-distance element is consistent with the idea of the spatial demand cone introduced in Chapter 3 and with the alternative formulation of demand discussed in Chapter 4. In fact there exists a family of such distance-decay functions, depending upon the manner in which customer patronage and quantities demanded drop off with distance (Taylor, 1971).

Huff (1963) was the first to build consumer utility functions of the form of equation (7.3) into a probabilistic "revealed preference" approach to store choice, an approach which includes the essential uncertainty of individual consumer behavior. By "revealed preference" is meant what consumers actually do, rather than what they say they prefer. Huff argued that the probability $P_{ig}$ of consumer $i$ visiting store $g$ is equal to the ratio of the utility of that store to the sum of the utilities of all the alternative stores considered by the consumer:

$$P_{ig} = \frac{\Lambda_{ig}}{\sum\limits_{g=1}^{G} \Lambda_{ig}} \tag{7.4}$$

where $g = 1, 2, \ldots, G$. As Craig, Ghosh, and McLafferty (1984) point out, equation (7.4) is based on the choice axiom stated by Luce (1959), and it belongs to the general class of market-share attraction models used in the larger discipline of marketing to study brand market shares (Naert and Weverbergh, 1981) and consumer brand choice (Batsell and Lodish, 1981).

Substituting equation (7.3) into equation (7.4), we obtain

$$P_{ig} = \frac{\Gamma_g^\sigma(f^{-1}s_{ig})}{\sum\limits_{g=1}^{G} \Gamma_g^\sigma(f^{-1}s_{ig})} \qquad (7.5)$$

This is what is now known as the "Huff model" with a general expression for distance-decay that can be replaced in any particular case by the actual pattern of decline with distance. Huff's model has played an important role in the development of store choice and retail market-area estimation models. An example of an application of a generalized form of the model is presented later in this chapter.

As this example will show, empirical studies using the Huff model support its usefulness in predicting the market share of shopping centers with reasonable accuracy. For individual retail stores, however, additional research has shown that several rather than one attractiveness variable need to be included in the utility function (Craig, Ghosh, and McLafferty, 1984). Other general forms of the Huff model that attempt to incorporate these additional variables include the Multiplicative Competitive Interaction Model (Nakanishi and Cooper, 1974) and the Multinomial Logit Model (Arnold, Roth, and Tigert, 1980). The reader is referred to the articles cited for exposition of these more complex versions.

## *MARKETING GEOGRAPHY AND STORE LOCATION RESEARCH*

"The choice of a store's location is perhaps the single most important decision a retailer has to make. . . . A good location is vital for a store's success. . . . Good locations allow ready access and attract large numbers of customers . . . even slight differences in location can have a significant impact on market share and profitability" (Craig, Ghosh, and McLafferty, 1984, p. 5). The store location process involves four interdependent decisions:

1. Selection of a market area in which new stores are to be located
2. Identification of feasible sites for new stores based upon land availability and land-use regulations
3. Choosing the sites most likely to optimize the company's performance
4. Determining the optimal sizes of the stores.

Following the publication of the Alexander Hamilton Institute's self-help book (Eastman and Klein, 1930), marketing geography emerged as a highly practical field of application to help businesspersons make these decisions.

The beginnings of the field of marketing geography are rightly traced to William Applebaum, who began work for a private supermarket chain at the very time in 1933 that Christaller was writing his book on central-place theory (Epstein,

1978). The work of marketing geographers went on for thirty years largely unnoticed by academia, however, until Murphy (1961) proclaimed that "marketing geography had come of age." At that time, Applebaum and his associates could cite a wealth of studies made within corporate marketing research departments seeking to answer such questions as: Where do we build new stores? How much business can we generate there? How can we measure a market area? How can we improve our market penetration? (Applebaum, 1954, 1965, 1966). These same questions are still asked today. Despite some significant theoretical breakthroughs, most marketing geography retains its practical applied focus, and this is reflected in the substantial literature that has emerged. A comprehensive volume on location by Nelson (1958) was the predecessor of the "how to" guide to supermarket location choice by Kane (1966), the volume of prescriptive contributions edited by Cohen (1961), and the updated procedures reported by Applebaum and Kornblau (1981). Contemporary with Cohen's 1961 work was a special issue of *Economic Geography* (Cohen and Applebaum, 1960), and a subsequent monograph on store location studies (Murphy, 1961), the largest concentration of applied marketing geography articles published in one place at the time.

In recent years marketing geographers have recognized that application must become more orderly and that theory must be developed and used (Davies and Rogers, 1976). Thus Epstein (1978 and 1982) has reviewed the problems facing location analysts. Root (1978) has unveiled some helpful hints. Rogers and Green (1978) have presented the first modernization of the analog method of analysis. There has also been recognition of the usefulness of the computer, but, for the most part, specific programs are treated as trade secrets (Green, 1984).

What, then, do marketing geographers do? Employed in business, they are faced with such questions as: "What shall we do in regard to location X"? Usually this is accompanied by, "I want the answer at the end of the day." Or perhaps the order will be, "Nothing fancy, just tell us what to do!" In keeping with the mandate of the last command, the remainder of this section will be concerned with a typical uncomplicated marketing geographer's approach to the solution of the following sample business problem: "Devise a retail location strategy for major metropolitan area *A* that will provide maximum market penetration (share of the market) most efficiently in terms of stores and investment." The problem as stated implies a client, and for the purpose of identifying key data sets it will be assumed that the marketing geographer is a consultant rather than a corporate employee. The attempt here is to show how the marketing geographer uses the applied craft in providing the answers. The presentation proceeds from client to final choice of site in the sequence outlined in Figure 7.1.

### *The Client Contribution*

Before the consultant begins work there is discussion and investigation of critical elements regarding the client's business. One cannot presume that "what is" will actually be the case. Obviously, a traditional (store-bound) retailer is likely to

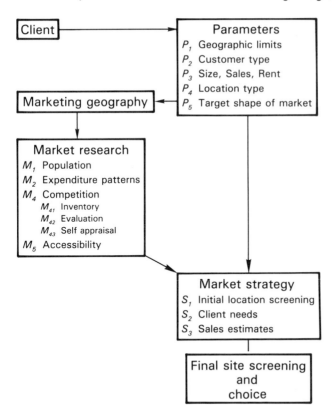

**Figure 7.1** The sequence of site appraisal and choice.

have existing distributional facilities somewhere, often within the market to be analyzed. Since retailing is open to the public, it is open to view and study by all who might have an interest. Despite this ready availability of observable characteristics, the client must articulate his or her perception of, as well as his or her knowledge about, the current business. What is the nature of the merchandise (or service)? Is it homogeneous or mixed? What are the proportions of various merchandise lines? What are the gross profit percentages? How are sales transacted (cash, charge, credit, or a combination)? Is the business a service or it is a self-service or a mixture of the two? Is there a nonstore component to the business? All the above questions relate to the present, and their answers will affect store size, rent and other occupancy costs, parking requirements, and the type of location (either free-standing or in shopping center).

What of the future? What are the parameters of the study as they relate to the stated mission of the marketing geographer? The solution to the retail distribution problem cannot be left solely to the ingenuity of the consultant. The corporate plan of the client has limits within which everyone concerned must work:

1. **Geographic limits:** Retail facilities must be supplied with merchandise and be supervised by corporate management. They must be part of a spatially

defined "market area" which can be served by a particular set of advertising media. Therefore, there will be an initial boundary line established which will relieve the researcher from probing beyond reasonable limits. This will also permit the establishment of a data base which ultimately permits an answer to the crucial question regarding share of market.

2. **Customer type:** The client often knows (or thinks he or she knows) the customer to whom the facilities and merchandise appeal. There can be an inability or unwillingness to serve all segments of a population. It is possible that the youth market or the elderly may be avoided. Or it may be the wealthy or the poverty-stricken or minorities or ethnic groups that the client may not wish to serve. If there is not an expressed desire to serve a market completely, the type of restrictions listed above may become critical for market segmentation (a step that is taken to pinpoint the specific clientele to be served).

3. **Size, sales, and rent:** The nature of merchandise determines space needs, sales productivity per unit area, and profit potential. Further, there are "critical masses" of retail space necessary to be competitive from the viewpoint of variety and depth of merchandise line. The business must have a competitive physical impression when compared with competitors. There is usually a size module with which a firm operates. There can also be more than one module. Size is thus keyed to some sales minimum and maximum that are governed by a great variety of operating characteristics which *may* be of little concern to the marketing geographer. Size and sales limits are in turn causally and reflexively related to rent (or occupancy cost). Therefore, size limits and minimum sales requirements must be set which are related to maximum occupancy costs. These parameters will determine ultimate site selection (or site abandonment) decisions.

4. **Type location:** It is possible for a particular business to have a variety of retail facility types, each of which may have different locational requirements. If all things are possible, analyses and recommendations can become cumbersome and time-consuming and too complicated. Therefore, this example will focus on one kind of retail facility—a supermarket or a warehouse food store or a convenience store or limited assortment store or some other type of retail facility. A store of a given type may need a particular retailing environment (such as a shopping center). Or it may be capable of drawing customers as long as access is possible. At the start, there has to be an appraisal of locational needs!

5. **Target share of market:** Although devising a retailing strategy may not result in a significant shift in market share, it should result in efficiencies which yield a "payoff." Ideally, the aim of this kind of research is to secure an increase in market share, which may not be articulated in specific dollar or percentage goals. Profit is what keeps a business alive, and if profits are increased, then the study costs are justified.

6. **Summary:** A clear understanding of the client's business is essential to meaningful analysis and planning. Often, the accomplishment of this phase of the study is very important to the client as well since it forces orderly thought and an unequivocal statement of objectives. This permits the marketing research to begin.

### The Market

The initiation of market research necessitates the establishment of a boundary line. Since this type of research is dependent on secondary data sources such as the census, a study area definition in terms of Metropolitan Statistical Areas (or at least, counties) represents a comfortable initial point of departure. Having established the outer physical limits of study, the next step is to determine the scale and level of detail necessary to solve the marketing problem. For most cases in retailing it is not necessary to seek resolution at less than census tract areal size or level of data aggregation. Block level data may be needed to analyze a very large-scale population distribution—often this is done for businesses which sell convenience goods and services. And although aerial photography can present a map base which indicates distribution of residential land use, it may not be sufficiently sensitive for analytical purposes. Many companies are now providing data at the zip code level, and their use is becoming increasingly popular. Using zip code data is convenient if the store plans to use direct mail promotion.

**Population.**    Since retailing is a response to individual demand in the provision of goods and services, population geography and demographics provide the first most critical measure of the market. The census tract provides the most complete reporting of census data, so it is most often the analytical unit of choice (Epstein, 1969). This census unit provides statistics on numbers of people, household characteristics, employment, age, sex, race, and income. These are all key variables in the assessment of market potential and the ultimate design of a marketing (location) strategy. If the consultant or the client has computer access and appropriate programs, it is possible to produce graphics (maps) from those data. Without easy computer access it is still possible to devise choropleth transparencies that can permit the map correlations necessary for market segmentation and analysis. Should there be a necessity for population data disaggregated from a census tract level, it is possible to use block data in urbanized areas to obtain a finer measure of distribution and density within the tract. It is possible that food stores, drug stores, restaurants, and other low threshold functions may need an accurately depicted population distribution. This may necessitate either a population map (such as Figure 7.2) or the type of surrogate that is available from large commercial data banks.

A combination of data sets from the variables considered above allows an initial market segmentation. This permits identification of the most desirable target areas based on the client's specifications regarding the nature of the business.

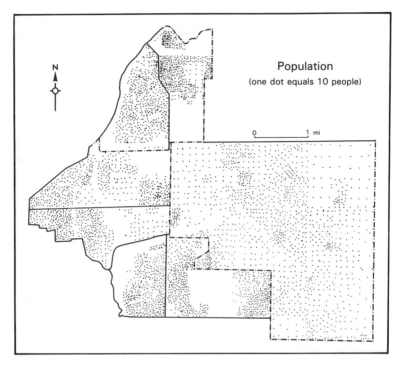

**Figure 7.2**  A typical map of population distribution.

But the validity and utility of the data is a basic difficulty in working with this initial segmentation. The Census of Population and Housing is held decennially in years ending in zero. The data of use to the marketing geographer are not produced immediately, however. For example, in 1983 very little detailed data from the 1980 census had been released. Therefore, census data are "old" when they become available and become progressively less reliable during the course of the intercensal period. This necessitates utilization of local sources for updating, and, in absence of that type of data, it is necessary to devise one's own scheme or to place trust in the data that private firms produce for a fee. This often forces the marketing geographer to make pragmatic decisions that could not be justified in an academic environment.

**Expenditures.**   How consumers spend their money and how much they spend is a vital measure in market appraisal and strategy determination. Individual trade organizations may have some data available, and large firms may produce a data base by means of survey research, but the major data source in the public domain is the Bureau of Labor Statistics (BLS), U.S. Department of Labor. Approximately decennially the BLS conducts a survey of consumer expenditures based on a national probability sample which permits at least a modicum of decomposition into meaningful regional data. It is possible, therefore, to determine household and per capita expenditures for a variety of commodities by region, by household size, by SMSA or non-SMSA location, by race, and by a few other useful breakdowns. These data can be arrayed to permit calculation of expenditures on a market-segmented geographical basis. These figures must then be adjusted for inflation. Of course, these data suffer from the same problem as census data, "aging" in the period between samplings.

As a check against the above data, it is possible to manipulate what is reported in the economic censuses, the Census of Retailing in particular. Here, from political units and from some census geographic units, it is possible to learn about sales transactions and retail stores by type for even relatively small political units. The larger the reporting area, the greater the level of sales detail. Combining these data with the "merchandise line" data that are also available, it becomes possible to check on the potential of the market area. These economic census reports provide detailed sales data which utilize four-digit SIC equivalents. Sales by line and sales by type of outlet are analyzed.

**Market potentials.** Market potential is the summation by geographic unit of potential expenditures adjusted for inflation multiplied by the number of people (buying units) in the geographical unit. Critical to this calculation is the derivation of a correct expenditure estimate. Many of the prescriptions for this kind of derivation are kept secret by their owners, typically consulting firms. If the client firm or its consultant chooses to use a system over which they have no control, they may purchase market potential data from the large market research and data bank firms that now are eager to sell their services. In this case, the data are available at a number of levels of generalization, and relevant data must be purchased for each instance of need. In sum, the degree of detail and desire for "control" determine which system is used. The larger the scale of the potential determination, the greater is the flexibility and sensitivity of the strategic plan for site selection and evaluation.

### Competition

If one were to judge competition on a technical definitional basis, different businesses like hypermarkets, warehouse stores, supermarkets, limited assortment stores, and convenience stores would all be competitors. An even less likely match would pit a local hardware store against Sears, Roebuck. Clearly, all outlets purveying a particular merchandise line vie for the same total dollar pool, and, equally clear, is the fact that each may do so in a different way. Consequently, the client must specify who in the market area is "in the business," that is, what other businesses seek a portion of total potential in the same manner and what businesses are likely to be affected by existing and future outlets of the firm. This evaluative decision must be made before an inventory of competing businesses is commenced.

**The competitive inventory.**    The inventory of competitive facilities is a field-generated data set. Often, the Yellow Pages or a city directory or a trade listing provides an initial list of facilities, but there is no guarantee of completeness or accuracy. Using a city directory and a map, a preliminary competition map may be prepared for use and verification in the field. Forms must be developed for recording field data, and these vary according to the key characteristics of the type of facilities being evaluated. In this research effort the client's facilities are subjected to the same measures as the competition.

Substantial amounts of the data are the result of observation, both within and outside of the facilities. In most cases both the gross area and sales area of retail stores are subject to measurement (but not by use of a tape measure). The most critical measure of competition is sales, and it is here that various devices come into play. A researcher who is experienced in a particular business can use a set of empirical measures to estimate sales. The researcher may simply ask the owner or manager about sales volume. The researcher may interview other competitors and the client's field supervisors for their estimates on particular stores. "Outside" suppliers may also be a source of this information, and sometimes sales-tax data can be quite useful. All of the above data lend themselves to manipulation and analysis. All the facilities in the inventory can be mapped, as in Figure 7.3.

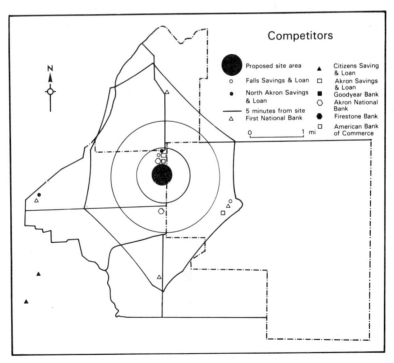

**Figure 7.3**    The inventory of competition.

**Competitive evaluations.**    The competitive inventory permits a "screening" evaluation of competitive market share. It also facilitates a rating of competitive facilities in terms of age and obsolesence. It rates efficiency in terms of sales per square foot, gross sales, sales per checkout, sales per employee, and over and under capacity. If deemed advisable, market areas can be inferred (using the client's experience or that of the consultant) or measured by license plate spottings. A competitor's customers can be surveyed with permission (usually with a sharing of data on a *quid pro quo* basis). Also useful, but not related to the inventory, is attitudinal and perceptual information that can be generated through telephone surveys. Finally, discussion with employees and management of the competition or with city planners and realtors can provide a measure of competitive plans for future stores or sales promotion. Many times the media reveal information as they get it, and release of such material may surprise the competitors who generate it! By means of inventory, evaluation, and investigation, an accurate appraisal of the competition can be accomplished. This action alone may influence the strategic decision of the client to pursue or delay further action. As a next step, self-evaluation for the client must be matched with the competitive analysis.

**Self-evaluation.**    The same data and measurements which were collected for the competition are more easily available for the client firm and its outlets. Sales data, customer count, exact measurements of area and equipment, exact age of equipment, profit-and-loss statements are available for each unit of the client firm. Such an inventory with maps can provide comparisons with competitors and also allow comparisons of location. Further, the client's sensitivity and readiness to adopt innovations are also evident.

Perhaps the most important data set in the whole study can be produced only for the client firm. Customer spotting can be done for all corporate units within the market study area and procedural details are discussed in Applebaum (1966), Applebaum (1968), and Epstein (1961) (see Figure 7.4). At the same time a customer profile can be developed, with an added possibility of obtaining income data. By plotting customer addresses it is possible to measure the market area as well as the market penetration of each store. Customer addresses can be plotted according to distance from the store and in relation to census tract. Per capita sales can be calculated and translated into an estimate of the share of market. And a separate count and market penetration calculation can be made by using the census tract.

The maps and data produced from customer spottings provide the basis for the development of analogs, whether by means of an experiential system or by means of a system such as that of Rogers and Green (1978), utilizing regression analysis to develop a weighting system. The breakdown by tract for each store permits an aggregation of client market share produced by all stores by tract. This identifys areas that are served well and those that are served less well. Not only does this system identify areas of opportunity, but also may present some caveats

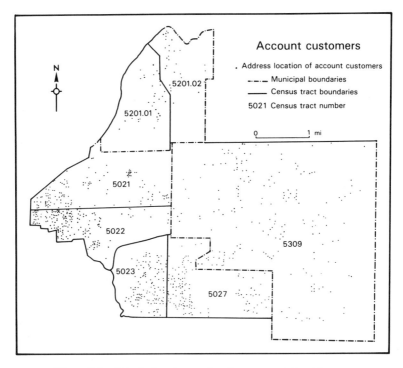

**Figure 7.4**  A typical spot map showing customers' residences.

in regard to future location activity. For example, what can be done when a firm does not serve a high-income clientele? Should the firm avoid that trade or recast a business in an attempt to appeal high-income clients?

**Accessibility.**    Although a road pattern does not show on any of the maps presented to this point, the traffic circulation pattern of the metropolitan area is what permits the consumer to travel to the store of choice. Location of retail facilities is sensitive to accessibility, but accessibility is more than mere highways. Roads can be both facilitators and barriers of accessibility. Likewise, railroads can be facilitators or barriers, as can hydrological features and steep slopes. The sum of the positives (facilitators) and negatives (barriers) helps determine the population that is likely to be served and generally is summarized in the map of land use (Figure 7.5). Micro accessibility (to a site) is considered a site selection criterion and is considered below.

**Summary.**    At this point in the market study, the basic data for decision-making are "in hand." The marketing geographer knows the character of the market, the sales potential and the distribution factors, and the distribution and effectiveness of the client's stores. Most important, the share of market belonging to the client and its apportionment by small geographic areas is now known. At

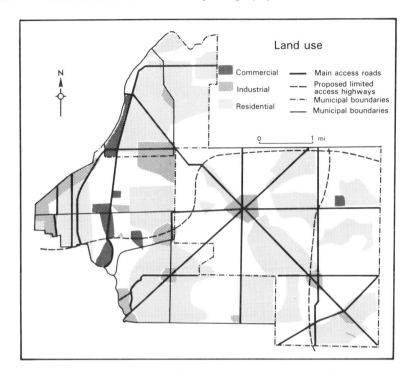

**Figure 7.5**  Details of land use for the marketing analysis.

the very minimum, this will permit recommendations in regard to which units to maintain, which units to enlarge or remodel, and which to close.

## Market Strategy

The major components of a marketing geography study are population, competition, and accessibility, all of which have been addressed above. By this stage these factors affecting the design of a market strategy have been described. The marketing geographer then turns to questions of strategy, and consideration is given to initial locational screening. At a relatively small scale, percentage shares of market can be written onto a census tract map, and a choropleth overlay can be produced using these data. A list of tracts with dollar sales potentials will be used following the first map analysis. First, one seeks "soft spots." These are areas with sales potential, little to no client sales penetration, and no competition. Or they can be areas with obsolete facilities belonging to the client or areas served by obsolescent facilities of the competition. Areas served by a good competitor (in which "head to head" confrontation may be desirable) can be identified. Next to be delimited are areas with little or no penetration, but with minimal potential. These are identified as future areas of concern (areas of "wait and watch"). Finally, areas which are served by strong competition may show a marginal penetration but insufficient potential to make a fight with a competitor worthwhile.

A combination of real sales potential, client share of that potential, proximity of competition, proximity of client units, and satisfactory accessibility determine where to seek new distribution facilities. It also shows where units which need upgrading are located or where there is no hope for location. "Ideal" sites may be chosen in the areas of opportunity and may be subjected to further detailed analysis in order to effect a finer screening, but in view of the combined knowledge of the market possessed by both client and marketing geographer, it may be more efficient to perform a preliminary site selection before proceeding with this time-consuming, costly analysis.

### Site Selection and Evaluation

Site selection is governed by sets of factors which may be classified as physical, psychological, legal, and economic (Epstein, 1971). In addition to the factors above, there are a few more, focused on the client firm, that must receive attention.

**Client needs.**   The client firm's self-image may keep it from an inner-city site, if the firm believes that it must maintain a "carriage trade" appeal. Or it may seek facilities with potential for "adaptive reuse" in preference to new space if it is to maintain a "good value for the dollar" and an "urban savior" stance. It may seek medium-sized (community) shopping centers with particular tenants if it believes that it needs help to draw trade. These site requirements or exclusions may be subject to change if it is shown that the consumer has a different image of the firm. This may become obvious from customer interviews or from a market survey (by telephone) which attempts to place the client in market perspective as compared with its competitors.

Further complicating a site selection process is the degree of flexibility possessed by the client in terms of the variety of "weapons" with which it "attacks" a market. This sort of complication may arise in the case of manufacturer-owned (or leased) facilities when there exists competition with independent dealers or purveyors of private label or "associated lines." Such is the case in the automobile tire industry. The sale of food at retail can have even greater complications. There are at least six ways to serve a food market: hypermarket, supermarket, convenience store, limited assortment store, warehouse store, and combination stores. In many instances a single firm will use more than one such facility to "cover" a market, and this strategy complicates a site selection process by permitting multiple options for particular sites. Or possibly more than one strategy (along with site selection) begins to be devised.

Finally, there is a decision to make regarding the firm's isolation from, or association with, other businesses. A map of commercial land use should prove helpful in making this decision. Shopping centers and districts can also be identified on these maps (Figure 7.4). A final decision may be determined by the character of the business or by hierarchical needs. "Footloose" facilities provide the greatest flexibility, but also create the greatest challenge in location. Dependent ("parasitic") facilities provide for the simplest search—the retail site necessary is either there or being developed. Or perhaps there is no possibility for action at the time. Once sites are selected, the marketing geographer is ready to make estimates of sales.

**Estimate of sales.** The data set on population (including the map) and the data set on competition and sales potentials provide independent variables which must now be manipulated by use of proprietary data. Customer spottings and physical and locational characteristics of client stores provide an additional data set which permit development of analogs. These data may be used as input in a proprietary model for site selection and sales estimating, or the experienced marketing geographer may perform the same analyses with his or her own models or techniques. The estimated sales produced by this system may be qualified with a confidence interval or may be "phased," that is, all other factors being equal, it is determined how much will be made the first year followed by $x$ percent annual growth. The sales estimate alone can serve as a decision-making datum, but total sales which are capable of being generated will be weighted heavily by business judgment.

**Final site screening.** Each proposed facility which has been placed in the study area for consideration is part of corpus which possesses a vast array operating data. Each facility also has a preferred module which is based on the client's way of doing business combined with the modern technology available. This makes it possible to produce a *pro forma* profit-and-loss statement in which the estimated sales of the proposed store are matched against gross profits. Gross profits, in turn, are diminished by such things as proposed and estimated occupancy costs, labor costs (wages and benefits), advertising costs, supply costs, transportation costs, maintenance costs, service costs, overhead costs, and taxes. Whatever remains is net profit. The fact that a store is potentially profitable is not sufficient to generate a recommendation or a commitment for a new site. New business undertakings always involve an element of risk. Return on invested capital should be at least equal to what the client could earn in a federally insured investment, although sometimes the client will settle for less, since growth is an integral need for most businesses. It is possible that the business growth generated by new facilities can "spin off" profits elsewhere.

## STORE-CHOICE MODELING

What was just described was the application of the marketing geographer's "checklist method," a systematic procedure for evaluating the relative value of sites compared with other potential sites within the context of a particular client's needs and aspirations (Applebaum, 1966). The checklists incorporate many subjective elements, and the relative ease with which such methods can be implemented (and the reliance on expert opinion) are seen as advantages by some

(Goldstucker et al., 1978). These methods are particularly useful when combined with the "analog approach" (Applebaum, 1968), which brings information on comparable stores to bear on the evaluation of sites. Analog methods have been generalized by the use of multiple regression analysis in which store performance is modeled as some function of store and market attributes (Craig, Ghosh, and McLafferty, 1984). These techniques can also be enriched by systematic application of store-choice models of the Huff type.

Let us now consider an example. In 1973, Lincoln Mall, a major new enclosed shopping center, was to be opened in the south suburbs of Chicago. Officials in neighboring communities were concerned. What was its impact on the older shopping centers in the south suburbs likely to be? In particular, what was the effect on the older shopping center in the adjacent community of Park Forest likely to be? An analysis by Margerum (1972) in a class of Brian Berry's in which he was studying helped to provide an answer. The analysis was conducted in several stages.

### Shopping Goods Expenditures by Residents

First, the information available in the Bureau of Labor Statistics' consumer surveys in the Chicago region was consulted. The data revealed that on the average in 1970, a low-income household spent $1313 on shopping goods, while middle-income households spent $2043 and high-income households $3375. The BLS income ranges were as follows: low (less than $3000); middle ($3000 to $10,000); and high (over $10,000). Next, the number of low-, middle-, and high-income households residing in each census tract in the south suburbs at the time of the 1970 census was tabulated. Multiplying the number of households by the appropriate average expenditure figure, and calculating total sums for the three groups, the total shopping goods expenditures in each tract could be estimated, as shown in Table 7.1. By finding the sum for the appropriate census tracts, the total shopping goods expenditures made by consumers residing in each suburb could also be estimated.

### Market-Area Determination and Calculation of Market Penetration

Where were these shopping goods expenditures made? In April 1972, on several Saturdays, surveys were made of the communities from which shoppers had traveled to four shopping centers with which Lincoln Mall was likely to compete: Park Forest Plaza, River Oaks, Dixie Square, and E. J. Korvette. A complete count of automobiles in each parking lot was taken, and the village-identifying windshield sticker was noted so that the number of automobiles traveling from each of the south suburbs to each shopping center could be recorded. The percentage of automobiles coming from each suburb could then be calculated for each center.

**TABLE 7.1**  SHOPPING GOODS EXPENDITURES BY LOW-, MIDDLE-, AND HIGH-INCOME CUSTOMERS LIVING IN EACH OF THE CENSUS TRACTS IN SOUTH SUBURBAN CHICAGO IN 1970

| Census tract | Number of families | | | Each group's shopping goods expenditures (in thousands) | | | Total expenditures |
|---|---|---|---|---|---|---|---|
| | L | M | H | L | M | H | |
| 8241 | 60 | 717 | 2622 | 78 | 1464 | 8849 | 10391 |
| 45 | 42 | 528 | 2541 | 55 | 1078 | 8575 | 9708 |
| 46 | 63 | 414 | 1476 | 82 | 845 | 4981 | 5908 |
| 47 | 74 | 731 | 1912 | 97 | 151 | 6453 | 6701 |
| 48 | 9 | 55 | 242 | 11 | 112 | 816 | 939 |
| 49 | 5 | 66 | 181 | 6 | 134 | 610 | 750 |
| 50 | 33 | 302 | 670 | 43 | 616 | 2261 | 2920 |
| 52 | — | 173 | 407 | — | 353 | 1373 | 1726 |
| 53 | 81 | 406 | 1351 | 106 | 829 | 4559 | 5494 |
| 54 | 6 | 186 | 551 | 7 | 379 | 1859 | 2245 |
| 55 | 34 | 320 | 2671 | 44 | 653 | 9014 | 9711 |
| 56 | 44 | 499 | 1153 | 57 | 1019 | 3891 | 4967 |
| 57 | 11 | 312 | 583 | 14 | 637 | 1967 | 2618 |
| 62 | 4 | 42 | 95 | 5 | 85 | 320 | 410 |
| 63 | 45 | 374 | 1567 | 59 | 764 | 5288 | 6111 |
| 64 | 93 | 420 | 2042 | 122 | 858 | 6891 | 7871 |
| 65 | 114 | 491 | 1358 | 149 | 1003 | 4583 | 5735 |
| 68 | 79 | 513 | 1263 | 103 | 1048 | 4262 | 5413 |
| 69 | 217 | 788 | 940 | 284 | 1609 | 3172 | 5065 |
| 70 | 41 | 412 | 849 | 53 | 841 | 2865 | 3759 |
| 71 | 28 | 182 | 329 | 36 | 371 | 1110 | 1517 |
| 72 | 26 | 110 | 214 | 34 | 224 | 722 | 980 |
| 73 | 77 | 463 | 633 | 101 | 945 | 2136 | 3182 |
| 74 | 93 | 496 | 831 | 122 | 1013 | 2804 | 3939 |
| 75 | 84 | 513 | 1108 | 110 | 1048 | 3739 | 4897 |
| 76 | 36 | 260 | 613 | 47 | 531 | 2068 | 2646 |
| 77 | 22 | 273 | 578 | 28 | 557 | 1950 | 2535 |
| 78 | 50 | 532 | 3393 | 65 | 1086 | 11451 | 12602 |
| 79 | 37 | 283 | 853 | 48 | 578 | 2878 | 3504 |
| 80 | 69 | 282 | 1026 | 90 | 576 | 3462 | 4128 |
| 81 | 70 | 392 | 1076 | 91 | 800 | 3642 | 4533 |
| 82 | 93 | 434 | 1456 | 122 | 886 | 4914 | 5922 |
| 83 | 36 | 279 | 713 | 47 | 569 | 2406 | 3022 |
| 84 | 97 | 515 | 1575 | 127 | 1052 | 5313 | 6494 |
| 85 | 10 | 83 | 605 | 13 | 169 | 2041 | 2223 |
| 86 | 56 | 298 | 2953 | 73 | 608 | 9996 | 10647 |
| 87 | 32 | 257 | 1455 | 42 | 525 | 4876 | 5443 |
| 88 | 40 | 322 | 1504 | 52 | 657 | 5076 | 5785 |
| 89 | 100 | 505 | 660 | 131 | 1031 | 2227 | 3389 |
| 90 | 204 | 705 | 329 | 262 | 1440 | 1110 | 2817 |
| 91 | 204 | 676 | 679 | 276 | 1381 | 2352 | 4000 |
| 92 | 73 | 545 | 1084 | 95 | 1113 | 3658 | 4866 |
| 93 | 113 | 562 | 1440 | 148 | 1148 | 4860 | 6156 |
| 94 | 39 | 482 | 1124 | 51 | 874 | 3793 | 4718 |

**TABLE 7.1**  (*continued*)

| Census tract | Number of families | | | Each group's shopping goods expenditures (in thousands) | | | Total expenditures |
|---|---|---|---|---|---|---|---|
|  | L | M | H | L | M | H |  |
| 95 | 69 | 461 | 775 | 90 | 941 | 2615 | 3646 |
| 96 | 34 | 268 | 502 | 44 | 547 | 1694 | 2285 |
| 97 | 165 | 494 | 458 | 216 | 1009 | 1545 | 2770 |
| 98 | 19 | 165 | 1336 | 24 | 337 | 4509 | 4870 |
| 99 | 30 | 204 | 928 | 39 | 416 | 3125 | 3580 |
| 8300 | 71 | 360 | 1187 | 93 | 735 | 4006 | 4834 |
| 01 | 6 | 40 | 1058 | 78 | 81 | 3570 | 3729 |
| 02 | 8 | 66 | 780 | 10 | 134 | 2632 | 2776 |
| 03 | 49 | 527 | 1328 | 64 | 1076 | 4482 | 5622 |
| 04 | 55 | 344 | 1057 | 72 | 702 | 3567 | 4341 |
| 05 | 9 | 63 | 224 | 11 | 128 | 756 | 895 |
| 8835 | 101 | 508 | 1847 | 132 | 1037 | 6233 | 7402 |
| 36 | 12 | 101 | 545 | 15 | 206 | 1940 | 2161 |
| 37 | 45 | 406 | 514 | 59 | 829 | 1734 | 2622 |
| 38 | 90 | 777 | 2108 | 118 | 1587 | 7114 | 8819 |

Next, an estimate was made of the sales derived by each shopping center from each suburb. To do this the total retail sales of each center were calculated for each of the suburbs using the same percentages as were calculated from the automobile counts. Then, the market share of each center in each suburb was calculated by dividing the sales estimated to have been derived by a given center from that suburb by the total shopping goods expenditures of the suburb. Finally, market shares were mapped to show the existing market areas of each center. Market shares were also graphed to show the manner in which market penetration decreases with distance of a community from each center. Table 7.2 shows the basic data for Park Forest Plaza and Figure 7.6 the resulting market penetration contours. Figure 7.7 shows the associated pattern of distance-decay. In contrast, Figure 7.8 shows the market penetration by River Oaks Shopping Center.

### Market Shares Summarized in a Market Penetration Model

The next step involved the application of a store-choice model to summarize the market penetration data. The model is broader than that of Huff, in that the parameters are specific to each center. The form of equation selected was as follows:

$$\Psi_{gy} = \frac{J_g T_g \exp(-b_g s_{gy})}{\sum_{g=1}^{G} J_g T_g \exp(-b_g s_{gy})} \qquad (7.6)$$

In equation (7.6),

$$\Psi_{gy} = \text{market share of center } g \text{ in community } y$$
$$T_g = \text{size of center } g \text{ (normally, square footage of selling area)}$$
$$s_{gy} = \text{distance from center } g \text{ to community } y$$
$$\exp(-b_g s_{gy}) = \text{the distance-decay element in the attractiveness or utility}$$
$$\text{of center } g \text{ to consumers in community } y$$
$$J_g = \text{a coefficient that is fixed for each center } g$$
$$J_g T_g \exp(-b_g s_{gy}) = \text{the attractiveness or utility of center } g \text{ to consumers in com-}$$
$$\text{munity } y$$

Thus the market share for a community $y$ derived by shopping center $g$ is equal to the attractiveness of $g$, relative to the combined attractiveness of all $n$ shopping center alternatives—the denominator of equation (7.6). The attractiveness of each

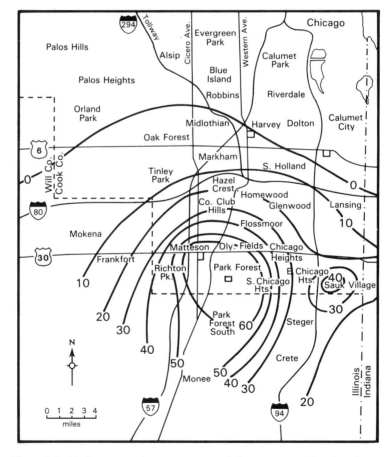

**Figure 7.6**  Market penetration contours reveal the percentage of trade going to Park Forest Plaza in 1972.

**TABLE 7.2**  PARK FOREST'S SHARE OF SOUTH SUBURBAN SHOPPING GOODS
EXPENDITURES

| Suburb | Number of automobiles | Percentage of automobiles | Expenditures in the center | Market share |
|---|---|---|---|---|
| 1 Park Forest | 1084 | 36.95 | 15690.1 | 0.68 |
| 2 Monee | 36 | 1.19 | 505.3 | 0.51 |
| 3 Park Forest South | 100 | 3.41 | 1448.0 | 0.67 |
| 4 Crete | 126 | 4.27 | 1813.2 | 0.21 |
| 5 Steger | 71 | 2.38 | 1010.6 | 0.21 |
| 6 South Chicago Heights | 76 | 2.55 | 1082.8 | 0.30 |
| 7 Chicago Heights | 299 | 10.24 | 4348.2 | 0.20 |
| 8 East Chicago Heights | 17 | 0.58 | 246.3 | 0.09 |
| 9 Sauk Village | 70 | 2.38 | 1010.6 | 0.45 |
| 10 Richton Park | 46 | 1.57 | 666.7 | 0.59 |
| 11 Matteson | 119 | 3.94 | 1673.0 | 0.67 |
| 12 Frankfort | 71 | 2.41 | 1023.3 | 0.14 |
| 13 Olympia Fields | 111 | 3.75 | 1592.4 | 0.50 |
| 14 Flossmoor | 100 | 3.37 | 1431.0 | 0.24 |
| 15 Homewood | 184 | 6.22 | 2641.2 | 0.14 |
| 16 Country Club Hills | 63 | 2.10 | 891.7 | 0.27 |
| 17 Glenwood | 56 | 1.87 | 794.8 | 0.15 |
| 18 Thornton | 2 | 0.06 | 25.5 | 0.008 |
| 19 Hazelcrest | 44 | 1.46 | 620.9 | 0.05 |
| 20 Lansing | 15 | 0.51 | 216.5 | 0.01 |
| 21 Tinley Park | 31 | 1.03 | 437.3 | 0.05 |
| 22 Markham | 8 | 0.27 | 114.6 | 0.01 |
| 23 Harvey | 8 | 0.27 | 114.6 | 0.005 |
| 24 South Holland | 3 | 0.10 | 42.5 | 0.003 |
| 25 Calumet City | 5 | 0.17 | 72.2 | 0.006 |
| 26 Dolton | 6 | 0.20 | 84.9 | 0.007 |
| 27 Burnham | — | | | |
| 28 Riverdale | 5 | 0.17 | 72.2 | .006 |
| 29 Phoenix | — | | | |
| 30 Dixmoor | — | | | |
| 31 Blue Island | 4 | 0.13 | 55.2 | 0.002 |
| 32 Robbins | — | | | |
| 33 Midlothian | 5 | 0.17 | 72.2 | 0.006 |
| 34 Posen | — | | | |
| 35 Alsip | — | | | |
| 36 Oak Forest | 21 | 0.74 | 314.2 | 0.025 |
| 37 Orland Park | — | | | |
| 38 Calumet Park | — | | | |
| Other | 148 | | | |

center varies directly with the size of the center and inversely with distance between the center and community. Table 7.3 summarizes the distances and the April 1972 market shares. Statistical estimates were made, using regression analysis, of the values of $J_g$ and $b_g$, and these are shown in Table 7.4.

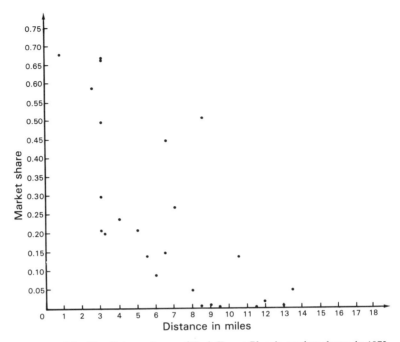

**Figure 7.7**    The distance-decay of Park Forest Plaza's market shares in 1972.

## The Market Penetration Model and the Impact on Other Centers

The market share model was used to compute the impact of Lincoln Mall on the four existing centers. Letting $\Gamma$ represent the attractiveness of a center, the market share $\Psi$ for each of the four centers is as follows:

For center 1,

$$\Psi_1 = \frac{\Gamma_1}{\Gamma_1 + \Gamma_2 + \Gamma_3 + \Gamma_4} \tag{7.7}$$

and for center 2,

$$\Psi_2 = \frac{\Gamma_2}{\Gamma_1 + \Gamma_2 + \Gamma_3 + \Gamma_4} \tag{7.8}$$

and similarly for centers 3 and 4. Adding a fifth center, we have

$$\Psi_1 = \frac{\Gamma_1}{\Gamma_1 + \Gamma_2 + \Gamma_3 + \Gamma_4 + \Gamma_5} \tag{7.9}$$

and similarly for centers 2 through 5. Lincoln Mall, with 1.2 million square feet,

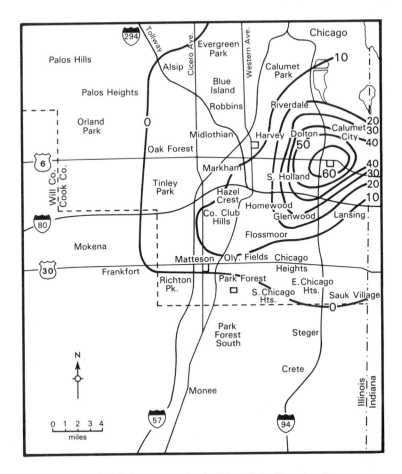

**Figure 7.8**  Market penetration by River Oaks Shopping Center.

was assumed to be most likely to have a similar market penetration configuration to its closest analog, similarly sized River Oaks (i.e., $J = 0.029$ and $b = 0.1759$).

Table 7.5 shows the predicted market shares resulting from the calculations with five centers, and Table 7.6 shows the dollar diversion of trade from the older centers to Lincoln Mall. The change in market shares is the difference between that observed in April 1972 and that predicted using the 5-center market share model. The dollar diversion effect is simply the dollar expression of the change in market shares. These predicted diversions were as follows: Park Forest Plaza (loss of $15,565,000, or 36.5%); Dixie Square (loss of $10,826,000, or 37.9%); River Oaks (loss of $2,367,000, or 3.9%); E. J. Korvette (loss of $3,948,000, or 46.3%); and Lincoln Mall (gain of $32,707,000).

Figure 7.9 shows the predicted market area of Lincoln Mall. It should be noted that the $32 million predicted for the Mall does not include potential sales

TABLE 7.3 DISTANCES AND 1972 MARKET SHARES SUMMARIZED

| | Distance to: | | | | April 1972 market share | | | |
|---|---|---|---|---|---|---|---|---|
| Suburb | Park Forest Plaza | Dixie Square | River Oaks | E. J. Korvette | Park Forest Plaza | Dixie Square | River Oaks | E. J. Korvette |
| 1 Park Forest | 0.7 | 8.5 | 15.0 | 3.0 | 0.68 | 0.006 | 0.008 | 0.09 |
| 2 Monee | 8.5 | 17.0 | 30.0 | 7.5 | 0.51 | | | 0.22 |
| 3 Park Forest South | 3.0 | 11.5 | 17.5 | 5.5 | 0.67 | | | 0.11 |
| 4 Crete | 5.0 | 13.5 | 15.0 | 7.5 | 0.21 | | 0.008 | 0.007 |
| 5 Steger | 3.0 | 12.5 | 14.0 | 6.5 | 0.21 | | | 0.02 |
| 6 South Chicago Heights | 3.0 | 11.5 | 13.0 | 5.5 | 0.30 | | | 0.07 |
| 7 Chicago Heights | 3.2 | 7.0 | 11.0 | 4.0 | 0.20 | 0.01 | 0.04 | 0.05 |
| 8 East Chicago Heights | 6.0 | 11.5 | 8.5 | 6.5 | 0.09 | 0.01 | 0.06 | 0.07 |
| 9 Sauk Village | 6.5 | 12.5 | 9.5 | 7.5 | 0.45 | | 0.02 | 0.03 |
| 10 Richton Park | 2.5 | 10.0 | 16.5 | 1.5 | 0.59 | | | 0.37 |
| 11 Matteson | 3.0 | 8.5 | 14.5 | 0.7 | 0.67 | 0.03 | | 0.30 |
| 12 Frankfort | 10.5 | 16.5 | 22.5 | 8.0 | 0.14 | 0.02 | 0.02 | 0.04 |
| 13 Olympia Fields | 3.0 | 7.0 | 12.0 | 1.5 | 0.50 | 0.009 | 0.12 | 0.13 |
| 14 Flossmoor | 4.0 | 5.5 | 10.5 | 3.0 | 0.24 | 0.01 | 0.15 | 0.05 |
| 15 Homewood | 5.5 | 4.0 | 9.0 | 4.5 | 0.14 | 0.009 | 0.16 | 0.02 |
| 16 Country Club Hills | 7.0 | 6.0 | 11.0 | 4.0 | 0.27 | 0.09 | 0.09 | 0.09 |
| 17 Glenwood | 6.5 | 7.0 | 7.0 | 7.5 | 0.15 | 0.01 | 0.22 | 0.009 |
| 18 Thornton | 8.5 | 5.0 | 4.5 | 9.5 | 0.008 | 0.01 | 0.44 | |
| 19 Hazelcrest | 8.0 | 4.0 | 8.5 | 6.0 | 0.05 | 0.06 | 0.09 | 0.007 |
| 20 Lansing | 13.0 | 8.0 | 3.0 | 13.0 | 0.01 | 0.002 | 0.14 | |
| 21 Tinley Park | 13.5 | 7.0 | 14.0 | 9.0 | 0.05 | 0.05 | 0.02 | 0.02 |
| 22 Markham | 9.0 | 1.5 | 7.0 | 17.5 | 0.01 | 0.55 | 0.04 | 0.01 |
| 23 Harvey | 9.5 | 0.7 | 6.0 | 9.5 | 0.005 | 0.55 | 0.04 | 0.01 |
| 24 South Holland | 11.5 | 3.5 | 2.5 | 11.5 | 0.003 | 0.04 | 0.50 | |
| 25 Calumet City | 16.0 | 6.5 | 0.8 | 16.0 | 0.004 | 0.07 | 0.68 | |
| 26 Dolton | 16.5 | 6.0 | 4.5 | 16.5 | 0.004 | 0.02 | 0.52 | |
| 27 Burnham | 17.5 | 7.0 | 2.5 | 17.5 | | 0.01 | 0.09 | |
| 28 Riverdale | 13.5 | 4.5 | 8.0 | 12.5 | 0.005 | 0.02 | 0.48 | |
| 29 Phoenix | 14.5 | 2.0 | 4.0 | 10.5 | | 0.26 | 0.21 | |
| 30 Dixmoor | 11.0 | 2.0 | 8.0 | 10.5 | | 0.16 | 0.05 | |
| 31 Blue Island | 12.5 | 3.5 | 9.5 | 12.0 | 0.002 | 0.05 | 0.02 | |
| 32 Robbins | 12.5 | 3.5 | 10.5 | 9.7 | 0.002 | 0.39 | 0.04 | |
| 33 Midlothian | 11.0 | 3.5 | 11.0 | 8.0 | 0.006 | 0.22 | 0.02 | |
| 34 Posen | 10.0 | 1.5 | 8.0 | 9.5 | | 0.46 | 0.10 | |
| 35 Alsip | 14.5 | 5.5 | 12.5 | 11.7 | 0.002 | 0.02 | 0.02 | |
| 36 Oak Forest | 12.0 | 6.0 | 10.5 | 9.0 | 0.02 | 0.03 | | |
| 37 Orland Park | 18.0 | 11.0 | 17.0 | 15.0 | 0.004 | 0.005 | | |
| 38 Calumet Park | 15.5 | 6.5 | 10.0 | 14.5 | | 0.07 | 0.05 | |

**TABLE 7.4** VALUES OF PARAMETERS USED IN THE
STORE-CHOICE MODEL

| Suburb | $J_g$ | $b_g$ | $R^2$ |
|---|---|---|---|
| Park Forest Plaza[a] | 0.0879 | −0.2808 | 0.74 |
| River Oaks[b] | 0.0293 | −0.1759 | 0.61 |
| Dixie Square[c] | 0.0274 | −0.2402 | 0.62 |
| E. J. Korvette[d] | 0.0813 | −0.2113 | 0.65 |

[a] 53 acres; 0.9 million square feet; 4800 parking; 83 stores; open 1949; majors: Sears, Marshall Field.

[b] 100 acres; 1.25 million square feet; 6000 parking; 54 stores; open 1966; majors: Sears, Marshall Field.

[c] 57 acres, 0.8 million square feet; 4400 parking; 68 stores; open 1966; majors: Penney, Montgomery Ward.

[d] 0.2 million square feet.

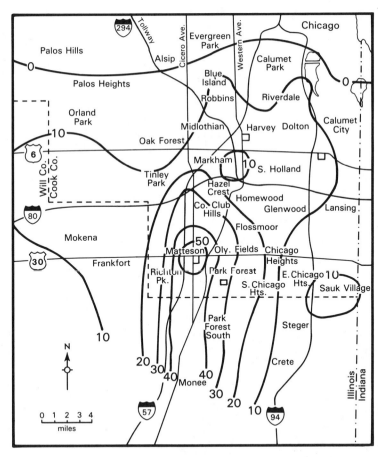

**Figure 7.9** Lincoln Mall: predicted market penetration.

**TABLE 7.5**   MARKET SHARES PREDICTED TO RESULT FROM THE OPENING OF LINCOLN MALL

| Suburb | Park Forest Plaza | Dixie Square | River Oaks | E. J. Korvette | Lincoln Mall |
|---|---|---|---|---|---|
| 1 Park Forest | 0.49 | 0.01 | 0.01 | 0.05 | 0.20 |
| 2 Monee | 0.02 | −0.02 | 0.03 | 0.07 | 0.42 |
| 3 Park Forest South | 0.48 | 0.01 | 0.01 | 0.06 | 0.21 |
| 4 Crete | 0.13 | −0.00 | 0.01 | 0.01 | 0.06 |
| 5 Steger | 0.15 | 0.00 | 0.00 | 0.01 | 0.05 |
| 6 South Chicago Heights | 0.23 | 0.00 | 0.01 | 0.02 | 0.10 |
| 7 Chicago Heights | 0.15 | 0.01 | 0.00 | 0.02 | 0.10 |
| 8 East Chicago Heights | 0.10 | 0.00 | 0.01 | 0.02 | 0.08 |
| 9 Sauk Village | 0.24 | 0.00 | 0.02 | 0.04 | 0.18 |
| 10 Richton Park | 0.42 | 0.01 | 0.01 | 0.12 | 0.41 |
| 11 Matteson | 0.32 | 0.01 | 0.01 | 0.12 | 0.52 |
| 12 Frankfort | 0.03 | −0.01 | 0.01 | 0.01 | 0.12 |
| 13 Olympia Fields | 0.29 | 0.01 | 0.01 | 0.09 | 0.33 |
| 14 Flossmoor | 0.17 | 0.03 | 0.01 | 0.05 | 0.18 |
| 15 Homewood | 0.10 | 0.05 | 0.01 | 0.03 | 0.12 |
| 16 Country Club Hills | 0.12 | 0.05 | 0.01 | 0.07 | 0.28 |
| 17 Glenwood | 0.16 | 0.04 | 0.01 | 0.03 | 0.12 |
| 18 Thornton | 0.14 | 0.13 | 0.02 | 0.02 | 0.12 |
| 19 Hazelcrest | 0.04 | 0.04 | 0.01 | 0.02 | 0.08 |
| 20 Lansing | 0.02 | 0.05 | 0.02 | 0.00 | 0.04 |
| 21 Tinley Park | 0.01 | 0.02 | 0.01 | 0.01 | 0.08 |
| 22 Markham | 0.10 | 0.27 | 0.01 | 0.04 | 0.12 |
| 23 Harvey | 0.09 | 0.36 | 0.02 | 0.02 | 0.10 |
| 24 South Holland | 0.07 | 0.30 | 0.03 | 0.01 | 0.10 |
| 25 Calumet City | −0.01 | 0.60 | 0.16 | −0.07 | 0.07 |
| 26 Dolton | −0.02 | 0.48 | 0.11 | −0.05 | 0.03 |
| 27 Burnham | −0.01 | 0.10 | 0.03 | −0.01 | 0.00 |
| 28 Riverdale | 0.03 | 0.30 | 0.04 | 0.01 | 0.10 |
| 29 Phoenix | 0.01 | 0.31 | 0.02 | 0.01 | 0.10 |
| 30 Dixmoor | 0.02 | 0.12 | 0.01 | 0.01 | 0.04 |
| 31 Blue Island | 0.01 | 0.04 | 0.01 | 0.00 | 0.01 |
| 32 Robbins | 0.03 | 0.21 | 0.02 | 0.02 | 0.12 |
| 33 Midlothian | 0.02 | 0.09 | 0.01 | 0.02 | 0.18 |
| 34 Posen | 0.08 | 0.31 | 0.02 | 0.02 | 0.01 |
| 35 Alsip | 0.00 | 0.01 | 0.00 | 0.00 | 0.01 |
| 36 Oak Forest | 0.00 | 0.01 | 0.00 | 0.00 | 0.03 |
| 37 Orland Park | −0.00 | 0.00 | 0.00 | −0.00 | 0.01 |
| 38 Calumet Park | 0.00 | 0.08 | 0.02 | −0.01 | 0.02 |

gains in communities south to Kankakee and west to Joliet, or gains from new community development along Interstate 57. How good were these forecasts? Figure 7.10 provides one insight. Three years after Lincoln Mall opened, Park Forest Plaza's retail sales had dropped by $16 million in real 1967 dollars, almost

**TABLE 7.6**  DOLLAR DIVERSION OF TRADE FROM THE OLDER BUSINESS CENTERS
TO LINCOLN MALL PREDICTED BY THE STORE-CHOICE MODEL

| Suburb | Park Forest Plaza | Dixie Square | River Oaks | E. J. Korvette | Lincoln Mall |
|---|---|---|---|---|---|
| 1 Park Forest | −4063 | −117 | −63 | −484 | 4728 |
| 2 Monee | 300 | 30 | −47 | −111 | 429 |
| 3 Park Forest South | −395 | −4 | −11 | −48 | 461 |
| 4 Crete | −490 | 3 | −26 | −62 | 575 |
| 5 Steger | −234 | −0 | −7 | −22 | 264 |
| 6 South Chicago Heights | −317 | −3 | −9 | −39 | 369 |
| 7 Chicago Heights | −1613 | −159 | −51 | −309 | 2133 |
| 8 East Chicago Heights | −184 | −5 | −13 | −42 | 244 |
| 9 Sauk Village | −316 | −2 | −26 | −62 | 409 |
| 10 Richton Park | −355 | −9 | −9 | −100 | 475 |
| 11 Matteson | −887 | −49 | −26 | −349 | 1313 |
| 12 Frankfort | −525 | 97 | −167 | −334 | 929 |
| 13 Olympia Fields | −733 | −68 | −22 | −240 | 1064 |
| 14 Flossmoor | −697 | −136 | −28 | −215 | 1078 |
| 15 Homewood | −1320 | −614 | −83 | −439 | 2457 |
| 16 Country Club Hills | −435 | −180 | −43 | −258 | 918 |
| 17 Glenwood | −448 | −117 | −38 | −89 | 693 |
| 18 Thornton | −167 | −149 | −26 | −31 | 376 |
| 19 Hazelcrest | −432 | −433 | −58 | −209 | 1134 |
| 20 Lansing | −161 | −338 | −153 | −6 | 659 |
| 21 Tinley Park | −90 | −353 | −114 | −163 | 721 |
| 22 Markham | −328 | −883 | −61 | −144 | 1419 |
| 23 Harvey | −447 | −1745 | −99 | −117 | 2410 |
| 24 South Holland | −240 | −953 | −112 | −48 | 1355 |
| 25 Calumet City | 41 | −1299 | −361 | 161 | 1457 |
| 26 Dolton | 29 | −526 | −125 | 63 | 560 |
| 27 Burnham | 0 | −1 | −0 | 0 | 1 |
| 28 Riverdale | −128 | −1054 | −163 | −25 | 1373 |
| 29 Phoenix | −2 | −84 | −6 | −5 | 98 |
| 30 Dixmoor | −33 | −161 | −12 | −9 | 217 |
| 31 Blue Island | −38 | −238 | −28 | −8 | 313 |
| 32 Robbins | −14 | −90 | −10 | −11 | 127 |
| 33 Midlothian | −189 | −614 | −72 | −145 | 1021 |
| 34 Posen | −20 | −76 | −5 | −6 | 108 |
| 35 Alsip | −2 | −38 | −7 | −2 | 51 |
| 36 Oak Forest | −106 | −258 | −61 | −88 | 515 |
| 37 Orland Park | 90 | −102 | −182 | 57 | 136 |
| 38 Calumet Park | −0 | −83 | −23 | 5 | 101 |

exactly the prediction. Soon thereafter, E. J. Korvette closed, no longer able to obtain threshold-level market penetration. The reader will note how closely the actual implementation of this store-choice model corresponded to key steps in the marketing geographer's checklist.

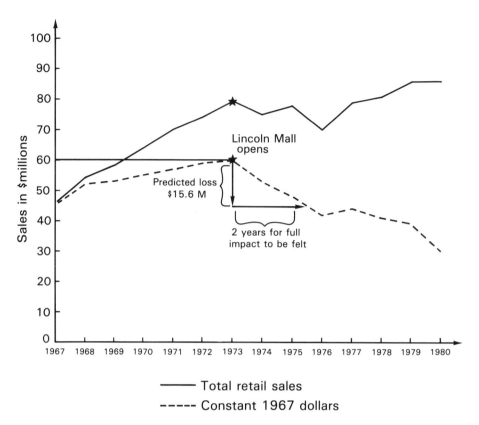

**Figure 7.10** Retail sales by Park Forest Plaza, 1967–1980.

## LOCATION-ALLOCATION MODELS

The particular Huff model used in the previous section is one example of what are termed in Britain "spatial interaction shopping models." It is in Britain, largely through the work of Wilson (1974), where such models have been recently generalized using "entropy-maximizing" techniques with much attention paid to problems of calibration and solution. The field is sufficiently diverse that we will not attempt a summary here, but the interested reader is referred to the excellent introduction by Openshaw (1975).

Another approach has been to use location-allocation models that involve the simultaneous selection of facility locations and the assignment of demand to these locations in order to optimize specified criteria. One recent example is the development of a multiple store location decision model, by Achabal, Gorr, and Mahajan (1982). Another is Ghosh and Craig's location allocation model for facility planning (1984). The advantage of such location allocation models is their ability to evaluate systematically a large number of possible locational configurations and select the one that maximizes the firm's performance.

Again, the pace of change is very rapid as marketing scientists make use of such models as decision support systems to aid in the difficult task of formulating a locational strategy and selecting good sites for retail outlets—a task in which analysis will continually need to be tempered with managerial judgment. More generally, there remains the formidable task of integrating central-place theory, marketing geography practice, and store-choice modeling. Enough has been accomplished to suggest that this integration is not simply desirable, but also probably within reach. The key elements in common are those of the spatial demand cone and associated patterns of distance decay as well as geometric constraints on the competitiveness of locations.

## REFERENCES

ACHABAL, D. D., W. L. GORR, and V. MAHAJAN (1982) "Multiloc: A Multiple Store Location Decision Model," *Journal of Retailing,* 58:5–25.

APPLEBAUM, W. (1954) "Marketing Geography," in P. E. James and C. F. Jones (eds.), *American Geography: Inventory and Prospect,* Syracuse: Syracuse University Press, 245–251.

APPLEBAUM, W. (1965) "Can Store Location Research Be a Science?" *Economic Geography,* 41:234–237.

APPLEBAUM, W. (1966) "Methods for Determining Store Trade Areas, Market Penetration and Potential Sales," *Journal of Marketing Research,* 3:127–141.

APPLEBAUM, W. (1968) *Guide to Store Location Research With Emphasis in Supermarkets.* Reading, Mass.: Addison-Wesley.

ARNOLD, S. J., V. ROTH, and D. TIGERT (1980) "Conditional Logit versus MDA in the Prediction of Store Choice," *Advances in Consumer Research,* 8:665–670.

BATSELL, R. R., and M. LODISH (1981) "A Model and Measurement Methodology for Predicting Individual Consumer Choice," *Journal of Marketing Research,* 18:1–12.

BERRY, B. J. L. (1962) *Comparative Studies of Central-Place Systems.* Washington, D.C.: Office of Naval Research, Geography Branch.

CLARK, W. A. V., and G. RUSHTON (1970) "Models of Intra-Urban Consumer Behavior and Their Implications for Central-Place Theory," *Economic Geography,* 46:486–497.

COHEN, S. B., and W. APPLEBAUM (1960) "Evaluating Store Sites and Determining Store Rents," *Economic Geography,* 36:1–35.

COHEN, S. B. (ed.) (1961) *Store Location Research for the Food Industry.* New York: National American Wholesale Grocer's Association.

CONVERSE, PAUL D. (1951) "Development of Marketing: Fifty Years of Progress," in H. G. Wales (ed.), *Changing Perspectives in Marketing.* Urbana, Ill.: University of Illinois.

CRAIG, C. S., A. GHOSH, and S. McLAFFERTY (1984) "Models of the Retail Location Process: A Review," *Journal of Retailing,* 60:5–36.

DAVIES, R. L. (1976) and D. S. ROGERS (1984) (eds.), *Store Location and Store Assessment Research*. Chichester: John Wiley.

EASTMAN, R. O., and J. KLEIN (1930) *Marketing Geography*. New York: Alexander Hamilton Institute.

EPSTEIN, B. J. (1961) "Measurement of a Trading Area," in S. B. Cohen (ed.), *Store Location Research for the Food Industry*. New York: National American Wholesale Grocers' Association, 55–61 and 125–134.

EPSTEIN, B. J. (1969) "Population and Income Distribution," in *Feasibility Reports for Shopping Centers,* New York: National Institute of Real Estate Brokers, 14–19.

EPSTEIN, B. J. (1971) "Geography and the Business of Retail Site Evaluation and Selection," *Economic Geography*, 47:192–199.

EPSTEIN, B. J. (1978a) "Marketing Geography and Retail Feasibility Studies: Data Projection and Problems," in J. W. Frazier and N. F. Henry (eds.), *Research in Contemporary and Applied Geography: A Discussion Series*. Binghamton, N.Y.: State University of New York, 1–20.

EPSTEIN, B. J. (1978b) "Marketing Geography: A Chronicle of 45 Years," in J. W. Frazer and B. J. Epstein (eds.), *Applied Geography Conference,* 1:372–379.

EPSTEIN, B. J., and E. SCHELL (1982) "Marketing Geography: Problems and Prospects," in J. W. Frazier (ed.), *Applied Geography: Selected Perspectives*. Englewood Cliffs, N.J.: Prentice-Hall, Inc., 263–282.

FETTER, F. A. (1924) "The Economic Law of Market Areas," *Quarterly Journal of Economics,* 38:520–529.

GHOSH, A., and C. S. CRAIG (1984) "A Location Allocation Model for Facility Planning in a Competitive Environment," *Geographical Analysis,* 16:39–51.

GREEN, H. L., and ASSOCIATES (1984) *Estimating Food Store Expenditure Potential*. Birmingham, Mich.: Howard L. Green and Associates, Inc.

GOLDSTUCKER, J. L., D. BELLENGER, T. STANLEY, and R. OTTE (1978) *New Developments in Retail Trading Area Analysis and Site Selection*. Atlanta, Ga.: Georgia State University.

HUFF, D. L. (1963) "A Probabilistic Analysis of Shopping Center Trade Areas," *Land Economics,* 39:81–90.

HYSON, D. D., and W. P. HYSON (1959) "The Economic Law of Market Areas," *Quarterly Journal of Economics,* 64:319–327.

KANE, B. J., JR. (1966) *A Systematic Guide to Supermarket Location Analysis*. New York: Fairchild Publications.

KORNBLAU, C. (ed.) (1981) *Guide to Store Location Research with Emphasis on Super Markets*. Reading, Mass.: Addison-Wesley.

LUCE, R. D. (1959) *Individual Choice Behavior*. New York: John Wiley.

MARGERUM, L. (1972) "Impact of Lincoln Mall on South Suburban Shopping Centers," Department of Geography, University of Chicago. Unpublished paper.

MURPHY, R. E. (1961), "Marketing Geography Comes of Age," in *Store Location and Development Studies* (a volume of reprints from *Economic Geography*). Worcester, Mass.: Clark University.

NAERT, P. A., and M. WEVERBERGH (1981) "On The Prediction Power of Market Share Attraction Models," *Journal of Marketing Research*, 18:146–153.

NAKANISHI, M., and L. G. COOPER (1974) "Parameter Estimation for Multiplicative Interactive Choice Model: Least Squares Approach," *Journal of Marketing Research*, 11:303–311.

NELSON, S. (1958) *The Selection of Retail Locations*. New York: F. W. Dodge.

OPENSHAW, S. (1975) *Some Theoretical and Applied Aspects of Spatial Interaction Shopping Models*. Norwich, U.K.: Geo Abstracts Inc. for the Institute of British Geographers.

O'SULLIVAN, P., and B. RALSTON (1976) "Sensitivity to Distance and Choice of Destinations," *Environment and Planning A,* 10:365–370.

REILLY, W. J. (1931) *The Law of Retail Gravitation*. New York: Knickerbocker Press.

ROGERS, D. S., and H. L. GREEN (1978) "Analog Modeling: A New Perspective on Store Site Selection," in J. W. Frazier and B. J. Epstein (eds.), *Applied Geography Conference*. Binghamton, N.Y.: State University of New York, 380–388.

ROOT, J. D. (1978) "Analog Data Bases," in J. W. Frazier and N. F. Henry (eds.), *Research in Contemporary and Applied Geography: A Discussion Series*. Binghamton, N.Y.: State University of New York, 20–35.

ROY, J. R., and B. JOHANSSON (1984) "On Planning and Forecasting the Location of Retail and Service Activity," *Regional Science and Urban Economics,* 14:433–452.

SCHWARTZ, G. (1963) *Development of Marketing Theory*. Chicago: South-Western.

SCOTT, P. (1970) *Geography and Retailing*. Chicago: Aldine.

TAYLOR, P. J. (1971) "Distance Transformation and Distance Decay Functions," *Geographical Analysis,* 3:221–238.

WILSON, A. G. (1974) *Urban and Regional Models in Geography and Planning*. London: John Wiley.

# 8

# Applications
# to Regional
# and National Planning

Even though central-place theory and marketing geography have yet to be satisfactorily integrated, urban and regional planners have made extensive use of central-place concepts in developing their prescriptive schemes for land use and spatial organization. Three examples should illustrate current practice.

As a first example, the Dutch planned settlements to serve farms newly established on polders reclaimed from the Ijsselmeer, they created a two-level hierarchy of market centers for the farmers. For another example, on the Lakhish plains running eastward from the Gaza strip, Israel built a system of new settlements in a three-level hierarchy (United Israel Appeal, n.d.):

1. "A" settlements (including protective border kibbutzim) absorbed immigrant settlers and Israeli pioneers, and served as centers of agricultural cultivation, containing facilities used daily by the settlers.
2. "B" settlements (rural community centers) were planned to serve four to six "A" settlements and to supply facilities and buildings used by them once or twice a week.
3. "C" settlement (regional center) is a town roughly at the geographical center of the region, providing administrative, educational, medical, and cultural facilities. It also provided factories for processing crops.

In yet another example, analysis of the pattern of shopping centers and identification of their service areas provided one of the main ingredients in the administrative reorganization of Greater London (Royal Commission, 1960; Carruthers, 1962). Again, when the village of Park Forest, Illinois, was laid out as a planned suburban community, residential areas were organized into neighborhoods, each served by a local business center, and the whole community was provided with one larger shopping center. Adjacent land was reserved for the administrative services of the village hall, the police, and the fire department. (For discussions of the planning and development of neighborhood, community, and regional shopping centers, see Baker and Funaro, 1951, and Burns, 1959.)

These examples are symbolic of the practical uses of the central-place *idea* by regional and city planners for locating business centers and market towns and for trying to engineer regional growth. More recently, work has been undertaken explicitly within the framework of the *theory*: in deliberations of the Royal Commission on Agriculture and Rural Life in Saskatchewan (1957); in understanding the settlement pattern of a nation (Reiner and Parr, 1981); in considering the needed changes in the urban structure of Ghana (Grove and Huszar, 1964); in developing models to aid the attack on commercial blight in the Chicago or Toronto regions (Berry, 1963; Simmons, 1966); and in constructing a general theory of regional planning (von Böventer, 1964; Friedmann, 1972).

## TWO NORTH AMERICAN EXAMPLES

The basic argument supporting use of central-place ideas in regional planning is that a system of centers arranged in a hierarchy provides an efficient way of arranging distribution, collection, and administration within regions. An appropriate system can avoid duplication and waste and make possible the realization of social benefits accruing from economies of scale. Identification of a network of centers and the scale of activities appropriate to each level makes possible the proper location of new facilities, or, where the scale of enterprise is changing rapidly, a systematic base for rationalization. Where an existing system is an integral part of the social and economic life of an area, it must be considered in any replanning efforts or those efforts are doomed to failure. Conversely, it can be argued that the very leadership of major central places as growth poles (growth centers) sets the pace of progress of their regions (Perroux, 1961; Boudeville, 1964; Gore, 1984; Darwent, 1969). There is, of course, no direct equivalence between the concepts of central place and growth pole (Parr, 1973).

### The Case of Saskatchewan

In Saskatchewan the distribution of population has changed rapidly as agriculture continues to mechanize, the mobility of farmers continues to increase, and the scale of business continues to change. The Royal Commission (1957) report argued that central-place concepts provide an understanding of the networks and hierarchies within which these changes are taking place. The report expressed the interdependencies among places that are of continuing significance for the provision of such public services as health, education, and municipal government. As the optimal scale of services shifts, the levels-of-centers concept provides an organized way of choosing new service locations and also specify places where inefficient services are to be terminated. For new programs, choosing the optimal size involves analysis of program objectives, planning requirements, administrative loads, public participation, and technical efficiency, but the central-place system then provides proper locations. Where administration requires several levels, the levels of the central-place hierarchy are available.

### The Case of Appalachia

Growth-center ideas played an important role in the plans made by the Appalachian Regional Commission (ARC) following its creation by the U.S. Congress in 1965 (Berry, 1973). Four basic assumptions were accepted as underlying the strategic principles for development fashioned by the Commission:

1. Substantial investment in human capital is required not only because the principal concern is the people of the region rather than geography, but also because without investments in the health and skills of the people, resources would remain inert and capital would never appear.
2. The location of the region between the major metropolitan regions of the East made it possible to integrate much of the Appalachian economy with the national mainstream by strengthening transportation linkages with major nearby centers.
3. Development of a well-articulated economy, particularly with respect to local services, required a growth strategy which recognized the relationship between urbanization and the potential for growth in a local area.
4. Public services and facilities provide the necessary supporting infrastructure for most private investments in manufacturing plants and services. A proper investment strategy would be attuned to that relationship and place highest priority upon those public investments in each area most likely to push the area economy over the threshold of growth.

These assumptions were synthesized in two general goals:

1. Social Goal—To provide the people of Appalachia with the health and skills they require to compete for opportunity wherever they choose to live.
2. Economic Goal—To develop in Appalachia a self-sustaining economy capable of supporting the people with rising incomes, improving standards of living, and increasing employment opportunities.

To achieve these goals, the Commission decided that it was necessary to understand the patterns of economic development in the United States and, to the best of its ability, to work with trends instead of against them so that ultimately the region could develop the capacity to contribute its fair share to national economic growth by offering competitive services and locations for new enterprise.

It was recognized that a selective strategy would have to be pursued to develop a self-sustaining economy. A self-sustaining economy was thought to be one that would be capable of fostering its own growth through continuing development of its own resources, market advantages, and internal economic structure. Growth was needed that does not require massive infusions of welfare and other transfer payments from the rest of the country to sustain its population at acceptable standards of living.

Obviously, to undertake such a strategy, it was necessary to understand clearly the pattern of economic growth that was occurring nationally and to help induce similar patterns in the region. Summarizing the Commission's discussions (Appalachian Regional Commission, 1970), the following recommendations were made:

1. Major employment growth in Appalachia, as in the nation, will be in the service sector of the economy, though this employment will rest on manufacturing and extractive activities which export to the rest of the nation and world markets.

2. This future employment growth, by definition, will be closely related to urbanization, though the form and character of that urbanization may differ in the future from what we know today.

3. The region is substantially underurbanized compared to the rest of the country. Therefore, it lacks both the service base and the concentrations of population required to support modern economic development.

4. Modern transportation and technology have substantially changed the economic geography of the United States (and therefore of Appalachia) enlarging effective markets, service areas, and the commuting radius around employment centers.

A principal component of the Appalachian strategy, therefore, became to strengthen selectively those urban centers, either existing or to be created, which on the basis of performance, location, and potential were the ones most likely to grow in service employment. The necessity of selectivity had been emphasized in the Appalachian Regional Development Act of 1965 where it was stated that ARC should concentrate its investments in areas with a significant potential for future growth and where the return on public dollars invested will be the greatest. A regional approach also was emphasized, so that rural jurisdictions could pool their resources in building quality schools and hospitals and in providing access for their citizens to nearby jobs.

In directing the Appalachian Regional Commission to take such an approach to regional development, the Congress made a dramatic break with past approaches to rural development. It recognized that the automobile and modern technology had drastically changed the conditions under which rural people live in the United States. It recognized that fewer people will be employed in agriculture and mining, that more will be employed in manufacturing and services, and that, thanks to the automobile, they can reach jobs and services each day many miles away.

The Commission decided that two aspects of urban development were of significance in constructing the new strategy. First, it was recognized that a certain degree of agglomeration of activity must occur in a given area if self-sustaining growth is to be achieved. Some minimum level of urbanization must take place if economic growth is to be supported. In Appalachia, there are many cases where this "critical mass" does not exist in any real sense, despite the existence of a large and densely settled rural nonfarm population. In such areas urbanization, perhaps of unique character, must be induced. The large populations of such areas in Appalachia may make such an approach feasible where, under other conditions, such a strategy would prove unworkable. Continued depopulation in these areas, voluntary or involuntary, would be the inevitable alternative if some such approach were not adopted.

The other characteristic of urban development which was taken into account is the tendency of urban centers, once they reach a certain size, to disperse into surrounding rural hinterlands. These forces create revenue problems for the centers and frequently impose higher costs for services on the metropolitan areas as a whole. But they could spell certain advantages for Appalachia where these forces are pressing into the region from the outside.

After careful consideration, the Commission therefore concluded that its major emphasis should not be on large metropolitan areas since it was going to attempt to divert the flow of rural migrants away from such areas. But on the other hand, it should not attempt to concentrate efforts in those communities least likely, because of location, topography, and other limitations, to respond to programs designed to increase economic growth.

By resolution the Appalachian Regional Commission adopted the following definition of growth centers and growth areas (ARC, 1970):

> By a "growth center" or "centers" is meant a complex consisting of one or more communities or places which, taken together, provide or are likely to provide a range of cultural, social, employment, trade and service functions for itself and its associated rural hinterland. Though a center may not be fully developed to provide all these functions, it should provide, or potentially provide, some elements of each, and presently provide a sufficient range and magnitude of these functions to be readily identifiable as the logical location for many specialized services to people in the surrounding hinterland. A "growth area" is an extension of the growth center itself. It is the adjoining area likely to experience residential and employment growth because of proximity to a center or location between centers. The hinterlands are surrounding rural areas which rely upon the growth center and growth area for services and employment. The hinterlands contribute resources and manpower to the

overall district economy. Some of the key relationships that should exist between centers and hinterlands include:

(1) Commutation patterns
(2) Wholesale and retail trade services
(3) Educational and cultural services
(4) Professional services
(5) Inter-firm and inter-industry trade
(6) Governmental services
(7) Natural resource and topographic considerations
(8) Transportation networks

Some investments may most appropriately be placed in rural hinterland areas. Most particularly, these investments would be in the fields of health and education, where such services and facilities must be located close to those they are designed to serve. In this way, the labor force of the hinterland can be upgraded to more effectively participate in the growth opportunities occuring in the growth area of the district.

The states first attempted to define the multicounty areas of Appalachia which tended to share common social, political, and economic interests and which tended to embrace common commuting and service areas. For planning and administrative purposes these areas then were designated as "development districts." Sixty such areas were identified, covering the entire Appalachian Region. Of the 60 districts, 37 with a population of 15 million encompassed important metropolitan or independent centers; 6 with a population of 750,000 were part of the commutation area of a major city either in or just outside of Appalachia, and 17 with a population of 1.9 million were outside the commuting fields of major regional or independent centers and were, therefore, dependent upon special approaches to development if their economy was to be made self-sustaining.

The next task was to clearly identify within each of the districts where, in state and local opinion, growth was most likely to occur. To guide this selection, the commission adopted a hierarchical definition of "urban centers" that emphasized the function which such centers play within each district and within the region as a whole. As defined by the Commission (ARC, 1970):

> Regional centers are important metropolitan centers providing specialized services and employment opportunities that extend well beyond the boundaries of the district in which they are located. Investments made in these centers are mainly "region-serving," i.e., they help improve services and employment prospects for a large area of the Appalachian Region embracing several state planning districts.
>
> Primary centers are communities or a complex of communities where preliminary analyses indicate a major portion of the future employment base of a district is likely to be located. Investments in these centers will develop their competitive advantages by providing the public facilities and services needed to make the area attractive to increased private investment and growth.
>
> Secondary centers are communities from which it is necessary to provide services to a large surrounding rural hinterland if isolated populations are to be given

the skills and training they need to compete for opportunities wherever they choose to live and work.

The next task the commission faced was to determine how public investments could be most effectively placed in these areas to permit development and improve the well-being of both the rural and urban communities. It was recognized that by developing an effective transportation network it could make it possible for people living anywhere in the area to commute to new jobs and services, providing they were placed at the right locations.

Those communities most likely to succeed in developing a level of employment growth that could support the surrounding rural populations with rising incomes and improving standards of living were to be chosen. In some cases, those communities might be declining at the present time, but because of highway improvement or other factors, the states might realistically expect them to be important centers of future growth. It was the potential for growth, not the lack of past growth, in which the Commission and the states were interested.

A variety of growth center strategies was envisioned depending upon the character of the area involved. Areas were defined as falling into the following categories (Berry, 1973, pp. 52–53):

1. Areas within the range of influence of major metropolitan areas outside of Appalachia where regional development programs can capitalize on development opportunities pressing outward from those metropolitan areas. Examples of areas under such influence in Appalachia are the Hagerstown area of Maryland and the extreme eastern part of the eastern Panhandle in West Virginia close to Washington and Baltimore; the area surrounding Atlanta; a small area in eastern Kentucky near Lexington; those portions of Appalachian Ohio near Cincinnati; portions of New York and Pennsylvania between Buffalo and Cleveland; and portions of eastern Pennsylvania and New York near New York City and Philadelphia.

2. Areas within the orbit of major Appalachian metropolitan centers such as Pittsburgh, Birmingham, or Charleston, where dual programs must be undertaken to reinforce the service base and employment opportunities in the city while at the same time the surrounding rural area is more effectively integrated and linked to the area economy through improvements in transportation, health, education, and resource development.

3. Areas unserved by any urban complex large enough to be capable of self-sustaining growth, but where there are many small towns close together. In these areas the program should help develop complementary services so that together they offer the same service advantages and employment concentration as a middle-sized city. The Pikeville-Prestonburg-Paintsville or Middleboro-London-Borbin areas of eastern Kentucky or the Dalton-Calhoun area of Georgia are representative of this kind of area.

4. Large Appalachian cities located in peculiar topographical situations where a "critical mass" of population and social overhead exists, but where further growth within the city as presently defined is unlikely for lack of available land. Here initial efforts should concentrate on alternative ways for such cities to join with surrounding

jurisdictions where growth will occur in order to preserve existing overhead in the city and make duplication of those services in the outlying areas unnecessary. Examples of such cities are Johnstown, Pennsylvania; Wheeling, West Virginia; and the central anthracite communities of northeastern Pennsylvania.

5. Areas with a dense, but rural nonfarm, population where there is no viable community and few urban services or urban centers. A combination of two approaches may be required in these areas; one may be similar to the third strategy above; the other is a "new community" approach in which an urban center is consciously induced based on analysis that indicates that access, market, and demographic conditions are such that a viable urban center can be created.

6. Areas that are sparsely populated but which have had conferred upon them unusual access and resource advantages which make it probable that development and emigration of population will occur. In such areas a planned "new community" approach may be indicated. A number of sites were identified where practically no community currently exists but where for many reasons the state believes a "new community" can be successfully created. Examples are the Midland new town site on Interstate Highway 64 near Morehead, Kentucky; the Lucasville, Ohio, new town site near Portsmouth, Ohio; the Fairdale new town site near Beckley, West Virginia; as well as a number of others still being studied in Pennsylvania and Georgia. In addition, a number of large employment complexes are being planned in areas along the development highways where no community currently exists, ample is the so-called Duffield industrial site in southwestern Virginia.

A final step in the growth center strategy was to select from among the 22 regional and 78 primary centers that had been defined those growth areas where investments were to be concentrated early in the program. Thirty places were selected, with the criteria for selection varying among the four major subregions of Appalachia:

Northern Appalachia that covers part of New York, Pennsylvania, Maryland, West Virginia, and Ohio, consists of many older industrial cities with problems of obsolescence and blight. Primary employment is in manufacturing. In Northern Appalachia, the states placed greatest emphasis on the strength of growth areas as centers of retail trade and employment with lesser emphasis on past population growth. The role of the community as a future service center with good sites for developing employment on the main transportation network was taken into account.

Central Appalachia covering parts of Kentucky, West Virginia, Virginia and Tennessee is far different from Northern Appalachia. Here the dominant employment is coal mining. The 1.5 million persons who live in this area are widely dispersed up the creeks and hollows near the mine heads. Topographically, it is the most rugged section of Appalachia in terms of developable sites. The states assigned greatest weight in Central Appalachia, therefore, to the role of communities as centers of retail trade and professional, educational, and cultural services, as well as to their location on the Appalachian Development Highway System and the availability of sites nearby for industrial expansion.

Southern Appalachia covers the valleys and plateaus of parts of Virginia, Tennessee, North Carolina, South Carolina, Georgia, Alabama, and Mississippi. This area is now making a rapid transition from an agricultural to an industrial and service economy. The states, in identifying the potential future centers of growth, gave primary weight to recent population and employment growth and in-commutation, as well as location on the Interstate of Appalachian Development Highway System.

The final subregion of Appalachia is the Appalachian Highlands, a sparsely populated, highly scenic recreation and resource region stretching from north Georgia to the Catskills of New York. There are relatively few growth centers in the Highlands. Instead, concentration was upon developing recreation complexes to serve the metropolitan markets to the south, east, and west in which local people will work. Those growth centers which have been designated are the centers of educational, health, and retail services or which have major potential as centers for serving the resort industry.

In addition to these more formal factors, the states also took into account more intangible ones such as the capability of local leadership to direct a successful program. Where such leadership exists, the probability of success is much higher.

## AN IMPLICIT GROWTH THEORY

Underlying the Appalachian Regional Commission's work was an implicit theory of regional growth, first outlined by Friedmann (1966, 1972). Briefly summarized, the propositions of this theory are as discussed subsequently.

**A regional economy is an interdependent part of a national economy.**   That differential regional economic growth has been, until recently, an expression of an open, highly dynamic economy, made up of an industrial heartland and resource-dominant hinterlands, is unquestionable. As long as demand and supply conditions change and regions have differing advantages for production, differences in regional growth must be seen as part of the total economic system. The same is true for regional differences in specialization and the division of labor. All the elements essential to national economic growth, therefore, are also essential to the economic growth of regions. Chief among these elements are development of natural resources, manpower skills, aggressive entrepreneurship, an elaborate infrastructure, and associated external economies. In such circumstances, the degree to which local decisions can shape the future of a regional economy depends upon the degree of self-sustaining local autonomy or "closure" of that economy. Greater closure implies greater autonomy of choice; greater openness implies greater dependency upon changes and choices in other regions and the nation. Clearly, the degree of closure is small in resource-oriented hinterland regions, and this, in turn, implies that sensitivity to external change centered in the national heartland remains substantial in such cases. The significant change noted later in this chapter is that all of the nation's major urban regions achieved substantial closure in the short run during the 1960s with the result that their growth rates converged on the national growth rate, whatever their economic specialization.

**Regional growth is externally induced.**    Basic to the growth of regions, according to the classical theory, is their capacity for attracting industries that produce goods for export to other regions of the country. Growth impulses in regional economies come from outside, according to this view, in the form of demands for regional specialities. The nature of these specialities, alternative sources of them, and changes in the structure of demand, therefore, determine in large measure the nature and extent of regional growth. Expanding national demands spark heartland growth which, in turn, directs differential hinterland growth through growing demands for hinterland specialities. What more recent evidence suggests, however, is that the growth of major metropolitan regions is based upon the exercise of innovative leadership as new specialities are invented, producing rapid growth based upon a favorable mix of new industries. Further, there is accumulating evidence that the heartland-hinterland "lever" no longer works by means of heartland demands for regional resource-related specialities, traditionally defined, but is rapidly being replaced by the "filtering" of older slower-growth industries from the metropolitan regions into the hinterlands as the principal source of hinterland growth.

For this reason, not all of the regions of a country can expect their economic activities and populations to increase at the same rate of speed. Yet, every region can hope to enjoy a high and rising per capita income as long as the nation's output and productivity continue to increase, as long as the filtering works smoothly, and as long as its people are willing to face up to the need for a degree of out-migration when the overall situation calls for it. In most such instances, significantly higher income levels within a lagging hinterland region can be achieved only combining effective economic development with substantial out-migration.

**Export sector growth translates into residentiary sector growth.**    Export industries need secondary support in the form of housing, public facilities, retail establishments, service facilities, and many other elements of local infrastructure. In the classical theory, export income supports these local facilities in a relationship that involves a simple multiplier linkage between export-industry fortunes and total regional growth.

The essence of the postwar transformation of regional economic relationships is, however, the changing role of the modern service industries. The export-base formulation relegates traditional services to a dependent role, with the magnitude of their growth determined strictly by a multiplier relationship to the export base. Recent evidence conclusively demonstrates that the modern service industries have become independent sources of growth.

**Economic growth takes place in a matrix of urban regions.**    The crux of the link between regional growth and growth centers is that cities organize economic life. They are centers of activity and of innovation, focal points of the transport and communication networks, and locations of superior accessibility at which firms can most easily reap scale economies and at which industrial complexes can obtain the economies of localization and urbanization. They encourage labor specialization, areal specialization in productive activities, and efficiency in the provision of services. Agricultural enterprise is more efficient in the vicinity of cities. The more prosperous commercialized agricultures encircle the major cities, whereas the peripheries of the great urban regions are characterized by backward lower-income economic systems.

There are two major elements in this city-centered organization of economic activities (Berry, 1972). The first element is a system of cities arranged in a hierarchy. The second element is corresponding areas of urban influence surrounding each of the cities.

Impulses of economic change are transmitted in such a system simultaneously along the three following planes:

1. Outward from heartland metropolises to those of the regional hinterlands.
2. From centers of higher-level to centers of lower-level in the hierarchy, in a pattern of "hierarchical diffusion."
3. Outward from urban centers into their surrounding urban fields, in radiating "spread effects."

Part of the diffusion mechanism has been shown to reside in the operation of urban labor markets. When growth is sustained over long periods, regional income inequality should be reduced because any general expansion in a high-income area will result in some industries being priced out of the high-income labor market. There will be a shift of that industry to lower-income regions, especially to smaller urban centers in more peripheral areas. The significance of this "filtering" or "trickle down" process lies not only in its direct but also in its indirect effects. If the boom originates in the high-income region, as is very likely, the multiplier effects will be larger in the initiating region, although the relative rise in income may be greater in the underdeveloped region. But the induced effects on real income and employment may be considerably greater in the low-income region if prices there rise less or if the increase in output per worker is greater. Both are likely, because of decreasing cost due to external economies stemming from urbanization of the labor force. If the boom is maintained, industries of higher labor productivity will shift units into lower-income areas, and the low-wage industries will be forced to move into even smaller towns and more isolated areas.

The net result is that the following properties should characterize such hierarchical urban-regional systems:

1. The size and functions of a central city, the size of its urban field, and the spatial extent of developmental "spread effects" radiating outwards from it will be proportional.

2. Since impulses of economic change are transmitted in order from higher to lower centers in the urban hierarchy, continued innovation in large cities will remain critical for extension of growth over the complete economic system.

3. The resulting spatial incidence of economic growth will be a function of distance from the central city. Troughs of economic backwardness will lie in the most inaccessible areas along the peripheries among the least accessible lower-level centers in the hierarchy.

4. The growth potential of an area situated along an axis between two cities will be a function of the intensity of interaction between them, which will be, in turn, a function of their relative location and the quality of transportation arteries connecting them.

It is easy to see how a logical progression of urban growth flows from such conclusions. This leads us to the final proposition.

**Economic growth results in progressive integration of the space-economy.**    If metropolitan development is sustained at high levels, rural-urban differences will be eliminated and the space-economy should be integrated by outward flows of growth impulses through the urban hierarchy and inward migration of labor to cities. Troughs of economic backwardness at the intermetropolitan periphery will thereby be eroded, and each area should then find itself within the spheres of influence of a variety of urban centers of various sizes. Concentric bands of agricultural organization and efficiency around metropolitan centers should be eliminated or reduced in importance. Agricultural organization should also introduce new specialities, taking full advantage of differences in local resource endowments.

It is this full integration of the national space-economy that constitutes the objective of regional development strategy. Essentially, what modern growth theory suggests is that continued urban-industrial expansion in major metropolitan regions should lead to catalytic impacts on surrounding areas. Growth impulses and economic advancement should filter and spread to smaller places and ultimately infuse dynamism into even the most tradition-bound peripheries. Strategies based on planned growth centers enter the scene if filtering mechanisms are perceived not to be operating quickly enough; if "cumulative causation" leads to growing regional differentials rather than their reduction (to be discussed below); or if institutional or historical barriers block diffusion processes. The purpose of spatially selective public investments in growth centers, it is held, is to hasten the focused attention of growth to lower echelons of the hierarchy in outlying regions and to link the growth centers more closely into the national system via higher-echelon centers in the urban hierarchy.

## *PLANNING IN THE ABSENCE OF "BALANCED" HIERARCHIES: COUNTER-MAGNETS, SECONDARY CITIES, AND RURAL SERVICE CENTERS*

Friedmann's model codified the U.S. experience (Berry, 1981). As the process of industrial urbanization ran its course in the later nineteenth century the northeastern manufacturing belt became the central driving force of the economy. The Northeast became a great heartland of industry and the national market, the focus of large-scale, national-serving industry, the seedbed of new industry responding to the dynamic structure of national final demand, and the center of high levels of per capita income. This core region became the lever for development of more peripheral hinterland regions, both in North America and beyond. This region reached to the hinterlands for their resources as its input requirements increased, stimulating their growth in accordance with its resource demands and the resource endowment of the hinterlands. Thus, standing in a dependent relationship to the heartland, radiating out across the national landscape, there developed resource-dominant regional hinterlands. Resource endowment became a critical determinant of regional comparative advantage and growth potential.

The result of core-centered patterns of growth was a high degree of regional specialization. Specialization, in turn, determined the content and direction of regional growth. Regional economic growth was externally determined by national demands for regional specialties. The nature of these specialties, alternative sources for them, and changes in the structure of demand therefore determined the nature and extent of regional growth.

Emerging systems of cities played a critical role in the whole process. Cities did become the instruments whereby the specialized subregions were tied together within the national economy. All the features of growth within a matrix of urban regions that have just been discussed in fact occurred. The growth processes produced and maintained an urban system comprising a few large metropolises, a larger number of intermediate-sized cities, and a still larger number of smaller towns. All shared in national growth and helped distribute its benefits throughout both heartland and hinterland regions.

Some planners argued that it was the "balance" of the urban system that made U.S. growth so efficient. But what exactly is a "balanced" urban system? Enter central-place theory and its relationship to the rank-size distribution noted in Chapter 4. A rank-size distribution exists if the plot forms a straight line when cities are ranked in decreasing order of size and plotted in a graph prepared on double-logarithmic paper with population on one axis and rank on the other. Zipf (1941) argued that such a straight-line relationship reflects the achievement of national political and economic unity. The presence of the distribution also indicates that the urban system has an underlying central-place component. The rank-size pattern emerges when all centers in the hierarchy share in a common growth process and have the same expected average growth rate.

When might an urban system be "unbalanced," and what are the consequences for economic growth? If the population of the largest city exceeds the figure that might be expected on the basis of the rank-size distribution, a condition of *primacy* is said to exist, and this is the principal circumstance said to lack "balance." Colin Clark (1967) used the additional term *oligarchy* to describe situations in which the towns over 100,000 population had a bigger share of the total urban population than would be expected from the straight-line relationship. The idea of primacy was initially formulated by Mark Jefferson (1939) and was very simple. He argued that everywhere "Nationalism crystallizes in primate cities . . . supereminent . . . not merely in size, but in national influence." He assessed the degree of eminence of cities within countries by computing the ratios of size of the second- and third-ranking cities to that of the largest place. But immediately after Jefferson's papers had appeared, Zipf (1949) directed attention to the entire system of cities. The rank-size distribution, he argued, was the situation to be expected in any "homogeneous socio-economic system" that had reached a state of "harmonious equilibrium."

It remained for discussants at a series of postwar conferences on urbanization in Asia, the Far East, and Latin America organized by the United Nations Economic, Social and Cultural Organization (UNESCO) to put the two together. Cases deviating from the rank-size distribution were said to arise from "over-urbanization" of the economies of lesser-developed countries because of "excessive" in-migration and superimposition of limited economic development of a colonial type. This created "dual economies" characterized by "primate cities" that tended to have "paralytic" effects upon the development of smaller urban places, to be "parasitic" in relation to the remainder of the national economy, and to be productive of social disorganization. Obviously, each of the words in quotation marks involves a value judgment, but their use reveals that the idea of the primate city became firmly established in many people's minds as a malignant deviation, with obviously pejorative connotations, from expectations about hierarchical organization derived from the rank-size rule and central-place theory. In the minds of planners and policy-makers, urban "gigantism" became a characteristic to be feared, even when the principal city was small in relation to cities in other areas. City-size distributions deviating from the rank-size rule were viewed as problematic. "Balanced" urban hierarchies became policy objectives, with plans taking three forms: encouragement of "counter-magnets" to primate cities, promotion of secondary city growth, and strengthening of rural service centers.

### Metropolitan Counter-Magnets

The counter-magnet idea first took form in France. In 1947 a young geographer, Jean-François Gravier, wrote a book entitled *Paris et le désert français* that attracted wide attention with its diagnosis that national ills were the result of Paris's dominance, creating a desert of the rest of France. Gravier recommended that a policy of decentralization be developed. Out of the debate that ensued emerged a progressive elaboration of planning tools, successive plans for restructuring the Paris region, and a national urban growth strategy focusing on the *métropoles d'équilibre*.

The planners' initial strategy was to try to halt the physical growth of Paris, reducing congestion at the center by massive improvement in the transportation infrastructure, and by diverting growth to major new nodes in the suburbs. Complementing these plans for the Paris region was an urban growth strategy, developed during the fifth plan of 1966–1969. The basic idea of this strategy came from the work of several French geographers. Among them, Pierre George argued that whereas in the past regions made cities, today cities make regions; and Hautreux and Rochefort (1964) identified eight metropolitan areas whose growth could offset the dominance of Paris. Thus, the urban strategy plans gave high priority to public incentives to spur growth in Lyon–St. Etienne, Marseille-Aix, Lille Roubaix–Tourcoing, Toulouse, Nancy-Metz, Bordeaux, Nantes–St. Nazair, and Strasbourg.

Other versions of the counter-magnet idea have been implemented in Turkey and in Colombia. In Turkey, there is a desire to achieve more "balanced" growth by stimulating development in the south and especially in the east. It includes the idea of trying to develop counter-magnets to the largest cities, that is, to encourage the growth of cities in the 20,000 to 100,000 size class. Incentives such as tax breaks, special amortization, and exceptions to corporate income laws have been given to industry. Professional salaries have been supplemented, and embryonic regional universities have begun. In fact, regional planning of this kind preceded the development of the current National Plan in Turkey. In Colombia, on the other hand, part of the national plan for development involved splitting the country into four major economic regions, each one having one of the four major cities as a growth pole: Barranquilla for the Atlantic coast, Cali in the southwest, Medellin in the northwest, and Bogota in central area.

### Secondary Cities in Regional Development

If there is primacy, city-size distributions also reveal a paucity of intermediate-sized cities compared to the rank-size rule. According to the accompanying regional growth theory, this insufficiency will inhibit normal filtering and spread of economic growth and, by that fact alone, the gap must be filled. Such is the basis of secondary city strategies now being promoted in many developing countries (Rondinelli, 1981; Belsky et al., 1983). Based upon a careful examination of 31 case studies from 17 developing countries, Rondinelli (1981) concluded that secondary cities (which he defined as those with populations of greater than 100,000) can or do perform at least 12 functions that are supportive of rural and regional development. These are enumerated below. See Table 8.1 for additional details.

**TABLE 8.1** URBAN FUNCTIONS AT DIFFERENT LEVELS OF THE HIERARCHY

| Services and organizations | Village centers | Market and district towns | "Middle level" and intermediate cities | Primate cities and metropolitan centers |
|---|---|---|---|---|
| Administration | Police post | District officer<br>District court<br>Police station (with jail)<br>Specialized officers (e.g., agriculture) | Provincial administration<br>Special government services headquarters | Seat of state/national government<br>Seat of judiciary<br>Embassies<br>Headquarters of government departments |
| Health | Dispensary | Physicians<br>Dentist<br>Health center/clinic<br>Drug stores | Regional medical offices<br>General hospital<br>Specialized physicians<br>Large drug stores | Specialized hospitals<br>Medical research institutes |
| Marketing and shopping | Small retail shops<br>Periodic market<br>Specialized shops rare | Larger retail stores<br>Specialized retail shops<br>Gas station<br>Small wholesale stores | Large retail stores<br>Retail of large consumer durables<br>Service station<br>Large wholesale and distribution<br>Warehousing | Luxury retail shops<br>Headquarters of chain stores and import-export houses |
| Industry | Artisans shops<br>Occasional agroindustrial plant | Larger cottage industry<br>Larger agroindustrial plants | Large agroindustrial plants | Heavy industry |

| | | | |
|---|---|---|---|
| Finance | Village money lender | Commercial/cooperative banks<br>Finance co. offices<br>Pawnshops | Banking<br>Insurance<br>Brokerage<br>Middlemen | Domestic and foreign banks<br>Financial headquarters<br>Chambers of commerce<br>Trade associations |
| Public utility | Branch post office | Electricity<br>Post office<br>Telephone service<br>Telegraph office | Electricity<br>Sewer system<br>Water supply | Full range of municipal utilities |
| Traffic | Not traffic junction<br>Unsurfaced/seasonal roads | Surfaced roads<br>District transportation focus | Regional transp. service headquarters<br>Regional road focus<br>Important railroad station<br>All-weather highways | Metropolitan transportation system<br>Riverine and ocean shipping<br>Airport |
| Education | Primary school<br>Small secondary school | Larger secondary school(s) | Secondary school<br>Technical schools<br>Colleges | Universities<br>Technical institutes<br>National research institutes<br>Scientific academies |
| Recreation | Coffee/tea rooms<br>Bar | Cinema<br>Cafés | Theater<br>Restaurant<br>Hotel with nightclub | Theater, ballet<br>Museums<br>Art galleries<br>Orchestra, opera |

Source: D. Rondinelli and K. Ruddle. *Urban Functions in Rural Development: An Analysis of Integrated Spatial Development Policy*. Washington, D.C.: USAID, 1976.

1. **Points for Decentralization of Public Services.** They can provide convenient locations for decentralizing public services through municipal governments, field offices of national ministries or agencies, or regional or provincial government offices, thereby creating greater access for both urban and rural residents to public services and facilities that require population thresholds of about 100,000 or more.

2. **Public and Social Service Centers.** They can offer sufficiently large populations and economies of scale to allow the concentration within them of health, education, welfare, and other services and often act as regional or provincial centers for a variety of basic social services and facilities.

3. **Commercial and Personal Service Centers.** They usually offer a wide variety of consumer goods and commercial and personal services through small-scale enterprises and through extensive "informal sector" activities.

4. **Regional Marketing and Trade Centers.** Many act as regional marketing centers offering a wide variety of distribution, transfer, storage, brokerage, credit, and financial services through their regularly scheduled and institutionalized markets or through periodic markets and bazaars.

5. **Centers for Small-Scale Industry.** They often provide conditions that are conducive to the growth of small- and medium-scale manufacturing and artisan and cottage industries that can serve local markets and satisfy internal demand for low-cost manufactured goods, and some of the larger intermediate cities also support large-scale industrial activities.

6. **Agro-Processing and Supply Centers.** Many act as agro-processing and agricultural supply centers for their regions and provide services to rural populations in their hinterlands.

7. **Centers for Promoting the Commercialization of Agriculture.** They often create conditions—through relatively high levels of population concentration, their advantageous locations, marketing, and agro-processing functions, and linkages to rural communities—that are conducive to the commercialization of agriculture and to increasing agricultural productivity and income in their immediately surrounding hinterlands.

8. **Centers of Off-Farm Employment.** They can be sources of off-farm employment and supplementary income for rural people and, through remittances of migrants, provide additional sources of income to people living in rural towns and villages in their regions.

9. **Regional Transport and Communication Centers.** They often serve as area-wide or regional centers of transportation and communications, linking their residents and those of rural villages and towns in their hinterlands to larger cities and other regions in the country.

10. **Centers for Absorbing Migrants and Providing Income Remittance.** They can absorb substantial numbers of people migrating from rural areas to urban centers, transforming a "rural-to-primate city" migration pattern to a "step-

wise" pattern, and offering long-term or permanent residence to some migrants, thereby creating a more balanced distribution of urban population.

11. **Centers of Social Transformation.** They can function effectively as centers of social transformation by: (a) accommodating social heterogeneity and encouraging the integration of people from diverse social, ethnic, religious, and tribal groups, (b) accommodating organizations that help to socialize and assimilate rural people into city life, supporting them during their transition and mediating conflicts among them, (c) infusing new attitudes, behavior, and life-styles that are more conducive to urban living, (d) providing opportunities for economic and social mobility, and (e) offering new economic and social opportunities for women.

12. **Centers of Diffusion, Linkage, and Integration.** They can be channels for the diffusion of innovation and change, the spread of benefits of urban development, the stimulation of rural economies, and the integration of urban centers and rural settlements within their regions through social, economic, and administrative linkages.

In any program of development, secondary cities can, it is believed, play a leading role in: first, increasing the productivity of agriculture; second, increasing the efficiency, productivity, and employment in commercial activities; third, increasing manufacturing employment and productivity; and fourth, increasing the efficiency in productivity and employment of service activities. If secondary cities are weak, however, this role will not be played and development will continue to concentrate in the primate city.

### Planning Rural Service Centers

A third level of planning involves providing basic human services to rural populations. In this case, the issue is less that of filtering of growth than of linking rural areas into the mainstream of the national economy and seeing to it that basic needs are met. As Friedmann and Weaver (1979, p. 175) write:

> . . . lower order centers do not generate socio-economic development; rather, they respond to the changes in agricultural production within their area of general accessibility. Nevertheless, they may be useful in helping to articulate the spatial organization of the rural economy through the location of services, the layout of transportation and communication networks, the establishment of public offices and governmental institutions and the development of rural industries.

Increasingly, location-allocation models of the kind used to solve retail location problems in the more economically advanced countries (Chapter 7) are now also being used to solve the rural service delivery problem in the developing countries. The reader is referred to Rushton (1984) for a review of these modeling approaches. Where rural incomes are low and populations are sparse, the periodic marketing system is being used for such service delivery. In the western highlands of New Guinea, a periodic marketing system was created to provide a network of locations at which there would be regular market meetings on a twice-monthly schedule. The activities at each of the sites include basic governmental services, banking purchase of agricultural commodities, sale of consumer goods, and provision of tertiary services and entertainment.

## NATIONAL SPATIAL STRATEGY

Counter-magnet, secondary city, and rural service center programs are all elements of what are now recognized to be the broader developmental concern of *national spatial strategy*—spatial planning designed for the national economy as a whole. This includes a *national urban growth strategy* (incorporating efforts at various levels of the central-place hierarchy), a concern for *implicit spatial policies* (general economic and social policies that have accompanying, and often unintended spatial impacts), and an explicit *regional policy* (directed at changing the spatial distribution of economic activity to achieve some predetermined goals) (Richardson, 1977).

An example is that of Kenya, discussed by Richardson (1980). Ever since the Second Development Plan (1970–1974), Kenya has been committed to giving priority to rural development. As part of this, there has been concern for rural service provision and for effective markets at the lowest level of the central-place hierarchy. But there is symmetric concern for the rapid agglomeration of people and activities in Nairobi; for implicit spatial policies, particularly the untended effects of import-substitution programs that increase the pull of the primate city and widen regional differences; and for weaknesses in the upper levels of the urban hierarchy, which are so critical for the efficient diffusion of developmental impulses.

The spatial strategy has at its core the growth-center idea, organized in a central-place framework. As Richardson (1970) notes, the justification for growth centers in Kenya is based on several interrelated arguments. First, there is the need to decentralize industry to reduce the attractive pull of Nairobi on migrants. Second, there is the need to strengthen regional urban hierarchies to improve public service delivery. There are needs for locations for some of the larger-scale agricultural and resource-based industries, which serve as incubators of small-scale industries for subsequent dispersal into the hinterland. These small-scale industries are needed to reduce migration loss from regions by offering alternative urban destinations for local migrants. At the top, the policy includes attempts to constrain Nairobi's growth. In the middle, the growth centers are to function as counter-magnets and to provide the array of secondary city activities. At the lowest level, the issues are service delivery and effective participation in the market economy. Some of the goals are to be achieved via an infrastructure allocation strategy. Others goals are to be achieved through the location of industry, through municipal fiscal reform, and through a new urban land policy. Each of the elements is designed to contribute to the achievement of a desired pattern of urban and regional development that reflects Kenya's goals, rather than to a structure inherited from the colonial past. A component of the national spatial strategy is, therefore, a new, balanced central-place hierarchy. In Kenya, as in many other parts of the world, central-place concepts are being used by planners to propose what ought to be. To the extent that the plans are realized, the image becomes reality, and central-place theory develops a life of its own, a self-fulfilling prophecy!

## REFERENCES

APPALACHIAN REGIONAL COMMISSION (1970) *The Urban-Rural Growth Strategy in Appalachia*. A Commission Staff Summary Report.

BAKER, G., and B. FUNARO (1951) *Shopping Centers*. New York: Reinhold.

BELSKY, E., R. HACKENBERG, G. KARASKA, and D. RONDINELLI (1983) *The Role of Secondary Cities in Regional Development*. Working paper: Clark University and the U.S. Agency for International Development.

BERRY, B. J. L. (1963) "Spatial Organization and Levels of Welfare." Paper presented at the First Economic Development Administration Research Conference.

BERRY, B. J. L. (1972) "Hierarchical Diffusion: The Bases of Developmental Filtering and Spread in a System of Growth Centers," in N. M. Hansen (ed.), *Growth Centers in Regional Economic Development*. New York: The Free Press.

BERRY, B. J. L. (1973) *Growth Centers in the American Urban System*. Cambridge, Mass.: Ballinger.

BERRY, B. J. L. (1981) *Comparative Urbanisation*. London and Basingstoke: Macmillan.

BOUDEVILLE, J. R. (1964) "Hiérarchie urbaine et aménagement des villes," *Revue d'Économie Politique*, 74:65–92.

VON BÖVENTER, E. (1964) "Spatial Organization Theory as a Basis for Regional Planning," *Journal of the American Institute of Planners*, 30:90–100.

BURNS, W. (1959) *British Shopping Centres*. London: Hill.

CARRUTHERS, W. I. (1962) "Service Centres in Greater London," *The Town Planning Review*, 33:7–31.

CLARK, C. (1967) *Population Growth and Land Use*. New York: St. Martin's Press.

DARWENT, D. F. (1969) "Growth Poles and Growth Centers in Regional Planning—A Review," *Environment and Planning*, 1:5–32.

FRIEDMANN, J. (1966) *Regional Development Policy. A Case Study of Venezuela*. Cambridge, Mass.: Massachusetts Institute of Technology Press.

FRIEDMANN, J. (1972) "A General Theory of Polarized Development," in N. Hansen (ed.), *Growth Centers in Regional Economic Development*. New York: The Free Press.

FRIEDMANN, J. and C. Weaver (1979) *Territory and Function: The Evolution of Regional Planning*. London: Edward Arnold.

GORE, C. (1984) *Regions in Question: Space, Development Theory and Regional Policy.* London: Methuen.

GRAVIER, J.-F. (1947) *Paris et le désert français.* Paris: Flammarion.

GROVE, D., and L. HUSZAR (1964) *The Towns of Ghana.* Accra, Ghana: Ghana University.

HAUTREUX, J., and M. ROCHEFORT (1964) "Les métropoles et la fonction régionale dans l'armature urbaine française," *Revue Construction et Aménagement,* No. 17.

JEFFERSON, M. (1939) "The Law of the Primate City," *Geographical Review,* 29:226–232.

PARR, J. B. (1973) "Growth Poles, Regional Development, and Central Place Theory," *Papers of the Regional Science Association,* 31:172–212.

PERROUX, F. (1961) *L'Économie du xx$^e$ siècle.* Paris: Presses Universitaires.

REINER, T., and J. B. PARR (1981) "A Note on the Dimensions of a National Settlement Pattern," *Urban Studies,* 13:87–118.

RICHARDSON, H. W. (1977) *City Size and National Spatial Strategies in Developing Countries.* Washington, D.C.: World Bank Staff Working Paper No. 252.

RICHARDSON, H. W. (1980) "An Urban Development Strategy for Kenya," *The Journal of Developing Areas,* 15:87–118.

RONDINELLI, D. (1981) *Developing and Managing Middle-Sized Cities in Less Developed Countries.* Washington, D.C.: USAID.

ROYAL COMMISSION ON AGRICULTURE AND RURAL LIFE (1957) *Service Centers.* Regina, Saskatchewan: Queen's Printer.

ROYAL COMMISSION ON LOCAL GOVERNMENT IN GREATER LONDON (1960) *Report of the Commission.* London: H.M.S.O., Cmnd. 1164.

RUSHTON, G. (1984) "Use of Locational-Allocation Models for Improving the Geographical Accessibility of Rural Services in Developing Countries," *International Regional Science Review,* 9:217–240.

SIMMONS, J. W. (1966) *Toronto's Changing Retail Complex.* Chicago: University of Chicago, Department of Geography Research Series.

UNITED ISRAEL APPEAL (n.d.) *Operation Lakhish, Stage 2.* New York: United Israel Appeal.

ZIPF, G. K. (1941) *National Unity and Disunity.* Bloomington, Ind.: The Principia Press.

ZIPF, G. K. (1949) *Human Behavior and The Principle of Least Effort.* Cambridge: Addison-Wesley.

# Index